NOT MY BLOOD

The Old Bus

NOT MY BLOOD

A STEPMOTHER'S STORY

A Memoir

LIETTE CORMIER

Liette can be reached at cormier.liette@gmail.com
ISBN: 978-1-7781701-0-2

I stand before you naked. Raw. Vulnerable. Okay, not literally, but it is an appropriate description of my state of being. Sharing my story with you terrifies me. A friend suggested I write it and then decide on the next steps. As you read the pages, I am sure you will understand why I tremble. While putting the words on paper, I laughed, I cried, but mostly I screamed. Writing the book was not therapy; it was a revelation. I am not an expert on domestic violence nor on stepparenting. This is not a how-to manual. It is a photograph of a part of my life. Hopefully, my experience inspires you. I changed a few names, but not all of them. My memoir is based on past events and how I remember them. I consulted my journals, and I had long discussions with my family and friends who helped me drift back some thirty years ago.

To Andre

Even after Oso threatened to slit your throat,
you did not run.

TABLE OF CONTENTS

PART ONE

The Old Bus

Summer 1986

The old orange school bus stared at me from across the wide field. I briefly wondered, was she daring me to come closer or warning me to stay away? As we ambled toward it, I drew a deep breath. I was twenty-four years old and an unemployed college graduate. I'd left behind my comfy parents' home to move into a crudely remodeled old school bus, with an older man, his two children, and a huge husky dog. As we approached, the kids hopped up from the picnic table where they hunched. They waved, their faces beaming. Jessi even clapped her hands. Over the next four months, I'd often spot them squatting outside on the table, waiting for one of us to get home. Oso locked them out during the day when we weren't home. He said it was to prevent them from getting into trouble. I'm not sure forcing them outside all day kept them safe. But the situation was temporary. We had both recently graduated from college. Soon, we'd find decent jobs and a suitable home.

The children hugged me, and I smiled. Jessi was twelve years old and Chris was ten.

After school loans ran out, Oso could no longer afford to rent a house. He loaded his bus and moved the family to a small local campground. The campground was tucked away behind a motel with trees bordering it on two sides. A road leading to the motel provided the primary access to the campsite.

Through the lush trees, we admired the majestic Bathurst Harbour. The extensive body of water connects to the sea across Chaleur Bay, which is part of the Atlantic Ocean. When the tide is in, and there is no breeze, the bay sparkles under the sun's brilliant light. On clear nights, when the conditions are right, one can observe an apparition that resembles a burning ship. Hundreds of people claim to have seen it in distinct spots on the water. Scientists suggest it's caused by decaying vegetation, undersea releases of natural gas, or a weather phenomenon like St Elmo's Fire. But those fortunate enough to have experienced it say it mirrors a blazing ship that sails away when they approach it.

Although beautifully located, the campground was not a busy spot. Visitors passing through pitched their tent or light camper for a day or two, then continued on their journey. Each campsite had a picnic table and an electric outlet. The owner was an elderly local businessman, and he offered us an affordable monthly fee.

Oso parked the old bus in the furthest corner from the facilities, near the trees, behind the motel. It was an ordinary school bus, not one of those flat-nose buses. Most of it still bore the bright orange colour of a regular school bus. Black paint covered the entire bottom of the vehicle, from half a meter below the windows to the edge of the metal. Oso fixed alloy rails on the top, spanning almost the total length of the roof. Within these rails, he secured a red canoe between wooden boxes of many sizes and colours. Almost everything the family owned was in or on that bus. Oso had proudly sketched the name of the bus, L'Arche, in black on a white panel above the front window. An enormous spare tire graced the front of the grill. The full television antenna rested on the hood, towering well above the canoe. Greyish curtains, covered with blue and white flowers, floated in every window.

Oso unlocked the door, and I stepped inside.

I noticed he had fastened an ample blue curtain from the ceiling in the middle, separating the area into two separate rooms. In the back room, behind the curtain, he had stacked pieces of furniture and chests of assorted sizes against the windows, almost reaching the roof. On each side of the limited space, the kids slept on mattresses, precariously balanced on the mounds. They shuffled sideways to get to the rear door. At night, I'd hear a thump and a moan as one of them tried to sit up in bed or turn around.

I had lived in the bus for a month during college. Then, it had seemed big. However, now that it was stuffed with all their possessions, we were jammed in like sardines in a can. Oso installed a table behind the driver's seat, and we sat on the original bus benches. At night, we lowered the table to prepare the bed where Oso and I slept. On the opposite side was a counter with six drawers full of dry food, pots, plates, utensils, and other kitchen necessities. In the upper corner, by the door, he installed a measly battery-run television. Handmade pouches of different colours and lengths covered almost every available wall space. We crammed them with many items, such as scissors, shampoo, and soap. My lone contribution to the décor was a small wooden cross my parents had given me. The pope, Jean-Paul II, blessed it when he travelled to Moncton in 1984. I stuck it on the wall beside the blue curtain.

The bus hooked up to the campsite electricity supply with a lengthy extension cord. We had lights but no running water and no toilet. We used the campground facilities. Oso purchased a cheap second-hand fridge and set it by the door, outside the bus. The fully loaded vehicle could not fit a full-size fridge. He covered it with a tarp to protect it from the rain. Since the entrance faced the woods, nobody could see it from the road. Oso locked the fridge door handle with a chain and key so nobody could steal our food. I suspect it was mostly so Chris would not devour our food supply. Both kids had very hearty appetites. We wedged our clothes and linens into colourful boxes in the back. Oso proudly grinned and opened an empty drawer. "For all your stuff," he said.

We cooked our meals outside on a portable barbecue or inside on a two-burner plate. Oso tied two ropes into clotheslines for our laundry. One end of each rope ran from the front driver's mirror to a tree behind the bus. We washed our clothes at the local laundromat and hung them outside to dry. A few socks or pairs of pants often dangled in the wind. When the weather allowed, we ate our meals on the campground picnic table. The huge husky dog, tied by the rear door, howled at the full moon, causing Oso to barge out in the middle of the night.

I was not in love with this man, but I did love him. Mostly, I loved how he loved me. He made me feel like the most beautiful woman on earth. His lips quivered when he gawked at me. I loved his cowboy hat and his proud demeanour. The promise of adventures and unknown territories drove me to pack up and leave my parents. He bought me teddy bears and flowers. He seemed unafraid of anyone. I devoured his colourful stories of his time in the Yukon.

Once settled on the bus, I wrote my parents a letter letting them know I was not coming back home. I was scared of their reaction. Would they be disappointed in me? These days, young adults meet on Friday and move in together on Monday. In the mid-eighties, in our modest village, it was not common to live together before marriage.

Growing up

I don't believe in luck. I think we create our own luck, and yet, I consider myself a lucky person. For starters, I was born a woman in Canada. I shudder to imagine being born in certain countries where being a female is far from a blessing.

Second, I had the best parents on this planet. On Mothers' Day and Fathers' Day, I read messages on Facebook from friends praising their parents, claiming they are the best parents in the world. I grin because I know mine were the best. Their parents are likely awesome, and I admit I might be biased. My mom and dad, like many of my friends' parents, were born and raised in Memramcook, a charming Acadian village in southeastern New Brunswick. They grew up within a kilometre of each other. My teenage mom developed a crush on my dad when he frequented the general store her family kept. She blushed and pretended to dust shelves, sneaking looks at him. She scribbled his name on a paper and hid it under her pillow. The Universe would know she yearned to marry him and would make it happen. Maybe my mom was lucky? My dad? Both of them?

In one respect, they were typical parents of the generation of the early 1930s. My dad worked two jobs for a while to support his growing family while my mom stayed at home to raise six kids. Yet in other ways, they were not typical parents at all. Although cooking was not my mom's favourite thing to do, she always had supper ready for my dad when he arrived home from work. We ate the last meal of the day together, sharing stories. My dad emptied his plate, patted his belly, smiled, and said, "Thank you for such an excellent dinner." They washed the dishes together while we worked on our homework. I'm not sure many men born in the late 1920s dried pots and pans with their wives. He was also the affectionate one in the couple, often embracing my mom, who shied away when the neighbours were around. My dad worked for thirty-seven years at the same company and my mom packed his lunch every day. She says he never complained once about what she fed him.

Third, my parents created me with no major deficiencies. Unless you consider being short a handicap. I don't. Although, it would be nice to not have to beg people at the grocery store to grasp that elusive bottle of ketchup. Oh, and I also have two uvulas, but unless I admit it, nobody can tell. My mom used to drag me to the window so people could gape at my wide-open mouth. I promised myself that once I became an adult, I would never expose my twin uvulas again. The doctor also noticed I had one cheek bigger than the other. I stare at the mirror, but I can't tell which one. If you meet me, please do not peer at my butt; the doctor meant my face cheeks.

Fourth, I entered this earth with average intelligence, sufficient to do well in school yet not be considered a geek. At times, I applied that intelligence well; other days, I'm not sure where it disappeared.

Fifth, I have five siblings, all of whom I adore. My parents planned for six kids, and they succeeded. First came the three boys (Gilles, Louis-Marie, Bert) and then the three girls (me, Camilla, Marianne). Yup, in that order. My life was simple as a child. We had no Internet or cell phones. What we had was lots of kids to play or fight with. We spent most of our time outside until our parents called us in for bedtime.

Finally, I almost stumbled into this life in a Beetle, my parents' first car. My mom says my dad was so proud of his car, her labour began the day he came home with it. He drove us to the hospital in the middle of the night. I was the first girl in a family with three boys. My arrival positioned me in a place of glory with my dad. Of course, he treasured his boys and his two other daughters, but I was his first little girl. We developed a special bond. Later in life, when Alzheimer's seized control of his mind and his barriers dissolved, he'd murmur to me, "You were always my favourite." Deep down, I always knew. After the doctors moved him into a home for Alzheimer's patients, Marianne accompanied him to the optometrist. While they relaxed in the waiting room, he asked her, "Pardon my ignorance, but are you Liette?"

My sister, unwilling to break his heart, said, "Yes, Dad, of course, I am." He blinked an eye and said, "Please don't tell the others, but you were my favourite." Shortly afterwards, she announced it during a family get-together and we laughed. We know our dad cherished all his children.

Camilla, my partner in crime, must've been in a rush to be born because thirteen months after I appeared, she popped out. I'd park myself beside her playpen and wait patiently for her to finish her milk bottle. I guzzled the leftovers she always left for me. My mother often dressed us the same and we could pretend to be twins. Growing up, she claimed she got the bad rap while I was the troublemaker.

In 1969, the world watched in awe when Neil Armstrong took his famous steps on the moon. I grabbed my parents' binoculars and peered at the moon, hoping to capture his silhouette. However, Marianne's arrival a few days later was more real and amazing to my seven-year-old self than a strange man flying in outer space. My parents brought her home from the hospital and laid her crossways on a living room comfort chair. I gaped at this tiny, amusing person. She was the cutest doll ever. Camilla did not share my enthusiasm. "Maybe we should get a cat instead," she said. I guess she didn't appreciate losing her place as the baby of the family.

Being born in the early sixties wedged me between the baby boomers and Gen X. We grew up watching violent cartoons like *Bugs Bunny* and *The Flintstones.* We didn't have computers or video games, and the television's only three channels reverted to snow at three o'clock in the morning while the CBC station played "Oh Canada!" Later, when we had boyfriends and our dates lingered late, my dad would tell us the next day, "I almost came down to sing 'Oh Canada' last night!" I'm amazed he never did because he loved to sing.

I enjoyed growing up in Memramcook, an intimate village of five thousand people. My friends and cousins lived in our community, and we played sports – hockey in the winter and fastball in the summer.

The competitive genes I have are from the Cormier side of the family. I was determined to do everything my older brothers could do. Sometimes, after much pleading, they agreed to teach me. For example, Bert showed me how to stick two fingers from each hand in my mouth, force my tongue inward, and whistle powerfully enough to startle anyone near me.

When he laid snares in the woods behind our house and caught himself a few hares, I begged him to take Camilla and me with him. We paid attention to how he wired his traps, and then we installed our own snares. He snickered at us because our snares were not round, nor the right height, but we forbade him to fix them. Early the next morning, we rushed out into the forest, and we were both jubilant and miserable to discover two dead hares hanging in our nooses. We handed them over to Bert to skin and clean while we scrutinized his work. Hare droppings collect in a straight row in their intestine, like a rosary. Bert held one end of the gut with his left hand and swiftly slid his right fingers along it, shooting the poop out like missiles. Of course, he aimed at us, and we sprinted for our lives. My mom cooked fricot with our trophies, my favourite Acadian dish.

Bert played hockey and as he approached the bench for a changeover, I watched him blow snot out of one of his nostrils. He pulled the same trick when we played outside. He'd seal one nostril with his thumb and force out the air from the other one, the snot shooting out like a bullet, clean and simple. Well, I could do that too.

One cool pleasant fall day, I drifted into the forest behind our house. I went almost every day and relaxed by a trickling creek, deep into teenage thoughts. It's funny because when I reflect on my teenage years, they seem so ordinary. Loving parents who trusted us and let us go out every weekend. A mom and dad who inspired us to thrive. Lots of friends, playing sports and performing well in school. Yet when I read my teenage diaries, I'm both amused and appalled at how dramatic life seemed.

The leaves had already turned crimson colours, and I wished the geese bon voyage on their journey south to escape the winter of the Maritime Provinces. I squatted on a narrow bridge, my legs dangling over the clear water. The chilly air caused my nose to run. I had neglected to bring tissues, but hey, no big deal. I've watched my brother deal with this condition. I stood up. One cannot blow out snot sitting down. I squeezed my right nostril with my right thumb. Leaning forward, I blew out from the other nostril. I hesitated. One should never waver while whooshing out unwanted fluids from one's body. The snot came out, but one end of it stuck to my nostril while the other end trailed down to my belly button. The wind hummed in the leaves around me as I hunched forward, a long string of gooey, thick, nasty, sticky, yellow snot dangling from my nose.

College

September 1984

I checked my watch: twenty minutes to eight, plenty of time. I hate being late. The imposing college stood perched on top of a steep hill. Drawing a deep breath, I grinned. A new chapter. Excited, I strode in and forced my way to the various lineups in the spacious auditorium. Pick up my class schedule; smile for my picture; collect my books; grimace at the photo on my student card. The whisperings and giggles from nervous first-day students filled the room as more people wandered in from the hall. I skimmed the hundreds of anxious and eager faces to spot a friendly one, but I didn't recognize anyone. No worries, I've always been good at making friends, and I was confident in my academic abilities.

Besides, it was not my first time away from home. After high school, I'd gone away to college for a one-year course learning to work with mentally challenged people. Bert had chuckled and stated that I would be homesick. "See you in two weeks." He was partly right. I cried for two weeks, blubbering at my parents' picture beside my bed. I did not own a cell phone. Heck, I didn't even have a telephone. To make a call, I had to use my landlord's upstairs phone and reverse the long-distance charges to my parents. I didn't wish to burden them with an extra phone bill, plus I knew my mom would worry if she realized how hard it was for me to be away from them. I not only inherited the Cormier competition gene, I inherited the pride. Desperate to prove my brother wrong, I completed the course and even enjoyed most of it. But when we had to do a workplace placement in the local psychiatric hospital, I became terrified of the patients after one of them attacked a fellow student. I quickly figured out it wasn't what I wanted to do for the rest of my life. When the course ended, I moved back home, and I landed a job at the local drugstore. I worked for three years at the Memramcook pharmacy, fell in love, and got engaged. Unfortunately, after three years of ups and downs, we broke up.

Heartbroken, I ached for a new beginning. I bawled for a few months, but after witnessing a friend struggle for years over an ex-boyfriend, I'd promised myself I would never allow a man such power over me. When the pain grew intense, I sank to my knees, and I scrubbed our kitchen's yellow linoleum floor.

So here I was, my second time in college. I was older than most of the other young adults struggling to find their bearings in a group of people. The school was a three-hour drive from home. I shared a basement apartment with another girl whom I had yet to meet. I chose this college not only because it was the only one in New Brunswick offering the environment course I was interested in, but because I yearned to get away from my village. Although I appreciated growing up in a small community where everyone knows everyone, the village just didn't feel like home anymore. Since I worked in the local drugstore, many people knew me or knew my parents or grandparents. I presumed the entire village knew why we split up. My fiancé was a decent man, but he was in love with someone else. As a young adult, my world revolved around me, and I became embarrassed about going out in public. I assumed everyone was mocking me.

I promised myself to stay clear of men for a long time.

Once done with the lineups, I drifted to my classroom and seized the front desk in the middle row. I'd learned from experience that if I sat at the back of the class, I'd be distracted by my neighbours, especially if one of those neighbours happened to be a cute guy. I picked up my biology book and carried it to my nose, inhaling its crisp new book smell.

I'd brushed off attending university because I believed I could learn in two years of college what they taught in four years of university. I liked school until I entered high school. Since we didn't have a secondary school in the village, we had to travel to the neighbouring town. Some students from the city sneered at us and called us hillbillies. I despised high school. But this was different. I'd chosen this college and this discipline. I hoped to get a job I'd appreciate and be paid a reasonable salary.

I deemed myself an average student. During school, I'd bring home my report card and most teachers had written: *Seems to try her best.* My dad would scrutinize my results, and he'd ask, "Did you try your best?"

I'd answer, "I tried my best."

He'd smile, "If you did your best, I'm proud of you." It wasn't a lie, although deep down, I knew I could've performed better. I was an extroverted teenager who played sports, liked to party and chase boys. My social life was as important to me as my school life; therefore, I shared my time equally between the two. I figured that with the limited time I had to study, I gave it my best. For an entire year, when I was seventeen, I had a job delivering the French newspaper *l'Évangeline*. I'd get up around five in the morning to drop my papers at neighbours' front door before school. A tough job since I hate getting up early. It paid thirteen dollars per week, plus tips. Once, after a party at our fastball coach's house, I was too hungover to walk the three kilometres in the snow for my paper route. I woke up my mom and told her I was not feeling well, which was true. She didn't ask questions, knowing I'd been a sickly child, but then again, maybe she knew the real reason. Camilla had to deliver my papers that morning. She was likely as hungover as I was, but she didn't dare confess to it. I heard from her later.

I smiled at the students stepping into the classroom. A few girls drifted in together, babbling as they slipped to the rear of the class. Others peered around the classroom, our home away from home for the next two years.

I noticed him right away. He strutted in, looking much older than everyone else. Proudly sporting a cowboy hat and cowboy boots, he looked rugged and handsome. He seemed out of place, yet he fit right in. He winked at me as he plopped his slender body in the chair right behind me.

I grinned. I turned around to face the teacher, ignoring the giddy feeling in my stomach.

Oso

Bears both fascinate and frighten me. I've had recurring night-mares about them. I've wasted countless waking hours in a tent at night, listening for the rustling sounds of these ferocious predators. While foraging for mushrooms in the woods, I'm constantly peer-ing over my shoulder. Yet I've travelled to the Canadian Rockies and the Great Arctic, hoping for a glimpse of the various bears prowling in Canada. I've seen several black bears, one huge grizzly bear, and three polar bears in the wild. Captivated, I forgot to be afraid, but of course, I admired them from a safe distance.

When I met Oso in September 1984, dark hair covered most of his face. His eyebrows, bushy and thick, merged in the middle of his forehead, appearing like one extended bushy brow. He claimed it gave him a mean look. A heavy moustache and beard, if not trimmed, would crawl over his cheeks, reaching under his eyes.

Oso is the Spanish word for bear, and since I'm on a lifelong quest to master Spanish, in my story, I call him Oso.

We both enrolled in the Environment Technology two-year program in the Bathurst, New Brunswick Community College. Most of the students had recently graduated from high school except Oso, who, at thirty-four years old, was twelve years older than I. He was the oldest student in our class and possibly even the entire school. A few of the teachers were younger than him. He grew up in Montreal, but he hadn't lived there since he'd turned eighteen. During the introductions, he told the class he was a single dad with three kids. They lived in the Yukon for a few years, then travelled to Newfoundland and Labrador in an old restored school bus. After three arduous years of fishing in the choppy seas, they crossed to New Brunswick so he could earn a college degree.

The instructors introduced themselves and shared their curriculum for the semester. It unnerved me to hear of so many chemistry courses. Our chemistry teacher looked the part, narrow rim glasses, grey hair and a long greyish beard. I soon mastered his courses. He lived and breathed chemistry, and he was an outstanding teacher. I also enjoyed the other courses, biology, microbiology and botany. I was in my element, and I studied hard. We didn't know what type of work we would get afterwards, but we hoped for a job in the environmental field. When the chief instructor handed out our first report card, he told me I had the second-highest marks in the class. One of the other girls had almost a perfect score. I studied many hours to beat her marks, but she always ended slightly ahead of me. The following year, she quit college for university.

Oso and I battled for the top place. He usually did very well, but we both grappled with the math material and teacher. When he delivered the results of our first math test, Oso gasped. I turned around, and he showed me his paper, *Fail.* He wrote the correct answers, but he hadn't applied the formula the teacher had shown us. The next day, our chemistry teacher shook his head, caressing his beard. "A student tore into the math teacher's office after school yesterday and banged his fist on the desk. The student insulted the instructor and brought him to tears. I understand the student was upset, but there are proper ways to handle this situation. If it happens again, please come see me." The class was silent. I assumed Oso had rattled the math teacher. I turned around, and he grinned sheepishly, raising his shoulders.

During a morning break, we headed out into the auditorium, babbling, creating new friendships. I glanced at Oso as he tackled a bag of chips. Butch, he had combated forest fires in the Yukon and trained workers on chainsaw safety, yet I watched him struggle, muscles bulging, trying to open the bag. "Do you mind?" I asked. He smiled, shrugged, and gave me the bag. I grasped each side and easily opened it. He stared at me with awe, and I noticed his eyes were a fine shade of brown, my favourite eye colour.

Most days, he wore jeans or brown corduroy pants and, of course, his cowboy hat and cowboy boots. The classes began at eight o'clock, but Oso was often late. We'd hear his boots as he stomped the corridor. The teacher would stop talking, chalkboard crayon in mid-air, and we'd all listen as he approached the classroom. Stomp! Stomp! Stomp! He'd stroll in, grin at the teacher, shrug and flop down on his desk chair. Laughter would erupt in the room. The teachers tolerated his tardiness because he had kids to take care of every morning.

He rented a two-story house in the Bathurst outskirts. When I got to know him better, I understood that only his two oldest children lived with him: Jessi, his ten-year-old daughter and his son Chris, almost two years younger than Jessi. The kids' biological mother lived across the country, in British Columbia, with their six-year-old daughter Catherine.

We became friends. I tried to make it to class early so we'd have time to chat before the instructors began their lessons. He also turned up earlier. I'd casually turn around, and we'd talk. He seemed engrossed in getting to know me. He gazed into my eyes as if he could see right through my heart.

Curious, one morning, I paid particular attention to my hair, and I applied black mascara and red lipstick. I appreciated the results, although I didn't think I was pretty. I'm short, barely over five feet tall, with no striking features. It's a constant battle to tame my fuzzy, auburn hair, especially in a damp and windy maritime climate. Friends often teased me because of my freckled face. When I was a youthful teenager, I asked this cute guy to be my boyfriend. Well, my friend asked him if he wanted to be my sweetheart because I was too shy to approach him myself. When I pressed her to know why he rejected me, she said, "He only dates pretty girls." I remember crying myself to sleep that night. A few years later, when my fiancé and I broke up, I thought maybe he couldn't love me because I was not attractive.

I slid into class, and I quietly sat at my desk. Oso was already there, chatting with the student behind him. When he turned toward me, his mouth fell open, and he stuttered, grappling to say hello. I saw the wonder in his eyes, and I was hooked. Nobody had ever looked at me that way. That day, he confided to a friend in class, "I'm going to marry that girl."

The school organized a Halloween party in October. Joanne, a girl in my class, shared an apartment with her sister, not too far from mine. We quickly became best friends. We dressed up in costumes in her apartment, and we drove to the party in my Datsun sports car. I'd won five thousand dollars scratching a lottery ticket the year before, and I'd bought a used car. When we arrived at the party, the golden flames of a bonfire shot miniature stars toward the black sky. Students danced and hovered around the warmth of the burning blaze. Everyone put on funny or scary costumes. We drifted to the crowd, and I paused in front of Oso. He had a mask, and he was unrecognizable. "Hello, Oso," I said.

"How did you know it was me?" His voice was baffled.

"Your smell," I answered.

"Oh God! Should I be insulted or flattered?" he responded.

I smiled. "Flattered." He smelled like a mix of musk and to-bacco, a sexy odour.

I guzzled too much alcohol that evening, and when people left, I offered Oso a ride home. I parked the car near his house and we talked for hours. He leaned in, and his lips brushed mine. I kissed him right back. He grasped at my boobs, but I stopped him. I was not that kind of girl, one who had sex on a first date. He gazed deep into my eyes, smiled, and murmured, "See you tomorrow, beautiful." He stepped out, and I very carefully and very slowly drove home.

Praise the alcohol; I plunged into a troubled sleep. The following morning, I wanted to stay home and bury myself under the covers. Oso had recently ended a relationship with a woman he'd picked up in Calgary on his way to Newfoundland and Labrador. I recalled my promise to steer clear of men, my heart still in pieces over my breakup. I had serious qualms about dating an older man with three kids. What was I thinking? I could list so many reasons last evening should not have happened. I had no intention of including a man in the first few paragraphs of my new life. Oso was older than me. He had kids, for fuck's sake. Oh my God, what had I done? I couldn't miss school, so I crawled out of bed and I showed up in class a few minutes before the bell. I feigned being busy reading my notes when he strode into the classroom, the memory of the kiss fresh on my mind.

During the break, I told him I was not ready for a relationship. He grinned, "Of course." The physical pull was there. I couldn't deny it. My body betrayed me whenever he stood near me.

My apartment was within walking distance of the school, so I'd race home for lunch. I watched *The Flintstones* on television while gulping down my food. I trotted back to school and climbed the stairs, where I knew he sat and smoked. They allowed smoking in many places back then, except in school. The teachers frowned and shook their heads when they caught us, but they usually ignored us. Oso rolled his cigarettes, and he taught me how to do it. We used a cigarette rolling machine. The machine made it much easier than rolling the cigarettes by hand. I opened the machine and stuffed the loose tobacco inside. I inserted the tip of an empty cigarette into the side and pushed the cylinder across the machine so the tobacco filled the tube.

I'd climb the stairs to reach the class, and I'd pretend to be surprised to see him.

"Hey, how are you doing? Can I bum a smoke? I forgot my pack at home."

He'd smile. "Of course, but only if you sit and smoke it with me."

"Oh okay, sure then."

I sat beside him on the steps, our knees touching, and I hung on to his every word as he boasted about his adventures in the cold and far away Yukon. He was mysterious and wild and sweet and sour all at once. I knew I should resist my attraction to him, but a part of me didn't want to. I giggled when he told me about the time his friend rode his horse straight through the Dawson City tavern doors and asked for a drink without even getting off his mount. He described the beauty of the northern lights dancing in colours in the glacial, arctic Yukon skies. "The temperatures were so cold," he said, "my pee froze before hitting the snow." Enthralled, I couldn't stay away.

Growing up in New Brunswick, I'd been to Prince Edward Island and Nova Scotia. I visited Disney World in Florida twice. The first time, I was seventeen years old when my girlfriend invited me to join her family. I went again with my fiancé, hoping to salvage our relationship. It didn't work. After my breakup, I needed to escape, and going to college allowed me to get away. I didn't know I would get so wrapped up in Oso's adventures. It felt like I had been living in a bubble for twenty-two years. I loved my life, but through his words, I discovered an entire new world out there. My fiancé and I had argued sometimes because I complained of being bored. We usually stayed home and watched TV.

A part of me I had yet to meet longed for adventures.

My basement apartment became an open house for my classmates. My roommate abandoned her course and moved back home, so I lived alone. One friend often showed up, and we worked on our math together and then we smoked pot or hash. I knew a few people who smoked cannabis, but I had never tried it until college. I didn't ask questions when my friend pulled it out of his bag. It would be another thirty-five years before it became legal in Canada.

After Oso and I agreed to be friends, we turned into buddies. We spent a lot of time together in school. On my twenty-third birthday in January 1985, the entire class went ice fishing. Oso drove many of us on his old bus. The outfitters pulled us on sleighs attached to their snowmobiles. We parked our frozen butts on benches in the middle of the lake, where they dug fishing holes. Oso brought his large husky dog, and he attached it to a sleigh. Someone snuck Baileys, and we poured the brown liquid in our coffee mugs. I enjoyed ice fishing, although none of us captured any fish. The ice glistened under the bright, sunny, crisp skies. Oso offered me a ride back to shore on his sleigh. I swayed in front of him as he yelled, "Mush, mush." The chilly wind in my face mingled with the booze inside me. I snuggled against him.

"Do you want to come over to my place tonight?" I asked. "I will give you a birthday gift." It would be our second date, and I resolved to let him kiss me again. He appeared at my apartment with flowers and chocolate. He later admitted to me he expected to get laid that evening. I was not a virgin, but I'd only had sex with my fiancé. I have to love a man to have sex with him. Oso was a gentleman about it. We kissed again without taking it any further. This time, I knew what I was doing, and I wasn't drunk. I lay in bed, a huge smile on my face.

We secretly dated. I didn't want anyone to know I was flirting with an older man. What would my friends and family think about me dating a thirty-four-year-old man with three kids? They had ample gossip material on me already, no need for more. Plus, I was not ready to meet his kids. I didn't expect it to amount to anything, but I relished the thrill of a new relationship. A relationship that seemed wrong, which made it highly exciting.

Toward the end of the first year of college, I came home to find my apartment door bolted from the inside. I hesitantly knocked on the upstairs door. Plopped on the stairs, my landlady was waiting for me. I knew her as a sweet elderly woman, but also prim and proper. She avoided my eyes when she handed me a piece of paper.

"We do not appreciate the funny smells coming from your apartment. The other day, you held a party, and we saw a guy peeing on our lawn. We drafted a list of house rules and you will follow them."

No more parties; no more visits after 10pm; you will inform us every time you go away for the weekend; you will keep your outside light on all the time so we can see who goes in and who goes out.

I've never liked conflicts, and I have no problems with authority or adhering to rules. But this time, I seized the opportunity to move out. I had a plan.

I called Oso, and I asked him if I could live on his bus for the remaining month of school. He heartily agreed. I packed my car with all my personal stuff, and I travelled home for the weekend. Of course, I hadn't told my family anything about my relationship with Oso, although I mentioned I was moving into the bus for a month in order to save rent money. I did not tell them about the circumstances of my moving out.

I turned into Oso's driveway. He stood outside, waiting for me. My heart was pounding, treading into unknown territory. I loved the idea of living on the bus. When I was fifteen years old, my brother built a home in Memramcook. Across from his land, there was a vast open field with a grey, rusted camper rotting in the corner. I remember wishing I could live there when I grew up. Oso grinned as he opened the rear door. He had cleaned the inside and had prepared a bed on the floor for me. He stuck an adorable teddy bear between the covers, and I melted from the romantic gesture. I was falling for him, and I tried not to overthink it. My parents taught me to follow my heart, and although my brain was very uncertain about this one, my heart betrayed me.

The June weather made it pleasant to stay and eat outside. I placed my food in his refrigerator and I used his kitchen to cook my meals. I've always appreciated my alone time, and I felt safe on the bus with him nearby. We kept our relationship from the kids until we knew for sure where it was heading. They hid behind the kitchen curtains and peeped at me through the windows. I waved at them. They shied away after throwing me a fleeting smile.

Oso often joined me, and we studied together. We'd often drop everything to make love in the back of the bus.

Other times, we pored over our material in the house. If the children's chattering disturbed us, he'd holler at them to shut up. I'd cringe. My dad only raised his voice at me once. He was talking to my sister at the table one day and I kept pestering him. Exasperated, he said, "Stop that!" I was eight years old. I froze, and then I lowered my head so he would not see my tears.

"Why are you so harsh with them?" I asked Oso.

He answered, "They have to learn to be quiet."

I smiled at them, hoping the affection in my eyes softened the verbal blows. Jessi had turned eleven in January. She was tall for her age, while her younger brother, Chris, was short and logged a few extra pounds. They seemed to get along well, and I over-heard them whispering after their dad ordered them to be quiet. Soon the noise level climbed up again, and Oso bellowed, "Shut up." I ignored the warning bells in my stomach. Of course, it was tough. He was raising kids alone.

We completed the first year of school, and I drove home for the summer. Camilla applied to a university in Quebec City, and she had to find an apartment. I offered to go with her, and we packed our brother's tent and headed out toward Quebec City, an eight-hour drive. I suggested we visit my college friends along the way. Not wanting her to realize it was Oso I wished to see, I arranged for us to have lunch with several of my friends. Oso and I sneaked looks and intimate touches under the table. I assumed our relationship was still a secret, although my friend Joanne knew about us. I'm now convinced the entire class knew.

Two hours before Quebec City, we stopped in a campground to put up the tent. We emptied the bag and its contents on the ground to realize the tent poles were missing. Our camping neighbours lent us a rope, and we tied the roof of the tent to nearby trees. The next morning found us trapped under the fallen canopy. We giggled, and since we had also neglected to pack juice or coffee, we drank a beer with our breakfast.

In September 1985, I drove to Bathurst for the second year of college. I was nowhere ready to move in with Oso and his kids, so I rented another apartment for the year. We continued dating. He introduced me to Cat Stevens' music, and we got stoned and made love while he murmured in my ear that I was his Hard Headed Woman.

The Dinner

In my family, dinner was a special time. When the entire family was home, there would be eight of us sharing a meal. My dad was always at the head of the table with my mom by his side. Gilles sat at the opposite end; he finished anything we left on our plates. We used to tease him and call him the human garbage can. Camilla and I sat across from my other two brothers. Marianne, secured in her highchair, snuggled between my parents.

Oso invited me for dinner to meet his children. I sat beside him on the rudimentary bench in his kitchen. Two pairs of brownish, inquisitive eyes gawked at me from across the table. I'd met them before on a few school excursions and during the time I lived in the bus, but I was now facing them as the girlfriend. I squirmed on the wood bench Oso had built to fit the table.

I observed the children eating in silence. I wondered if they, too, always sat in the same spot around the dinner table. Oso had likely warned them to be on their best behaviour. They seemed almost reluctant to speak. What were they like? Still confused about my feelings toward Oso, I prayed this was a good idea, meeting the kids. I cared about him – hell, I think I'd fallen in love with him – but he came with not one, not two, but three kids, even if his youngest daughter lived thousands of kilometres away. I was apprehensive, and yet...

Oso had an outspoken personality, and he was not afraid to voice his opinions. It was such a contrast to anyone I knew. He could be intense and coarse around the edges. For reasons I did not fully grasp, it fascinated me. I doubted my parents would be thrilled. Most Acadians are humble and reserved, at least in my family. My dad and I went to the wharf once to buy lobsters from the fishermen. We had to push our way through a crowd, as they only sell a limited amount to onlookers, needing to reach their quota. Once, a few Quebecois were ahead of us, and we weren't confident we would reach the boat. I told my dad we would have to force our way in. He replied, "Yes, but they are Dobermans and we are Poodles."

Oso beamed and said he invented the recipe he expected us to eat. He called it glop, and I understood why when he dropped a generous spoonful on my plate. He blended ground beef and a brown sauce together and boiled it for a while in a pot on the kitchen stove. It looked like a mix between a stew and chunks of oatmeal. I bravely took a bite, and I exhaled a sigh of relief when I discovered it was edible. The taste was between an original version of a hamburger helper meal and spaghetti sauce. The kids ate slowly, and I smiled at them, hoping to win their confidence and friendship. I could tell Oso was nervous; he was trying to have everything perfect. He even had a bouquet of autumn wildflowers in the centre of the table. I suspected Jessi picked them outside, where they grew plentifully around the house. They spoke politely, saying yes please and no thank you. Jessi wore a delicate pink blouse and blue jeans. Chris had a black-and-white chequered shirt with black corduroy pants held up with vivid red suspenders.

I gobbled a few bites before asking them about their friends and school. They answered my questions, a twinge of a smile on their lips, but they did not ask me anything. I loved their thick medium brown hair and, of course, brown eyes like their father. Jessi's eyes were a dark, beautiful brown, whereas Chris' were brownish with a green tinge. Her hair was lighter than Oso's, and she wore it shoulder length. They both had his full eyelashes and bushy eyebrows. Their faces were softer than Oso's, still innocent. Jessi's look was curious and kind, while Chris's eyes sparkled mischievously. I noticed a few freckles on their noses, and a tender feeling swelled over me.

After a pleasant, although slightly awkward, dinner, the kids got up to clear the table and wash the dishes. I offered to help, but Oso would not let me, stating it was their responsibility. Chris had to stand on a chair to dry the plates. My heart reached out to him. Our parents did not give my sisters and me many chores while growing up, preferring that we spend our time studying and playing sports. My brothers complained because they had chores, telling us girls our parents spoiled us. I prefer to think we were pampered.

Oso and I watched television in the living room. I listened to the kids whispering to themselves, "She's so tiny." An immediate glow of warmth overflowed my heart, and I hoped they liked me too. I couldn't see myself becoming an instant mother. These kids had a biological mother, even if she lived across the country. I had no idea when they had seen her last. I didn't dare question Oso about it too often. His lips hardened, and gloomy shadows filled his eyes whenever I brought up her name.

After the dishes were done, the kids relaxed with us before heading to their room to do their homework. "I think they like you," Oso said. "They seem sweet," I answered. Around ten pm, he told them it was bedtime. They kissed him on the cheek and grinned at me before bolting upstairs.

I'd always dreamed of having a big family, although I was not the little girl who fantasized about a huge, fancy, white dress wedding. My plan was simple: I would grow up, fall in love, get married, have six kids and stay home to care for them while my husband worked. That's how my parents did it, and it turned out well for them. Of course, their path was filled with bumps and detours, but love overcomes all, doesn't it?

In grade seven, I decided I'd become a veterinarian. I loved animals, and I yearned for a pet. I told Bert, and he said, "A vet, hey? Do you realize what kind of work vets do in the country? Your arm up to your elbow in a cow's ass." Well, I scratched veterinarian from my list. Then I informed him I wanted to be an archeologist, and he replied, "Well, forget about having a family. You'll be in faraway places in the middle of nowhere with nobody." Okay then, scrape that off my list as well. I then decided I would work with mentally challenged people.

At midnight, I kissed Oso goodbye and drove back to my apartment. I lay awake for hours. Can I do this? Do I want to do this? To answer these questions, I needed to understand what *this* was. What does it mean to become a full-time stepparent? I loved their dad, and I knew he adored me. He insisted I was the most beautiful woman in the world, and he was nuts about me. When he looked at me, I saw the love and wonder. I adored being loved by him. I almost felt like a groupie whose idol had chosen me. But was I ready for this? I'd broken up with guys before, when I'd realized it was not a solid fit. But this was different. He had kids. From the beginning, I figured that if I committed, it would be forever.

I used to love babysitting Marianne. I'd offer to my parents to stay with her so they could attend my brother's hockey games on Friday nights. We worked on assorted projects, such as melting wax into candles or building cute cabins out of popsicle sticks. I'd babysat a few times for my cousin, but this was not babysitting. This was not a Friday evening project. This was a full-time, permanent, non-refundable, long-haul career. This was daunting. But I felt the indomitable strength of youth. I could do this. This was exciting.

I watched the clock tick away, then I suddenly sat upright. Oso was twelve years older than me. His oldest daughter, Jessi, was twelve years younger than me.

Montreal

I spent most weekends at Oso's house. The kids and I got acquainted, and we got along well. Twice a week, I remained at my apartment for my alone time. I finally admitted our relationship to my family.

My parents' reaction was as I expected, loving but wary. My dad's father had four kids with his first wife before she died in childbirth. He then married my grandmother, and they had seven additional kids, including my dad. My father felt his dad preferred his kids from his initial marriage, and he feared that if Oso and I had children, he might do the same. My mom's mother passed when my mom was eighteen years old. Her father quickly remarried, and my mother was not overly fond of his second wife. Maybe Oso's kids would not appreciate me either.

I tried to reassure them as best I could, and I promised to bring the family for a visit soon.

I liked the kids, and I knew they trusted me. It began with subtle behaviours – Chris leaning over me to read a paper, gently resting his head on my shoulder; Jessi picking a bouquet of wildflowers for me on her way home from school; Chris drawing a picture for me to put on the refrigerator; Jessi asking me to sign her homework. Then the kiss happened. Every evening, when their dad ordered them to bed, they'd get up and give him a goodnight kiss on the cheek. They smiled at me and ran upstairs.

Bidding her dad goodnight, Jessi kissed him, turned around, and shyly planted a quick kiss on my right cheek. She tried to appear casual, as if it was part of the routine. She grinned and bolted upstairs. Chris did not hesitate to follow suit. I glanced at Oso with wonderment in my eyes. He beamed.

Before I started grade one, I already loved learning. Once in school, I'd hurry home after class and ask Camilla if she wanted to play school. I would then teach her everything I studied that day. When she began grade one, the teacher wanted to place her in second grade since she'd already learned everything. My parents thought it wise to keep her in first grade so we would not be in competition.

Oso had limited patience in helping the kids with their homework, so I offered to take over. He gladly surrendered. Jessi liked school, and she learned quickly, so homework was fun for us. We giggled while studying algebra, a subject she found useless. She preferred English; she loved to compose poems and stories. I offered her my cookbook, as it still had many blank pages in it. She treasured it and scribbled on the cover, *If any little brother of mine reads my diary, he will have a broken neck.*

I still needed my recipes, but she didn't want me to read her journal. So, I asked her if I could get it back. She reluctantly handed it over after tearing up the intimate pages. I then offered her what I was hiding behind my back. She shrieked with delight. I had bought her a diary that locked with a key. She snatched it and hugged me.

Chris had a learning disability. He mixed letters and con- fused numbers. His attention span was also very poor. I had never heard of dyslexia. I'm not convinced the term existed yet. Learning was laborious for him, but I noticed he loved to draw, and he excelled at it. He also wanted to learn to cook. I tried to incorporate art and creativity into his homework. I also showed both kids how to do housework and self-hygiene. Although Oso was strict about the kids pulling their own weight with chores, his years in the Yukon had left him with cleaning standards well below mine. I've always appreciated a neat, uncluttered house. I tend to not get attached to material things. When I had moved into the bus, I had asked him if I could clean the bathroom. "The toilet stinks," I'd said.

He'd replied, "Well, just flush it."

Oso grew up in Montreal and his family lived there, so we travelled to the big city for Christmas. It was my first time in Montreal, my first time away from home for the holidays, and my first time meeting his family.

The kids were excited to see their grandparents and cousins. We took Oso's car to drive from Bathurst to Montreal. I'd sold my Datsun sports car because my cash was getting sparse. We drove the nine hundred kilometres' trip in one day, arriving in Montreal after sunset.

We brought a few gifts, handmade stuff the kids built. It was fun to see them so cheerful and chatty; they fidgeted in the car. "Are we there yet?" They described their grand-papa and grand-maman and all their cousins. I had no idea what to expect, and I tried to share their enthusiasm. Jessi and Chris cared for their relatives, so they must be okay. I held my breath as Oso swerved in heavy traffic such as I'd never seen before. Vehicles rushed around us, honking and screeching tires. The noise of the city, even in the winter, blew my mind. The city was alive. I strained my neck to peer up at the buildings. They seemed to reach the clouds. Many forms of graffiti marked many of the building facades. Montreal boasted a population of almost three million people. In comparison, the entire province of New Brunswick didn't even have one million habitants. I grew up in a village of five thousand people. To say I felt overwhelmed is an understatement.

We approached Oso's parents' house. The kids became agitated, and this time, Oso did not rebuke them. With all the hustle and bustle of the city, I forgot, for a few minutes, my cautious anticipation about meeting Oso's parents. Would they like me? Would I like them?

Oso parked the car in front of the family home, and Jessi and Chris bolted to the door. He smiled at me, "Are you ready?" When he'd told his family that he was dating a young Acadian woman, his oldest sister became furious and scolded him, alleging he was going to destroy me.

"Why would she suggest such a thing?"

"I don't have a clue," he said. I'd assumed it was because he had kids.

I nodded to Oso, and I opened the car door. He wrapped his arm around my shoulders as we wandered to the house. The kids were already inside. The door was wide open. A horde of people besieged us. Oso's parents and his two sisters dragged me inside and fluttered around me like I was a circus clown. Oso's mom grabbed my shoulders, laughing. "Cacarisse (her favourite curse word), you're almost as short as me. Come in, come in." She kissed me on both cheeks, leaving vivid red lipstick smiles on my face. Oso laughed, and he proudly introduced me, his new girlfriend. "Oh my, what a delightful accent you have," they said. The French in Quebec differs from the French in New Brunswick.

His parents reminded me of a couple from an original gangster movie. His dad stood tall, strong, and proud. He grasped my hand and shook it vigorously. "Welcome, welcome." His thick moustache tickled when he kissed me. He passed his hand through his generous, wavy black hair. I could tell where Oso got his handsome looks. He had gained wealth in the construction business, and he now appreciated his retirement. His fingers were constantly clutching a glass of whiskey or liquor. Oso's mom was short, even smaller than me. Her laugh vibrated in the house as she grabbed my shoulders.

I adored her reddish curly hair, although I presumed a recent visit to the hairdresser. Her pretty red and white dress matched her red lipstick. She smoked one cigarette after the other, often lighting her new cigarette with the one she was about to crush. I'd never met anyone like her before.

Oso's mom was tiny and vociferous. A person easy to love. She blurted out whatever crossed her mind, and often, it related to sex. A few years later, I almost ducked under the picnic table at the beach when guys cruised by and my sweet, little, old mother-in-law, with her shiny red lipstick, shouted, "Look! He wears it to the left!" Toward the end of her life, when dementia imprisoned her mind, she'd often lose her dentures. She'd laugh about it and claim she could suck easier without teeth.

Oso grew up with two older sisters, and like their parents, they drank hard, partied solid, and loved their family ferociously. There were nephews and nieces to meet as well. They soon pressed a glass of wine in my hand, and I felt at ease, surrounded by such an endearing family. Jessi and Chris ran off with their cousins.

I'd told Oso I looked forward to meeting his family. But I also had three separate requests: ride the Metro, see a prostitute, and watch a stripper dance. My wishes appalled my mom, but for a naïve country girl who had no real-life experience, these lifestyles intrigued me greatly. Oso chuckled when he mentioned this to his family. Even today, when I travel, I try to get off the main tourist track and greet the people in their environment.

The following night, we drove to a Metro station. The former mayor of Montreal, Jean Drapeau, inaugurated the Metro in the 1960s. It has continued to expand, with now over sixty stations covering almost seventy kilometres.

We parked the car and wrestled our way through a crowd of people. Men and women pushed ahead, knowing where they had to go and how to get there. As we strolled down to reach the Metro tunnel, the many noises infiltrated my senses. Sounds echo differently underground. People hustling, scrambling to catch the train. Buskers played their guitar or sang with a hat in front of them. But it was the rip-roaring sound of the engine that caused my stomach to flutter. As we reached lower platforms, my nose picked up an orchestra of smells, a distinct mix of oil, sweat, heat, and humidity. I peered at Oso and his sister, and they both appeared unfazed, so I figured this must be typical.

I heard the train coming from a significant distance, well before I saw it. The entire platform vibrated with energy as the train's electrifying noise approached from the dark tunnel. My eyes bulged, looking at the sharp light raging toward us. People lined up on the side, ready to bolt into the wagon when the doors snap open and then slam shut. The lengthy train appeared at a phenomenal speed, and I watched in trepidation as the conductor stopped it in time for the crowd to pack in, elbowing their way against the horde coming out.

These sights, smells, and sounds invaded me like a magnificent culinary experience. I grinned and clapped my hands, causing Oso to laugh. We hopped into the wagon, and as the train picked up speed, I spotted a man slouched over a green garbage can, rummaging through its contents. Having been raised in a small village, the closest to a destitute person I had come across was a hitchhiker on the road across from my parents' house. Barely a teenager, I peered out the kitchen window and noticed a stranger with his thumb out trying to hitch a ride. His worn-out black coat flapped in the wind. Long grey hair hid parts of his face. A person I'd never seen in our peaceful village. "He must be hungry," I told Marianne. I prepared him a grilled cheese sandwich. I hoped not to humiliate him by bringing him food. However, before the cheese melted, a car stopped and picked him up. Marianne shook her head. "Liette, always trying to save the world."

The train jumped forward. I could not save this man either. I glimpsed his shaggy beard when he turned slightly. He clung to an iron trolley packed with what looked like all his belongings. He didn't pay attention to the trains or the surrounding people. Before we disappeared into the tunnel, I saw him pluck an unfinished sandwich, partially wrapped in paper, and stuff it into his wide pocket. My stomach churned, and I collapsed in my seat, fighting to control the tears from rolling down my face. All the exhilaration of the Metro evaporated in an instant. Oso and his sister didn't bat an eye.

We disembarked the train and reversed direction to return to our initial station. The hungry man was gone, but my heart was heavy. I couldn't imagine what it was like to not have a home, to not have a mother who prepared our meals every day. I didn't understand why someone had to live like that. There must be programs in place to support these people. The beauty of the city quickly lost its appeal.

We left the Metro station, and I sat in the car as we drove to a neighbourhood known for prostitutes. Oso and his sister were used to seeing homeless people. I'm not sure they understood why my heart hurt.

I noticed her first, a young prostitute, a girl, standing on a deserted Montreal Street corner. She wore a short, tightly fitted black skirt and black tights with high-heeled boots. Her thin jacket, partially covering her flimsy silvery blouse, was open to reveal her cleavage. Her fake bleached hair swirled in the hostile breeze, and she hugged herself while rubbing her arms. The temperature had dipped well below freezing, and snowflakes danced in the air. She shivered and turned her pretty face away from the icy gusts of wind. She worked hard to appear sensuous to the indifferent men speeding by. I broke down, and I wept. Oso squeezed my hand.

We ended the evening in a strip club. Although I managed not to cry, I'd seen enough.

Oso's sister hugged me when we got home. "Welcome to Montreal." I lay awake for hours that night, questioning my judgment but also trying to understand the different realities I'd witnessed. Why did I want to see a prostitute and a stripper? People usually go to Montreal for a hockey game, to tour the botanical gardens or, like my sister Camilla, to enjoy shopping. What did I expect to gain? From reading books and watching movies, I'd built this romantic notion in my mind of prostitutes and strippers. These girls, did they practice these jobs by choice? They could do like the old man in the station, dig for food in dumpsters. Is that better? Is that worse? Where did he sleep at night? Could they not attend school and work at a better job? I didn't understand all the complexities of mental health issues or family abuse. I'd grown up with approximately five television stations and no internet. My upbringing had shielded me from the inhumanities of the world.

On Christmas Eve, everyone dressed up. Oso looked dashing in his brown jacket and pants, white shirt, and black tie. Jessi wore her favourite striped blue and purple dress and proudly sported massive red earrings. She had her hair cut for the occasion, and she looked stunning, with her high cheekbones. Chris put on his nicest large red sweater and baggy black pants. Everyone insisted he looked swell. It warmed my heart to see them so happy. I wore the unique dress I owned, a black and blue three-quarter length dress. I completed the look with a beaded necklace and black earrings. Nobody mentioned going to midnight mass, and although I usually attended church on Christmas Eve, I didn't dare say anything. After a delicious, rich dinner with the entire family, cousins and all, the music resounded in the house. And oh, how these people loved to dance. The decorated house came alive with music and booze. Oso twisted and twirled with his two sisters to the blaring sound of disco. I'd never been much of a dancer, but I admired Oso swinging his sisters across the floor. During a break from dancing, he relaxed across from me in the living room. His eyes wet, he looked at me and mouthed, "I love you." My cheeks turned a crimson red.

Oso's father disappeared for a few minutes and then showed up, dressed as Santa Claus.

The kids delighted in spending time with their grandparents and cousins. Oso's family did not speak much English, but Jessi and Chris grew up speaking that language. Their biological mom was an Anglophone and since they moved to Newfoundland and Labrador after the Yukon, Oso had always spoken to them in English. I am bilingual, so it was not an issue for me. Both kids attended French immersion in New Brunswick. Despite the language barrier, they adored their relatives, and they had a splendid time. Oso mocked his sisters when they tried to communicate in English. His oldest sister smirked and showed him the finger. "Fuck you, Jack" is about all she could muster.

I fell in love with Oso's family and their feistiness. They cursed at each other as easily as they confessed their love. The family worshiped Oso's dad. I didn't understand why. He could be ruthless with his words, especially when he had a few bottles of booze in him. He mostly directed his strong words at his wife. But then he'd shed a few tears while speaking about his mom dying when he was a child. A brute with a tender heart.

The family danced and partied for a week. My folks always get together at Christmas, but we never dance. My family plays cards. You can always spot a few decks of cards at a Cormier reunion. After each family get-together, my mom says, "I'm so happy, everyone got along." We tease her because there have never been any fights.

Following a week of eating, drinking, and partying, we drove home, exhausted but filled with holiday love. We arrived in Bathurst to discover we no longer had a driveway. The snow had piled in its place. Oso parked on the street and tried to step out, but his dancing caught up with him, and his back froze. We crawled on top of the snowbank to the house where he remained on the floor, moaning. The kids and I shoveled until late in the night so we could squeeze the car into the driveway. I made a game of it – how many shovels of snow can you throw in five minutes? How far can you pitch it? It granted us some courage after such a long day.

The Family's Dramatic Side

Jessi and I were both born in January, me the twelfth, her the thir-tieth. A few days after she turned twelve, I stepped into the kitch-en to find both her and her father weeping. "What's wrong?" Grinning through his tears, Oso said, "Jessi started her period. My little girl is a woman now." Wait, what? I mean, I knew it was going to happen one day, but now? I was not ready for this.

She was twelve years old. What did she know? What did I know about educating her on such matters? I began my period at the same age. And, yes, it is a big deal. When I caught sight of the blood on my white cotton panties, I got this uneasy feel-ing in my stomach. Relieved to be upstairs, I yelled from the top of the stairwell, "Mom, my panties are red." Of course, she had explained the menstruation cycle to us. She said it was the most natural thing in the world for a woman to menstruate each month. I remember her saying that if we didn't have our peri-ods, it would not be healthy. Still, my face must've matched the colour of my panties when she told me where the pads were. It's overwhelming to realize one is going to bleed between the legs for a week every month for the next thirty or forty years. She described how babies develop inside our uterus, but not how they are conceived. That discussion happened in school. The priest showed up one day when we were barely teenagers and displayed slides of the woman's reproductive system, explaining the ovulation process. Then he ordered the girls to exit the classroom. The guys remained in there for an additional thirty minutes. I was nosy and jealous. When they finally walked out, I'd demand to know what had transpired in there. But they sneered at us, *we know something you don't.* I learned about sex in a magazine I discovered in my cousins' bedroom.

Jessi and Oso both leaned on the counter, one at each end of the kitchen. I looked at her.

"Do you understand what is happening?"

"Yes, Dad's previous girlfriend described it to me." She lowered her head, barely looking at me.

"Do you have anything for the blood?"

"No," she replied.

I smiled gently at her. "Come upstairs with me." I asked her if she preferred a pad or a tampon.

"Pads are gross," she said. I tore the cover off a tampon and told her she needed to insert it in her vagina.

"You can crouch or sit on the toilet. You introduce the bigger end inside your vagina until the applicator is fully in. You pull out the applicator, being careful to leave the short cord hanging out." She stared at me, her eyes huge and round.

"Does it hurt?"

"It can initially, but you can rub Vaseline jelly on the applicator to help slide it in."

"How long do I leave it in there?"

"Maybe two or three hours. You can decide, depending on how much you bleed." I handed her the box of tampons and I grinned at her. "Are you okay?"

"Yes," she said, "I'm glad you're here."

Once in a while, I took the train to visit my family. One weekend while I was away, Oso prepared to go out. He was in the bathroom getting ready and he splashed on cologne. Jessi asked him where he was going. He explained he was going out to a club. She replied, "That is not fair to Liette, is it?" Even at the youthful age of twelve, she was concerned with right and wrong. She was constantly reading self-help books from the library and writing journals. Much later, when she became a mom, she'd fill a thermos full of coffee and take her daughter downtown to offer cups to homeless people during the holidays.

In early spring of 1986, I arrived home from shopping (I called it home now), and I found Oso pacing the floor. He and Chris had a fight and Chris was gone. He was ten years old, and he'd run away.

As a kid, I'd run away from home a few times when my mom refused to bend to my demands. I'd climb up my favourite crab apple tree behind the house and sit on a branch, hidden from view. I'd wait for what felt like hours. *She will be so worried; she will grant me my wishes.* I'd come down and I'd walk into the kitchen, my head high, expecting her apologies and her begging for forgiveness. She either had not noticed I had gone or pretended she didn't. I'd be disappointed but then shrugged it off. I learned early on that I could not manipulate my mother.

We did get lost in the woods once. When darkness engulfed the forest, my parents organized a search party. I was with my cousin and my brother, Bert. He professed to know where we were, but when dusk fell and the shadows threatened, I doubted and became anxious. After two hours of bleak darkness, we heard shouts and saw lights in the distance. Our parents and neighbours turned the car's headlights toward the forest and yelled and honked. I had picked wildflowers for my mom, and I hid them behind my back to surprise her. When we finally made it home, she was very relieved but also very pissed. While she gave Bert a loud thrashing, I discreetly threw the flowers under the deck.

Chris had been missing for three hours. I felt confident that he would be back soon. However, when the darkness settled in, we began the search. Jessi helped us. We looked near the house, calling his name, but to no avail. Chris was a mischievous kid with a heart of gold. When Oso and Jessi fought, she yelled back at him. When Oso and Chris argued, he winced and holed up in his body. Oso suspected he might be hiding in an old barn not too far on a neighbour's land. He suggested we let him be and retire to bed. Chris would prefer to come back on his own terms. Oso left a note on the door, *Welcome home, my son, I love you and all is forgiven.* He fell asleep right away, but my eyes and my ears remained open. I imagined a frightened young boy sheltering in a barn, in the dark, and I craved to rush to him. He was just a kid, likely terrified by the darkness but also scared of what his dad's reaction might be when he came home. At three o'clock in the morning, the stairs creaked. He gently closed his bedroom door, and I struggled to imagine what he was going through. Should I get up and go hug him, tell him it's okay? I'd never been a parent before; I had no clue how to handle this situation. I stayed in bed.

As specified on the note, the next morning his dad hugged him, and nobody alluded to the fight.

I don't remember what the fight was about. I'd noticed that Oso could get upset about petty stuff like the dishes not being washed on time or the kids spending too long in front of the television. If they disobeyed him, he'd get mad, and he'd scream at them. He grounded them often. I imagined it was difficult to raise kids as a single parent, and I didn't dare step in. I grappled to determine my role within the family.

My parents invited us for Easter dinner. I was nervous about them meeting Oso, recognizing they were already skeptical. The kids were respectful and reserved. They played in the sunroom, and Jessi drew a gorgeous Easter card for my mom. My mom and dad stayed cordial with Oso, and the evening progressed better than I had hoped. As we drove home, I felt peace. Everything was going to be okay.

Toward the end of college, we applied for jobs in our related fields. We quickly realized that environmental positions were rare. I posted my CV to Environment Canada to become a National Park interpreter. They called and asked me if I was interested in a weather-related position. I jumped on the opportunity to apply for a federal job. Since I knew nothing about meteorology, I asked my physics teacher to teach me. He devoted the afternoon to preparing me for the exam, coaching me on waves and lows and high-pressure systems. I owe him a debt of gratitude because thanks to his help, I succeeded in both the exam and the interview. When the results came in, Tony, the representative for the department, informed me I was number thirteen on a list of twenty-five Canadian candidates. The list would remain active for the next eighteen months. When my turn came up, they would telephone me. Although the environment course did not cover meteorology in its curriculum, my mom told her friends that I was going to broadcast the weather on CBC radio. For her, environment meant Environment Canada, and Environment Canada meant the weather forecast. Mothers always know.

Oso and I discussed moving in together after college. "The kids have loved and lost a lot of mothers," he said. "If you move in with us, you have to promise to never leave because they can't go through another heartbreak, another goodbye." He added, "I can't promise you much, but I promise you a roller coaster ride."

When school ended, I drove back to my parents' house, not ready to make the huge step yet. I needed to speak to them, justify my decision. The truth was, I was terrified to tell them.

My mom told my dad that the relationship would end after college. "Just give her time," she said. However, the telephone continued to ring.

Oso begged me to come back. "Jessi and Chris miss you, and so do I." I missed them. I'd grown attached, and the thought of them missing me was painful. I doubted I was in love with Oso, but I certainly was in awe of him. He had a hold over me I did not understand. However, the idea of confronting my parents caused my heart to beat faster. Oso called, and I stalled. I knew they hoped it was over between us and that I was home for good. I could sense it.

"I need to tell you something," I said as we relaxed in the living room. My mom and dad were ardent Catholics, and living together before marriage was a sin. They had met Oso, and they were not sure what to make of him. He seemed nice enough, but he was older and had kids. What were his intentions?

"I'm going to see Oso." There, I said it. I looked them in the eyes while they stared at me, dumbfounded. They did not want me to leave. I listened as they attempted to talk me out of it. They respected our decisions, trusting they raised us well.

But my dad frowned and gently squeezed my shoulder. "Raising children is a lot of work, and it's even harder when they are not yours."

My mom added, "Maybe he's just hoping for a mother to raise his kids."

"He's had several women in his life, and it never lasted. Maybe something is wrong with him," said my dad.

I hated to see the concern in his eyes; he was worried about his little girl.

I grew up with loving parents whose most precious gift to their children was to love each other for over sixty-five years until my dad's death from Alzheimer's at eighty-nine. I imagined a similar life for myself, a devoted family with several kids.

My mom always keeps an open mind on life. I get my curiosity and love of people from her. She is alert and curious, and she asks me questions about my friends, even those she has never met. My mother is a wise person. She had us drinking lots of water before the health community preached about the eight cups of water per day. She blamed (and still does) most of our illnesses on either not drinking enough water or our body's response to stress. A superb listener, she's been advising us all her life, *You have to zip your lips and just listen. Do not offer recipes or advice. People will discover their own way.*"

My dad was my hero. He was an introvert and often set in his ways. But he was affectionate where my mom was not. I recall sitting at the table as a teenager, working on my homework. He would lovingly grip my shoulders, saying he loved me. He was usually the one to order Camilla and me to bed. We'd ignore his commands until he'd had enough and would chase us upstairs, running on all fours. We'd squeal, laugh and dive under the cover before he could catch us. "A story, a story," we'd plead.

"Okay," he'd say, "which one?" We'd answer, *Boisseau de Sel.* It was the same story he'd told us the night before, and the night before that one, and the night before that one. "Don't you want another one?" he'd ask.

"No, that one." He would sigh and give us a resigned look. Then he'd jump right in, altering his voice, acting the parts, and we'd hang on his every word.

He would tuck us in. Before closing the door, he'd say, "Now, girls, be quiet and go to sleep." Of course, as soon as the door closed, we'd sit in bed and whisper to each other.

If only my parents could see what I saw, they would understand the extent of the love Oso had for me.

I also felt that their own experience of having parents who had remarried clouded their judgment. I valued their opinion, but Oso needed me.

Pretending a confidence I did not feel, I packed a few summer clothes and a few personal items in an old blue suitcase. My parents drove me to the station, and as the train left, I waved to them, choosing to ignore their sad smiles. My stomach fluttered as I headed for this new chapter in my life.

I exhaled a sigh of relief when the seat next to me remained empty. Normally, I love to meet people and chat, but that day, I needed to be alone with my thoughts. A new adventure. In three hours, I would go from being a careless and happy daughter to becoming a full-time partner to Oso and stepmom to two pre-teenagers.

The train pulled out of the Moncton station, the nearest station to our village. Memramcook is within twenty kilometres of Moncton, in the countryside where the taxes are lower, the people are friendly, and the sunsets are spectacular. I'd always grin and wave back when I'd go for a walk and anyone driving by honked and waved.

The train picked up speed. I could hardly wait to see the look of joy on Oso's face when I stepped off the wagon. It didn't occur to me that I was excited about his reaction, not mine. I settled in my seat for the three-hour ride to my new life.

The train stopped at its final destination in Bathurst, New Brunswick. I clutched my blue luggage, and I hopped onto the platform. Oso stood there, an enormous grin on his face. I noticed he'd combed his hair and trimmed his beard. Although the sun was blazing, he wore his usual blue jeans and a lumberjack shirt. I smiled and hugged him. He gave me a splendid bouquet of twelve red roses and grabbed my suitcase. "Let's go home."

Stepparenting

I've always enjoyed camping, and I appreciated living on the bus...for a short while. I was a minimalist before minimalism was in vogue. Most days, the kids played outside. Oso would not let them hang inside during the day. He worried they could get in trouble. I wondered, could they not get in greater trouble locked outside all day? I kept my mouth shut. It was neither my job nor my place to raise these kids. Jessi had many friends, and she often lingered at their houses, but Chris, always a loner, disappeared all day, doing whatever a ten-year-old can do to entertain himself.

I adjusted to my role. I picked up a part-time job at the local drugstore, and Oso entered into a few contract jobs in forestry. Work in our fields was sparse, and we considered leaving the province to seek employment in Quebec or Ontario.

I honestly hadn't given stepparenting much thought. Although the idea of moving in with a man and his two kids was daunting, I figured I would wing it. I was plowing my way into this new chapter of my life, giddy with excitement. I often blurt out what is on my mind without thinking. Not much of a filter,

Camilla once said. So, I jumped right in. I dove into the deep end of a pool, barely knowing how to swim. How hard could it be?

I'd been living stress and rent free with my parents since I'd come back from my initial time in college. I kept my room cleaned, and I did my laundry, but that was pretty well the extent of my contribution at home. After three years of working at the drugstore, I could do my job blindfolded. I devoted my spare time to my fiancé and my friends.

During the one and a half years Oso and I dated, I'd gotten to know the kids. We'd become comfortable with each other, and I wasn't worried about getting along with them.

The impact was brutal, the learning curve more than steep. I had to learn to live in a cramped space with three other people and a huge husky dog. The vehicle measured slightly over two meters in width and less than seven meters in length. Since the curtain divided it in half and most of the back half was full, four people shared a space of just over seven and a half square meters. This space included the table, the counters with all our kitchen supplies, and the driver's seat. Privacy was a rare commodity with two pre-teenagers and only a curtain between both rooms.

I had to learn to buy groceries for four people on a stringent budget. Without a kitchen, I had to learn to cook dinner for the family. I had to purchase clothes for others, mend cuts and bruises, patch broken hearts, drive kids to their friends' houses, and pick up kids from their friends' houses. A few of my friends were married and had babies, but life flung me without mercy into the parenting havoc of raising teenagers.

The biological mom, not in the picture, was both a blessing and a curse. We did not have to negotiate two sets of rules, child support, fights with the ex, etc. But the kids had a visceral need for their biological mom. An absent mother can grow into a sanctuary in the minds of children.

I suppose it could've gone several ways. I could've hated them, and they could've hated me in return. When I looked at them, I saw two messed-up kids desperate to be cared for. And I had tons of love to give. After all, I wished for six kids. I opened my heart, and I gave it to them. That part was easy. They were good kids with kind souls. A friend once explained to me that kids cannot resist love. Oso's kids craved love from a woman.

I didn't know them when they were born, and I didn't know them when they left the Yukon. I often wondered what it was like. Jessi was seven years old, and her brother five when their parents split up. Their dad thought it was appropriate to leave the Yukon with his two oldest kids and drive more than eight thousand kilometres to the other side of the country. He renovated an old school bus, making it into a rudimentary livable vehicle, and left for a different scene. Did Jessi and Chris understand they would not see their mom again until they became teenagers? Did they realize they were leaving their three-year-old sister Catherine behind? Were they scared or excited, or both? Did they grasp what was happening? Maybe Catherine raced after the bus, pleading to be with her siblings and her dad. *Come back, come back, wait for me.*

We spoke to Catherine on the phone, and I tried to imagine what she was like. Jessi and Chris grew up together, yet they had differing personalities. Was she outgoing like Jessi or timid like Chris? Was she happy living with her mom? Did she miss her siblings? Did she even remember her dad?

I never understood the decisions he made so long ago. For example, why did he only take the two oldest kids? Why did he take them away from Susan, their biological mother? When I asked him about it, he said if he had grabbed all three, their mom would have gone mad. Maybe he didn't want a baby in diapers. And why would any mother allow her kids to stray so far? Did she have a choice? Jessi always felt her mom had deserted them. Was Susan relieved they were gone, or did she grieve for years? Did she willingly let them go, or were they taken from her? Oso told me her boyfriend stood in the doorway, trying to prevent him from taking them. He threatened the boyfriend, who backed down.

My brother-in-law once accused me of being a pickpocket of the soul. It was his polite way of calling me a nosy person. His comment flattered me. My mom keeps telling me I missed my vocation. She says I should've been a shrink. People confess their secrets to me. Friends often tell me, *Wow, why did I tell you that? I haven't shared that with anyone.*

I acted the same way with the kids. I asked questions. And we chatted. We grew into a family. Jessi could blab on for hours about her friends, boys, school, her dreams. Chris was shy and secretive; I had to pull hard to get him to open up. He wished to be a chef when he grew up.

I didn't have access to resources on the internet; we didn't even have a computer. The internet was emerging, but not readily available. Oso and I hadn't debated my role as a stepparent other than him saying he would support whatever decisions I made. It took me more than a year after I moved in to scold Chris when he misbehaved. I was utterly terrified to step in. I had no clue how to assert myself in this family. Other than my parents' experience with reconstructed families, I didn't know anyone who was a stepparent. And I certainly didn't want to consult my parents. I came home from work one day to find that Chris had stuffed himself with our whole dinner. We had a strict budget for food, so I was furious. I knew his father would be livid, and that was never good. I frowned at him. "What were you thinking? What will we eat for dinner now?" He lowered his head and muttered an apology. He seemed so contrite. I couldn't stay mad at him.

We shopped in thrift stores, and I let them choose their own clothes. Jessi always found clothes that looked perfect on her. Chris favoured clothes too large for him. He was aware of his excess weight and tried to conceal it with oversized sweaters. Jessi had a smile that could melt hearts. She was a passionate girl like her father. Chris was the opposite. He had a coy smile and a face full of freckles. An introvert. Because of his weight and shyness, I suspected some kids bullied him in school, although he never complained about it. He appeared to not have many friends. He'd often fib to avoid getting caught when he did something wrong, which, of course, brought him more trouble. Despite their differences, the kids got along with each other, but they were not close.

The relationship between parents and children can be frustrating and complicated, wonderful and rewarding. What is it supposed to be between a woman and another mother's children? They barely had any contact with their biological mom, and I was too young to be a full-time mother.

Jessi cautioned me, "Dad's previous girlfriend was severe with us, but especially with Chris. She hit him with a wooden spoon and locked him up in a closet for hours." My heart shattered to imagine anyone brutalizing a sweet kid like Chris – or any child. I worked especially hard to be kind to him. His gorgeous eyes always bore a twinge of sadness.

Kids do stupid things once in a while, so when I got angry, I'd stop talking to them. I didn't think of it as sulking; I simply didn't know how to communicate my frustration toward them. I did not carry them for nine months; I had not raised them. Years later, Jessi admitted to me it was torture when I went quiet. They were accustomed to screams, not silence. They would bend over backward to make it up to me. I was twelve years older than her. What did I know about being a mother to pre-teenagers? I was scared of their reaction if I disciplined them. Every stepparent dreads to hear those famous words: *you are not my mother and you cannot tell me what to do.*

During the following years, these kids challenged us in more ways than any parents should endure, but they never uttered those words. Years later, I'd often say, "These kids have done everything you do not want your kids to do. I mean everything, other than killing someone."

Skipping Rocks

I had spent a lot of time with the kids during college, but it felt like visiting friends. Now, it was different. We lived together as a family. I was a full-time partner and stepmother. Because we settled in a campground, I pretended it was a camping holiday. School was out for the summer, the weather pleasant, and I adapted to this strange life as best I could.

Soon, however, I needed more breathing space, so I drifted to the shore. Nature and water always have a soothing effect on me.

Jessi was often away with friends, but Chris tagged along with me. I didn't mind; he was an introvert, and he said little, plus I appreciated him. The kids didn't choose this life, moving more often than I can count, adapting to different stepmoms and living thousands of kilometres away from their biological mother and sister.

"Do you know how to bounce a rock on the water's surface?" I asked Chris.

"What?" he said. "Rocks don't bounce."

"Find a nice roundish flat rock, then hold it between your thumb and index finger like this," I said as I showed him. "Then it's all in the flip of the wrist. You throw it hard, sort of sideways." Soon, we were having skipping rock competitions, and he'd jump up and down when his rock skimmed the water, five, six or even seven times. He must've been practicing while I was at work because he quickly exceeded my rock-skipping abilities. I chose to not teach him how to blow snot from his nose.

We strolled on the beach, and I watched him stuff his pockets with colourful shells and rocks. He was ten years old and a bit on the pudgy side. No longer a boy, yet not quite a teenager. He seemed content to walk with me along the shores of the Atlantic Ocean. He proudly showed me his treasures and carried them to the bus. Days later, we had to throw them out because of the rotting odour of some miserable sea creature trapped in the shell.

Chris and I relaxed on a log, and we marvelled at the tide. Mud and rocks blanketed the beach. It was not a great nor safe place to swim. The waves trickled in, the water tickling our feet. Chris removed his shoes and rolled up his pants. He chased the waves, then quickly leaped back, trying to keep his toes dry. "Try it, Liette, try it." I removed my sandals, and the two of us danced with the waves. Our laugh echoed over the open water, and by the time we stopped, we were both soaked up to our thighs.

Broken Promise

We'd been living in the bus for a month when I snapped. It was a combination of circumstances that threatened to drive me insane.

There was the cramped space the four of us called home. My bedroom in my parents' house was bigger than our current living area. I was the rare teenager who kept her bedroom spotless. Everything in its place. I hate when things are not where they should be. Inside the limited space on the bus, we jammed everything into any available spot. We had to cook, eat, watch television, play games, read, sleep and have sex within a space of five square meters.

There were the non-existent appliances. Cooking meant stepping outside to get the food out of the refrigerator. It restricted our diet to food that could either be barbecued or boiled. We dined outside on the picnic table as much as we could.

There was the extra work we had to do every morning and every night. Pull down the table, get our bedding from the back, and make our bed. Each morning, store the bedding away and remount the table for breakfast. The camping novelty quickly wore off. Living became one massive chore.

There was the lack of hygiene facilities. We had to walk two hundred meters to use the bathroom, take our shower or brush our teeth. Hence, when I woke up in the black of the night, I grabbed a sweater, rushed outside, squatted in the woods, and did my thing. The next morning was a Sunday, and I attended mass on Sundays. The morning was cool, so I snatched the same sweater and off I went. I sat beside an old lady and throughout the service, I resisted the urge to plug my nose. The poor old lady smelled like shit. I wondered why she stared at me with pity in her eyes. Maybe she was ashamed. Driving home, I could still smell it in the car, and I figured I captured the stink in my nostrils. But this gnawing thought crept into my mind, and I was horrified when Oso said he could also smell it. "Is that the sweater you wore last night?" It's only then that I spotted the large brown stain on my sleeve.

There was the lack of intimacy. I held my breath and tensed my body, desperate to not make a sound every time we had sex. I was raised in a Catholic home, and sex was never talked about. We used to joke that we had no clue how our parents had six kids. It was only later in life that my mom and I discussed sex. I was very timid about anyone hearing me doing it. We waited for the kids to be asleep, and even then, I'd cringe if we made any noise. Oso wanted sex every day, so he ordered them to take off for at least an hour. I enjoyed having sex, but I averted my eyes when they showed up again.

One day when the rain had been coming down for two days, Oso was getting frustrated. We played cards when I felt his foot moving up my leg. A sign that he was horny. I nodded toward the kids. Jessi sat at the table with us, browsing a magazine while Chris played in the back. "Go for a walk and do not come back for at least an hour," Oso said.

Jessi peered up from her reading and waved her hand toward the window. "It's raining. We can't go out; we have nowhere to go."

Oso stood and his voice climbed up a notch. "You're not gonna melt. Out now." They glared at each other.

Jessi gripped the bus door handle and swung it with the full strength of a pissed-off twelve-year-old girl. She stomped down the step, flounced toward the road, shaking her head. Chris was slower to react. He dropped his toys and dragged his feet to the door. I heard him sigh, watched his shoulders slump. He covered his face with his forearm and plodded through the trees.

Oso smiled at me and lowered the table. I was stunned. Had he gone mad? "What are you doing? What is wrong with you, pushing them out in the rain? They'll catch pneumonia. Where will they go? You seriously think I'm in the mood for sex now?"

His eyes turned black. "We haven't had sex in two days," he said. "Don't you love me anymore? What is wrong with me? What is wrong with you? If we don't have sex, they will get wet for nothing, and it will be your fault."

We were still arguing when the children came back. I had no experience with couples fighting, but it didn't seem like a fair fight. Oso did most of the talking. I tried to slip a word in, to justify myself, but his tone went up an octave every time I opened my mouth. I'd never been yelled at, so I had no clue how to defend myself. "Please stop," I begged.

"Tell me why you don't want to have sex anymore? Is this how it's gonna be from now on? Don't you know how important sex is in a relationship?"

"Yes, but it's just –"

"There is no excuse; you love me or you don't."

"But I –"

"Shut up and listen when I'm talking to you." I collapsed. "What? Now you're gonna cry? You have no reason to cry."

A wave of despair shoved me out in the rain. As the kids approached, I kept my eyes on the wet ground. I sprinted to the facilities, where I huddled in one of the shower stalls. I bawled. What had happened? I didn't understand. Who was this man? Had I done something wrong? How was I going to fix this? Eventually, I headed back to the bus. Where else was I gonna go?

When my parents got married, they promised each other they would never argue in front of the children. It was a wonderful way to grow up, but it did not prepare me for the cruel realities of living with a man who used his voice to control others.

Oso was cooking dinner, and Jessi and Chris were playing in the back when I entered the bus. He smiled sheepishly at me and kissed me on the cheek. His eyes were back to normal, and the kids had changed into dry clothes. We sat at the table, but I couldn't eat. I didn't understand what had just happened. I pretended I was okay. It was our first actual fight. I'd cringed many times when Oso chided the kids, but he had never gotten mad at me before. I saw rage and hate in those eyes. And it scared me.

My biggest frustration was that I had no chance to talk, to explain my side of the story. Every time I tried to get a word in, Oso would cut me off. It was so frustrating. That evening, when I brought up the fight, he stopped me. "Why are you still talking about that? It's done. Get over it."

That night, as I lay in bed awake, I made excuses for him. I blamed the rain, the cramped bus, the kids. I blamed everyone and everything except Oso.

The next day, I confided in a friend at work. She offered me a place to stay for a while. When I got home from work, I found my old blue suitcase, and I packed my things. Jessi cried, and I felt terrible, but I had to get out of there. "I will be back," I told them. "I need time away for a few days."

"Is it our fault?"

My heart shattered as I looked at their gloomy faces. I hugged them and reassured them, "Of course not."

I waited outside on the picnic table for Oso to come home from work. He spotted my blue suitcase. His face dropped. "Where are you going?"

"I need a break, I need space. I hate it when you shout or swear at me or the kids. It breaks my heart, and you scare me."

He said, "I don't yell. But they need to obey. You don't know how hard it is to raise kids alone. Plus, I'm not like your father. You didn't grow up in a normal family. This is life. People fight, couples fight." He softened his tone. "Please don't go."

Shaking my head, I walked away without glancing back. I didn't want to see the kids' sad faces in the bus's windows.

I stayed away for one week. I missed them, and I was worried. Was Oso taking his frustration out on them? I knew Jessi could escape to her friends, but I imagined Chris alone on the shore, with no one to compete with for the most rock bounces. They had lived without me for a long time, but I'd grown attached to them, and I felt responsible for their plight. So, when Oso begged me to return, I remembered my promise, and I followed him back to the bus.

We played cards and board games when rain kept us inside for long stretches. Jessi loved to read, and she was always writing in journals. Chris was not much of a reader, but they both enjoyed drawing, so I bought them drawing pads and crayons with my drugstore discount.

I decided I needed a kitten. The bus was not mine; the kids were not mine, even the dog wasn't mine. Except for my personal items, the only object I owned was the small wooden cross on the wall. We adopted Sam from the pet store. She was such a cutie, orange and white. She chased after the little ball we threw on the floor. We lay the litter box under the kitchen table, which meant I had to eat with my feet in the litter. To this day, I still wonder why I thought I needed a kitten on a bus already jammed with four people and a big husky dog.

The Small Cottage

In late October, I woke up one morning to frost on the grass. We needed to find accommodations for the winter. We discovered a cute cottage for rent by the ocean in a neighbouring village. The cottage had three tiny bedrooms, a narrow kitchen, and a charming living room. My favourite spot was a rocking chair beside the two enormous windows looking out on the sea. We had plenty of room to park the bus beside the chalet and lots of space for the husky dog. I tried to take him for walks, but he must've weighed over a hundred pounds, and I couldn't control him.

After living on a bus for four months, the cozy cottage was a luxury. The kids had their own room. We could go to the bathroom and take a shower without having to step outside. And we had an oven.

Fall temperatures always give me the urge to bake muffins. Muffins are the perfect food. Not too sweet; I can pretend I'm eating healthy food. I always add fruits to further support this belief. I've never been a fruit person, so I bury them in muffins, smoothies, and my favourite, chocolate fondue.

"Hey, do you want to help me bake muffins?" I asked the kids.

They looked up, "Yes, yes. What kind? Can we put chocolate chips?" They hovered around me, eyes glowing, excited.

"Of course," I replied. Jessi grabbed the flour and sugar while Chris reached for the chocolate chips.

"What else do we need?" asked Jessi.

"Bananas," I answered. "Let's bake banana and chocolate chip muffins."

By the time we stuffed the muffins in the oven, Chris had flour up his nose. Jessi wiped her hands on her pants. "How long do they need to cook?" asked Chris. I put the timer at twenty minutes, and we giggled, staring through the oven window as the muffins rose. The delicious scent invaded the small cottage.

Oso arrived home from work just as the buzzer beeped. He sniffed the air. "Sure smells good in here."

Chris shot up. "Can I take them out?"

I handed him the oven mitts. "Be careful."

We let them cool for a few minutes and then set them on two metal racks. "Can we take a picture? They're gorgeous," asked Jessi. I grabbed the camera. It would be another few years before digital cameras became the norm. We did not have cell phones either. The kids each seized a rack of muffins while I shot the picture.

We had to wait until the camera roll was done, twenty-four pictures, and then bring the roll to the drugstore to have it developed. The staff mailed the rolls to a laboratory, and we received the pictures two weeks later. I chuckled when I saw the muffin picture. Each kid is holding a tray. Chris is showing off his muffins with a wicked smile and beady eyes. You'd think he's holding seven stinky bombs and not seven muffins. Jessi's face is partly cut off from the picture. All we see is her proud smile as she shows off her muffins.

I love Halloween. It's the one day of the year when I can dress up and not get arrested. It was our first Halloween as a new family. I took the kids shopping for their costumes. Even with a limited budget, we could afford a few basic make-up necessities. Jessi wanted to dress up as Catwoman, and Chris picked up what he needed to transform into a vampire.

They prepared at home while I was at work. I wore Oso's hat and jean shirt. Jessi drew me a large black moustache and beard on my face, and when I got to work, I realized I had dressed up as Oso!

Oso herded the kids around to trick or treat and they showed up at the drugstore, pretending they didn't know me. Gosh, they sure had done a good job with their disguise, and their proud smiles made the money spent well worth it. Jessi wore a Zorro mask and black clothes. She drew whiskers on the bottom part of her face and a white patch on her chin. Her full lips glowed with bright red lipstick. I stared at her. She was twelve years old, hovering between a child and a teenager, but she looked sensual and older in that costume. Chris wore black pants and a black cape over a white shirt. He painted his entire face white with large black shadows around his eyes that drooped on his cheeks. He added two long black lines around his smile, and a few drops of blood drooled out of his mouth. A set of vampire fangs completed his look. Jessi strolled around in a suave motion while Chris growled and pretended to bite me. They showed me the meagre content of the large pillowcases they were dragging from house to house. "We're not done," they said in unison. When I got home from work, candies of all sorts covered the entire living room floor. They must've been trick or treating for hours because they had enough candies to last until spring.

It was late November. I rested by the window, knitting mittens for Chris. The kids worked on their homework, and Oso listened to the news. I set down my needles and gazed outside the window. The ocean had gone mad. Even as the darkness of the evening descended, I watched the gale force wind blowing fiercely across the bay. Gigantic waves crashed on the shore, spitting salty mist on the cottage windows. The heavy rain and sleet came down hard as if God was outraged and throwing buckets at us.

Amid this craziness, I noticed people wandering on the beach. They were holding on for dear life to their coats. They trotted on, picking objects and sticking them in pails. "Chris," I said. "Can you please go see what's going on out there?"

He looked at me as if I'd gone mad. Oso repeated in a stern voice, "Chris, go!"

He reluctantly put on his raincoat and his boots and forced the door open. I felt guilty, asking him to go out to investigate in the dreary weather. He ran out and rushed back in, waving a small lobster in his hand. "They're all over the place, tons of them." Jessi and I threw on our raincoats and boots and grabbed large buckets. The gigantic waves plucked up small lobsters from the bottom of the sea and flung them on the shore. The blizzard assailed us, but we laughed, and we picked up buckets of baby lobsters. I briefly wondered if this was legal, but the thought of fresh lobster quickly erased any concerns. Either way, they would not live long lying upside down on the cold beach. We enjoyed a feast that night. We spent all evening boiling them and then taking out the yummy meat from the shells, freezing it for later.

Chris's school planned a Christmas concert, and he joined the band, playing the xylophone. He loved music, and he practiced at home, little Christmas jingles. Oso, Jessi, and I attended the concert and cheered for him. He scanned the crowd, and his face beamed when he spotted us.

It was our first Christmas as a reconstructed family. Although the year before, we had gone to Montreal, we had not been living together yet. Even though I knew my parents were not pleased with my relationship, I asked them if we could spend Christmas Day with them. After we opened our gifts, we drove to Memramcook and arrived for lunch, which was our family Christmas meal. Jessi and Chris built thoughtful gifts for my parents. Their gestures moved me. My parents received them graciously. My dad seemed more comfortable with Oso, and we had a pleasant time with the family. We left after dinner and made it home by midnight. I felt confident that we'd reached a turning point in our relationship with my family. As always, the kids behaved well and politely, convincing me their father was doing a good job.

I did not know it would be my last Christmas home for fifteen years.

Winters can be fierce in the Maritimes and even more so by the ocean. The cottage we rented was at least half a kilometre from the road. Blustery winds came from the wide-open sea, bringing walls of snow with them. It wasn't long before we lost control of the driveway. We cleared a narrow area by the street so we could park the car. The kids snowshoed from the house to take the school bus. They hid their snowshoes in the ditch, under the white powder, and then walked back with them when they returned. Oso and I did the same to get to work.

It was my day off, and I was home alone, preparing my lunch. I noticed an enormous tractor blower clearing the snow from our driveway. I stared in awe as he cleared a pathway, the walls of snow on each side as high as the bus. An airplane could land in our driveway. He stopped near the house, and I observed him eating a sandwich. I pulled on my coat and stepped outside. "Excuse me, sir, we did not ask anyone to clean our driveway." Every month, we calculated our pennies to pay rent and buy food.

He smiled. "Oops, I must've done the wrong driveway." I resisted the urge to throw my arms around him.

I worked part-time, earning slightly above the minimum wage. Oso grabbed temporary work contracts when he could. After having paid the rent and utilities, we hardly had any money for food. Oso reached out to the social security office and explained our dilemma. They handed him a few food coupons. I don't think they have those programs in place anymore. Food stamps were temporary help for families going through a rough patch without having to apply to what we used to call welfare. I didn't feel poor. I mean, of course, we were struggling, but I was an optimist. After all, we were college graduates; we would secure good jobs. Still, I lowered my eyes to the floor when we handed over the coupons to the cashier. The cashier glanced at us when she rang the case of beer through her cash register.

Since Christmas had gone well, we visited my family for Easter. This time, they invited us to spend the weekend. The kids slept in the sunroom, and they offered Oso and me the spare bedroom. We slipped the mattress on the floor so the bed wouldn't creak when we had sex.

Dog vs Cat

Chunks of ice floated near the shore, competing with the whiteness of the fresh snow surrounding the cottage. The house was quiet. The kids were in school, and Oso was at work. I enjoyed the calm as I savoured my morning coffee. Hmmm, snowshoeing today?

A loud ring jolted me out of my reverie. It was my mom. "Your dad woke up with chest pain, so we rushed him to the hospital. He's okay for now; he's resting while they're running more tests."

"Oh my God, should I come home?"

"No, he isn't in any immediate danger. I'll keep you posted."

Home was a three-hour car ride. I called Oso at work. "Do you need me to come home?"

"Not right now, but be on standby."

Worried, he left work early in the afternoon and found me bawling on the couch.

"Oh, no," he said. "Your dad?" He sat beside me. I glared at him.

"My dad is fine; it was a false alarm. He suffered indigestion, and he's home." I stood up. "Your dog ate my cat."

I let Sam, our cat, play outside. We lived far from any neighbours and away from the road.

She playfully teased Yukon (the big husky dog) by resting near the end of his restraint. He'd howl and twist and turn, trying to get at her. She'd sit quietly, licking herself, barely acknowledging him.

After my mom told me my dad was okay, I stepped outside, breathing the fresh air, my snowshoes in my hands. I squinted against the bright snow glare. A messy patch of red fur contrasted with the white snow near the husky. Sitting proudly, he licked his chops. I knew what it was even before I recognized Sam's two back paws and tail.

I dropped the snowshoes. I screamed. He stood up and wagged his tail.

I slowly approached, and he got up to sniff her remains. "What have you done? Oh my God, what have you done?" He didn't even give me the courtesy of appearing guilty.

Her blood and guts trailed on the snow.

I ran to grab a shovel, needing to salvage what he left of her. I pushed him away with my body and picked up the pieces he had dropped. A bit of fur, two paws, the tail and the guts.

Oso's face filled with sympathy. "It's a husky trait," he said. I was inconsolable. To be honest, she wasn't a great cat. She used to lie on my lap, and I'd pet her until she decided she had enough. Instead of jumping off, she'd turn and bite me, often drawing blood. Still, she was my cat, my Sam. And she certainly didn't deserve to be viciously devoured. The only thing I had left of my own was the wooden cross on the wall.

When the kids came home, we dug the snow and buried Sam. Yukon lived a ripe age, and we found him dead one winter morning, lying on his side. He perished alone.

Birthdays

I love birthdays. It's the one day of the year that's your own special day. Okay, I admit it; I enjoy being the centre of attention.

My birthday is in January, and I'd come home from school, all excited. My mom acted innocently, but I detected the sweet smell of chocolate cake that had baked while I sat in class. She hid all the evidence, but I searched the garbage and always found the cake mix box. Dad would come home, and we'd all sit at the table for dinner. I'd wait anxiously for her to fetch the cake. She'd stroll into the kitchen to everyone singing happy birthday. Thrilled, I'd blow out the candles, always making a wish. Dad would grab a paper bag from the closet, and I'd get my small gift. I always liked it, no matter what it was. It certainly was not like birthday parties these days when most kids receive tons of presents. We all enjoyed the same treatment, and I felt like a queen on my birthday.

It was natural for me to do something special for the kids. Chris' birthday was in November, and Jessi's was in January. We bought them a small gift, and I baked a cake. Chris loved chocolate cake; Jessi liked anything but chocolate. It became a joke throughout the years because I always confused the two. I would make Jessi a yummy chocolate cake. I baked it while they were in school and then hid all the evidence until after dinner. We sang and the birthday person made a wish and blew their candles.

I invited their friends when possible and cooked their favourite meals, which involved fries with hotdogs or hamburgers. But no matter how hard I tried, the kids wore long faces all day until the phone rang. Then they would bolt and grab the receiver. Their biological mother, Susan, called to wish them a happy birthday. At first, I thought this was good. It made their day. It made them happy. But eventually, I began to resent that call, and yes, I even became jealous of it. Jessi and Chris had put their biological mom high on a pedestal. But she was not there when they got sick at night or when the school called, and I had to go meet the principal. She was not there when they didn't come home and I was worried sick.

Every Christmas, she promised them they would visit her during the summer in British Columbia. As summer approached, they got restless. They could hardly stand still. And every summer, she broke their hearts by changing her mind at the last minute. There was a new boyfriend, not enough room in her new apartment, she was sick. We picked up the children with a spoon. Devastated, it took them all summer to recover, and even then, I don't think they ever did. And each time, in the depth of my soul, I hated Susan.

Yet every birthday, the same scenario repeated itself. I used to think she had the best and certainly the easiest role. She didn't have to nurse a sick kid or mend a broken heart; all she had to do was remember their birthdays, and she was a queen.

The Phone Call

1987

The pharmacy intercom blared my name. "Liette, line two, please, Liette, line two."

I remembered giving my work number only to my parents and Oso. It was a July Friday afternoon, at four pm. The cottage owners had kicked us out in the spring because they planned to sell the cottage. We moved onto the bus again at the same campground. Cell phones had been on the market for a couple of years, but they were not widely available, and besides, we couldn't afford such luxury. I hastily reached for the receiver.

"Hello?"

"Hello, Liette, this is Tony from Environment Canada. How are you?"

I gulped. "I'm fine. Thank you, and you?"

Tony and a colleague had interviewed me for a job at the end of our last year in college. The interview had taken place more than a year before, and I'd almost given up on the possibility of landing the job.

Tony continued, "We had a cancellation for a course starting next Monday. If you want to take the five-month basic weather technician course, you have to be in Cornwall, Ontario, by eight o'clock Monday morning."

I had no clue where Cornwall was, and honestly, I barely knew where Ontario was. But I knew we would be there Monday morning.

He added that while on the course, I would not be considered an employee, but if I stayed at the establishment, the government covered my room and food. Plus, I would get one hundred dollars per week for expenses.

"I can't live in the school because I have a family now."

"That's okay. If you don't stay there, we will grant you one hundred and seventy dollars per week. If you graduate from the course, we will likely offer you a job."

Although they had recruited me within the Atlantic region, the Ontario region was interested in bilingual female candidates, and he asked me to think about transferring between regions.

I knew the drugstore appreciated my work. I liked my job and the people I worked with. But the salary was barely above the minimum wage. This was an opportunity I could not pass up.

With three hours left on my shift, I immediately called Oso. He was working on a forestry contract, which was ending within a week. I said to him, "Pack the bus, we're moving to Cornwall." He agreed since both of us struggled to find work in our field of study. We had already discussed leaving New Brunswick.

I told my boss. "I'm sorry. An opportunity has come up with the federal government. I have to be in Cornwall by Monday morning. I quit."

"You can't quit without giving us two weeks' notice."

"I know, but I can't, so thank you for everything. Here is my name tag and my smock."

His shouts echoed across the pharmacy as I walked toward the exit, waving my hand in the air in a goodbye gesture. I explained to my co-workers, who assured me they would drop by that evening.

Putting money into a payphone, I called my parents to tell them we were leaving for Ontario. We would not have time to drop by to say goodbye. My dad was home alone. Later, my mom told me that when she got home, he sat her down and said, "I have good news and bad news."

Oso drove the car to work, so I was on foot. I usually took my time to walk home, enjoying the peacefulness before getting to the tumult of the bus. But this time, I skipped and hopped all the way. As I turned the corner, I froze. The kids were sitting at the picnic table.

I observed them for a while. They were playing cards, waiting for us to come home for dinner.

Once again, they would be forced to leave their friends and change schools. They started school in the Yukon, and then got homeschooled while moving to Newfoundland and Labrador. Now, after three years in New Brunswick, they would have to do it all over again. A new school, new friends, new home, new town, heck, even a new province. Then five months later, when the course finished, who knows where we would end up?

I walked over to the table and sat with them. They smiled. "Hey, how was your day?" Excited about this new opportunity, I'd forgotten the impact it would have on them.

I was never good at hiding my feelings. "What's wrong?" Jessi asked.

"Do you remember last year I had that interview with Environment Canada? Well, they called me this afternoon and offered me a job. But we have to be in Cornwall by Monday morning."

"Where is Cornwall?" Chris asked. He was suddenly alert.

"Somewhere in Ontario, I'm not sure," I replied. "It's far."

Tony had told me it would take us about twelve hours to drive from Bathurst to Cornwall. The kids tried to put on a brave face, wanting to congratulate me, but their eyes told the truth.

"Do we have to go?"

"When do we leave?"

"Early tomorrow morning, so you can go say goodbye to your friends this evening."

I added, "I'm sorry."

Our friends gave us an impromptu going-away party that evening. The kids tearfully said their goodbyes to their friends. We secured our possessions on the bus, and with the sun barely up on Saturday morning, we began our long and exciting journey toward Cornwall.

PART TWO

Cornwall

1987

The distance between Bathurst, New Brunswick, and Montreal, Quebec, is approximately eight hundred kilometres. The first hundred and forty kilometres, conceived as a secondary logging and mining road, cuts across the northern area of the province. With evergreen trees on both sides, the loaded bus trotted along at a turtle's pace, and I followed it in our compact used Aspen. It took over three hours of swerving around potholes to reach the Quebec border. The kids rode with me for that part, and we played road games. Games such as trying to name all the provinces' capitals or all the states.

Our plan was to arrive in Montreal by the day's end. The kids entertained themselves as best they could, alternating between riding in the bus with their dad and sitting in the car with me. On the bus, they could move around or draw or play cards. After we crossed into Quebec, the road became wider, and the driving got better. The bus proceeded at a maximum speed of fifty kilometres per hour. Our games shifted to counting dogs or red houses, a game we used to play on Sunday drives with our parents. Our dad couldn't help but compete with us, making our mom nervous. "Alphonse," she would say, "eyes on the road."

We'd been driving all day, and I forced my eyes to stay open. Afraid I would doze at the wheel, I signaled for Oso to stop. We were within two hours of Montreal, but even pushing it, I couldn't drive another kilometre. We parked the car on a side road and travelled the rest of the way on the bus.

Early Sunday morning, Oso and his brother-in-law recovered the car.

It was a brief visit with the in-laws since I had to be in Cornwall by Monday morning. We had to find a place to sleep once we got there since we could not afford a motel. Besides, why waste money on a motel when we had the bus? Everyone agreed it would be easier to leave the kids in Montreal. Oso drove the bus, and I tailed him with the car. We reached Cornwall early on Sunday afternoon. Our pockets and bank accounts were near empty, and we had nowhere to stay, but we were thrilled for this opportunity.

If I hadn't been nervous, I would've appreciated the beauty of the town. Cornwall lies on the splendid St. Lawrence River in Eastern Ontario. In the 1980s, a substantial paper mill factory highly supported the local economy. It was a quiet, industrial city with a population of forty-seven thousand people.

Oso parked the bus at an almost empty mall lot. We drove through the city in the car, searching for a place to spend the night. We found what seemed like an abandoned warehouse. Wooden boards covered the decrepit building's windows, and tall grass stretched around it. Oso swerved the car behind the warehouse, and we noted a few aged barrels by a back door. A spacious yard extended behind the building, backing into a swamp. The place was deserted.

We fetched the bus and maneuvered it behind the old building. The unforgiving summer sun scorched down on us. We had no electricity, no running water, no toilet, and only a few dollars in our pockets. But we had hope.

With our limited cash, Oso bought a pizza and beer for dinner. He also purchased a bag of ice for the cooler and bread and milk for breakfast the next morning.

We sat outside on worn-out lawn chairs we had stored on the bus. Oso handed me a second piece of pizza. "How are you feeling?"

"I'm not sure, overwhelmed, I guess, excited, scared." I pointed at the swamp. "What should we use for a toilet?" Oso grinned and pulled out a bucket from under the bus. I glanced at the rusty metal bucket. I could pee in there, but I'd wait to be in school for anything else.

We settled in for our first night. Classes started at eight, so I set my alarm for six am. I didn't need the extra stress of fretting about being late. My insomnia was at full force, and I remained awake for hours. We couldn't open the bus windows because of the millions of bugs flourishing in the swamp. Hot sweat dribbled between my boobs. I wondered if the kids were having a great time with their grandparents. We didn't have cell phones, so if we wanted to talk to them, we had to call from a payphone and reverse the charges to Oso's parents.

Early the next morning, I washed up in a basin of lukewarm water. I tugged on my newest blue jeans, cleanest t-shirt, sneakers, and I grabbed a light, almost empty backpack. Oso dropped me in front of the school. As he drove away, he gave me a thumbs up. He was going to spend the day hunting for work and for a place for us to live.

Transport Canada Training Institute

The Transport Canada Training Institute, or TCTI as we fondly called it, was a considerable facility set on beautifully groomed grounds. It had an indoor swimming pool, a bar, classrooms, a tennis court, and a full cafeteria. Each student was assigned a modest bedroom with a private bathroom. They ate at the well-stocked cafeteria equipped with cooks and salad bars. A maid cleaned their rooms every day. Each student collected one hundred dollars per week for their personal expenses. Until we completed our training, we were not treated as employees of the federal government. Since I did not live in the school, my weekly allowance was one hundred and seventy dollars.

I stared at the school for a few minutes. I'd moved my family across two provinces, with no guarantee of a job. My heart thumped loudly in my chest. Tony had informed me I was the sole student not living in the school. Would I be the outsider? I drew a heavy breath and raised my chin. The central door opened freely when I pushed it. I felt none of the confidence I'd displayed on the first day of college. The lady at the reception, who looked to be in her forties, greeted me with a kind smile. She had rolled up her brown hair in a bun on top of her head. Her glasses hung at the tip of her nose, and her cheerful face put me at ease.

She helped me with the various forms I had to fill. I hesitated at the question regarding my home address. "It's because, like, uh, we, uh, we are sort of between homes right now."

"Well, you can write your address here in Cornwall," she said.

"Huh, it's sort of, well, huh, we haven't found a place to stay yet." I blushed. I told her about the bus behind the warehouse. She suggested I use the school address. The five-month course was called the Basic Weather Technician Course.

Once all the paperwork was completed, I shuffled through the narrow corridors to the classroom. It was early, and only three other students sat at their desks. I smiled at them and grabbed the first empty chair near the front of the class. The other students had showed up on the weekend and had shared a few beers at the bar. They acknowledged each other as they came in. I remembered sitting in the classroom three years earlier in college. But this time, it felt different. Anxious, I prayed I'd made the right decision.

At eight o'clock, the classroom was full. An instructor stepped in. He must've been near retirement because his hair was completely white. Tall, he looked professional, wearing a white shirt and black pants, no tie. He peered around the classroom and introduced himself as being the chief instructor responsible for the five-month program. He had been a meteorologist for several years, working for Environment Canada. The other instructors walked in, eight men and two women. They introduced themselves as either meteorologists or technicians. Meteorologists have a university degree, whereas technicians do not. If we succeeded in the course, and they hired us, we'd become weather technicians.

It was our turn to present ourselves. I was relieved to discover a few guys were from Atlantic Canada. I counted twenty guys and four girls, including myself. The instructor described the various climates we have in an immense country like Canada. He asked me if it was cold in New Brunswick in the winter. I'd lived nowhere else in Canada, so I replied yes, it is quite cold. Laughter erupted in the class, and someone replied we Maritimers have mild winters because of the impact from the ocean. I had a lot to learn.

The instructor explained the grading. The passing mark for each exam was seventy per cent. If you failed once, you could redo the exam. Failed twice, and you were gone.

He introduced common words like high and low pressure systems, cold and warm fronts. Then words I'd never heard before, foreign words like troughs, Coriolis effect, wind shears, Stevenson screen.

When the class broke for lunch, I followed my classmates to the cafeteria. A gigantic snack bar provided a choice of hot lunches, an extensive fresh salad bar, and tons of fruits and desserts. The students presented their ID card to receive their free food. I stood in line with my tray, acutely aware of the few bucks in my pocket. "Do you mind if I sit here?" I asked a friendly group.

"Of course, please do," they said. "Did you not get your ID? You shouldn't pay for your food."

I hesitated. They would find out anyway. "I have my family with me, and we live on a bus." I must've earned their sympathy because they went back and brought me more food. They slipped me an apple and a banana under the table. They also offered to share their bathrooms with us so we could shower. I exhaled an enormous sigh of relief. Most of the students were my age, some older, a few younger.

When school ended at four, I found Oso parked outside, waiting for me. Overall, I had a good day, although I still felt overwhelmed. Oso had purchased bread and tuna, and we made ourselves sandwiches for dinner. During our meal, the warehouse owner showed up, demanding to know what we were doing there. After we explained our predicament, he generously offered to let us stay as long as we kept the area clean.

In New Brunswick, we often had a cool breeze flowing in from the bay. Here, the bog offered no relief from the sweltering heat. It was mid-July, and the line on the thermometer in the old bus could not go higher than one hundred degrees Fahrenheit, or thirty-eight degrees Celsius. For the next two weeks, the red mercury line stalled at the highest mark, so we didn't know the actual temperature inside the bus. I left a chocolate cookie on the counter, and within an hour, we had chocolate milk.

A week after classes began, we had our first quiz. We had to identify pictures of various clouds, as observed from satellite photos. I had tried in vain to study on the bus, but the heat was unbearable. If I sat outside, the bugs feasted on me. I hardly slept because of the hot and humid weather and had reached a point where I could barely walk straight. I stared at the satellite pictures, and I gulped. I would not shed tears in front of my peers. How could I know the difference between a cumulus or stratus cloud? I guesstimated most of my answers. I had graduated from college with the highest marks in our class, but I had been in a completely different place, and I had seriously studied.

The next day, the instructor handed out the results. I tried to appear nonchalant as he called my name. Rooted in my chair, I held my breath. The instructor grinned as he gave me my quiz. He had written *Well done, seventy-three percent*. Relief rushed through my veins, and I swore to myself I would never be that close to failure again. Afterwards, I studied at the library every evening. If I failed the course, where would we go?

After several weeks of theoretical learning, the instructors ran mock training where we pretended to work in a real weather office. Outside the school, we observed and then reported the weather. Everyone in the class would begin their careers as weather observers. We learned to identify the clouds, their heights from the ground, and what percentage of the sky they covered. We measured various weather elements, such as the temperature, the wind, and the pressure, and then coded the numbers on a gigantic paper form. I enjoyed the course, except for one day when the instructor stood at my desk and glared at my numbers. Without uttering a single word, he reached for his fat red marker and wrote in huge bold letters across my form: *367 dead in airplane crash because of observer error!*

Cockroaches

While I attended school, Oso hunted for a job and a place for us to live. Each morning, he dropped me off at the air-conditioned school. In the afternoon, he picked me up, and we drove to the swamp to devour the food the other students stole for us. After dinner, we rushed back to the school where I studied in the library. Oso played in the pool and made friends at the bar. Each night, we returned to the searing bus to sleep.

After two weeks, Oso grinned when I hopped in the car. "I found an apartment. The owner agrees to give us first month rent free if we clean it."

"Oh, have you seen it yet?" I asked.

"Nope, we're heading there now." We drove to a run-down part of town and stopped in front of a three-story, red, dilapidated brick building. The apartment was on the second floor. I clung to the wobbly rail as I climbed up the frail stairs.

We weren't wealthy growing up, but we weren't poor either. We lived in a nice, tidy two-story house. Each Friday, my mom cleaned the entire house from top to bottom. She vacuumed, then washed all the floors, dusted every piece of furniture and trinkets, scrubbed the bathrooms and changed all the sheets on the beds. In the spring, she whipped up all her cleaning tools and organized her spring cleaning, which meant washing the inside of every cupboard, every closet, ceilings and walls. Sometimes, I'd find a chocolate bar tucked away in the bottom of a drawer, and I'd pull it out. "What is this?" I'd ask. We rarely had such treats in the house.

My mom would say, "That's for me, a reward for my cleaning." She is now ninety years old, and she lives by herself in an apartment. She still gets on her hands and knees to scrub her floors. With six kids using a tiny bathroom, it didn't take long for the sink to get dirty. Halfway through the week, I'd offer to wash the downstairs bathroom. My mom never said no. Then, I'd line up the sixteen boots/shoes in pairs against the wall. I've always loved order, everything in its place.

The owner unlocked the old grey wooden door. I resisted the urge to plug my nose from the fetid smell. We walked into the apartment, which comprised a narrow kitchen/living room, two minuscule bedrooms, and a puny bathroom. I didn't remove my shoes as I trudged on the nasty, torn linoleum floor. I tugged at my feet as I stepped into a layer of slime. The walls were coated with smoke and grease so thick a person could scribble on them with a broomstick. "Here is the bathroom," said the owner. He opened the door to a windowless, foul-smelling room. I jumped back. I stared at Oso, panic in my eyes. The previous tenants had clogged the toilet, so they used the bathtub instead.

"We'll take it," Oso said. I shook my head, trying to block the bile coming up my throat. We slept in the bus that evening and the next day, Oso drove to Montreal to pick up the kids. I refused to put another foot into the apartment until he cleaned the bathtub. Then, armed with all of our cleaning supplies, the four of us spent the weekend scrubbing and disinfecting the place.

The owner approved our work, and we moved in on Sunday. Oso and I snatched the biggest bedroom while Jessi claimed the other one. Chris laid his mattress in the single closet of the apartment. I wore sandals to take my shower.

That night, I turned on the stove burner to cook dinner. The rusted element turned red, and when I approached to put a pot of potatoes to boil, the ugliest creatures I'd ever seen spewed from under the heat. The evil bugs scattered in all directions. I shrieked and dropped the pot on the floor. Oso rushed over and chuckled when he discovered the cockroaches.

I grew up with five siblings in a four-bedroom house. My parents slept in the largest bedroom, and the rest of us shared three bedrooms. In the beginning, I shared a room with my two sisters. As my brothers grew older, my father renovated a bedroom in the basement. Camilla and I were thrilled to move into our own space. My father brought our twin beds downstairs, set them side by side, and we settled for the night. A few minutes after we shut off the light, I picked up a clicking sound. I turned on the light, and we found a black beetle wriggling on the floor. They'd crawl on the ceiling and fall on their backs on the wooden floor. Click, Click. We grabbed our shoes and squished them without mercy. Searching for more bugs, we knelt in bed with the light on. I asked, "Do you hear something?"

"No," she replied. I inserted my finger in my ear to scratch an itch and a bug slipped out. I gasped, and we sprinted upstairs. I dozed on the couch while Camilla tried to get comfortable on the carpet floor. The next day, Bert took over the bedroom basement, but he didn't like it because of the lack of windows. Eventually, Louis-Marie moved in there and stayed until he got married.

In our shitty apartment, I had nowhere to hide from the cockroaches. I had never seen one before. They have an ugly tiny head and a shiny striated flat body. Apparently, they can survive a few minutes without their head, but I never tried it. We trampled them without pity, but no matter how many we killed, more came.

Geography being a crucial part in understanding meteorology, I taped a wide map of Canada on the wall in our bedroom. Each morning, I woke up before dawn to study before the kids got up. As soon as I turned on the lights, these beastly creatures darted in all directions, scrambling to hide behind the map. I'd look at them in despair. At night, I closed my mouth tight and buried my head in my sleeping bag. The kids didn't seem perturbed by the cockroaches. I surmised this was not their first encounter with them. Maybe they simply accepted whatever happened to them, knowing that complaining would change nothing.

None of us had beds; we slept on the mattresses we used on the bus. One night, I heard a loud noise followed by a dull moan. A piece of the ceiling tile dropped on Jessi's bed. Thankfully, she was a sound sleeper, and she didn't even stir.

I attended school every day while Oso searched for work. The kids spent a lot of time alone, exploring the town. The neighbours were friendly. Oso said the woman living on the first floor danced as a stripper. I guess he'd been doing more than chasing a job. The couple who lived in the apartment above ours persuaded us to join them in the yard for a bonfire. The guy had long grey hair and a shaggy white beard. He was as skinny as a stick, while his wife was obese. They shared a joint with us and laughed and fought together. He tugged her t-shirt over her head. She giggled, so he ripped off her bra. She clutched her sagging boobs to cover them while her whole body shook from laughing. I peered at Oso, resisting the urge to roll my eyes.

The school administration agreed to let us park the bus in their wide parking lot since we had no room at the apartment. Oso registered the kids in a new school for September. I walked to the store one day and realized how lonely I was when a car drove by, and the driver honked and waved. It was our landlord. It moved me that a person acknowledged me. I wept. Oso secured a three-month contract in forestry when the kids started school. We reminded them we would have to move again once I completed the course in November. We just didn't know where yet.

The course went on for five months, and we lost three or four students along the way. They either flunked their exams and were sent home, or they dropped out. I worked extremely hard to succeed, not only because I had brought the whole family with me, but I was also proud and determined.

Two weeks before the course ended, in November 1987, the lead instructor strode into the classroom with a list. We waited in anticipation. Many students were told to go north, to isolated places like Resolute Bay, Alert, and Mould Bay. A few were excited about the northern experience; others dropped their head on the desk and moaned. I waited, biting my nails, to see where our next adventure would take us. The instructor smiled at me and said, "Liette, you're moving to Ottawa."

Oh my God! I jumped with joy. Ottawa is the capital of Canada: a place of opportunities, both for Jessi and Chris and their father. I later learned that being a bilingual woman had a lot to do with their decision to station me in Ottawa. Cornwall is approximately one hundred kilometres to Ottawa.

The government offered us two days off and paid our way to Ottawa to find a place to live. We discovered an old farmhouse for rent in Richmond, Ontario, which is thirty kilometres southwest of the Ottawa airport, where the Ottawa Weather Office was located. We signed the lease and enrolled the kids in the local Richmond school.

When the course ended in late November, we packed the bus and headed toward Ottawa. We had bought used furniture for our apartment, and since the government covered the fees for our move, we hired a moving company. I had yet to receive the advance cheque to cover their fees. Direct deposit did not exist yet. I fretted all the way to Richmond; we had no money to pay the movers. I drove nonstop to the Ottawa airport. I took a deep breath and nervously stepped into the office. Three people, two men and one woman, sat in a corner, waiting for me. Unbeknownst to me, the Cornwall lead instructor had prepared them. "We're sending you a new employee. She and her boyfriend live in an old school bus with two kids, a huge husky dog, and a red canoe on top." They expected a checkered-shirt, hard-tip-boots, braided-hair hippie to turn up for work. When I walked in with my tight blue skirt, white blouse, and the only pair of high-heeled shoes I owned, they gaped at me. I barely had time to say hello when the manager in charge came out and said, "Let's talk in my office. I will introduce you to these yahoos later."

As soon as the office door closed, I blurted to my new boss, "I have a problem; the movers will be here in one hour, and I don't have any cash to pay them."

The office manager asked me how much I needed to cover the movers' fee. I lowered my eyes. "Twelve hundred dollars." He reached out for his personal cheque book and wrote me a cheque for the total amount. I knew I was in a good place.

The Old Farmhouse

While I visited the bank, Oso continued to Richmond with the bus and the kids. Jessi and Chris had not seen our new home yet, and they anxiously stared out the windows as Oso drove through the village.

The bus pulled up the eight-hundred-meter-long driveway to the old farmhouse. Chris shook his head. "Will we have to walk to the road every day for school?"

"It will be good exercise for you," his father said.

The ordinary house looked like any other two-story house with white vinyl siding. Two small porches, one in the front and one facing an adjacent barn, seemed to have been added as an afterthought. Attached to the back of the house, facing the Jock River, an old summer kitchen served as storage.

The kids stepped out of the bus. "What's that smell?" asked Jessi, pinching her nose. She quickly discovered the stink emanated from the many cows grazing between the house and the river. The strong odour reminded me of my brother Bert when he'd come home from working in a butcher shop. I didn't mind it, but Camilla hated it so much, she could not even finish her meal. I remember once, he teased her and rubbed his hands on her head. Although he had scrubbed his hands before dinner, she wailed and bolted upstairs to take a shower.

The kids darted up the dark, rickety stairs lodged between the dining and living room. "The biggest bedroom is ours," said their father.

"I claim this one," said Jessi.

"Then I guess I will take the other one," said Chris. Nobody wanted the smaller bedroom.

To the right of the house, there was an old barn full of dry hay, which was often frequented by a gigantic owl. Oso and I holed up in the loft of that barn to smoke pot and have sex. I always worried about lighting a joint, lying on bales and bales of dried hay.

We mostly came into the house through the side door, which opened into a long corridor. We purchased a freezer and stored it in that narrow room. At the end of the hall, a door opened on the right to a summer kitchen and on the left to a rustic dining room. We used that primitive kitchen to store and chop our wood for the winter. Oso installed a majestic woodstove he had brought from the Yukon and had stored at his parents' house in Montreal. He mounted it in the corner of the dining room, near the kitchen, where it stood proudly on the torn flowered linoleum floor. I loved the warm glow that extended to the room. The smell of fresh baked bread or home-cooked beans masked the fragrance of manure. After a few weeks, we hardly noticed the cows' smell anymore.

We mounted a dartboard on the old wood-panelled walls, and we threw darts in the dining room. There was an electric stove and a refrigerator in the teeny kitchen, but we didn't use the electric stove much. We barbecued in the summer and cooked on the woodstove in the winter.

In the fall, we parked the car a few kilometres north of the Jock River near a bridge where we launched our canoe and drifted downstream. The gentle river flowed near a golf course. Chris hunched in the middle of the canoe; his eyes fixed on the bottom of the river. "There! there!" he pointed. We manoeuvred the canoe, and he swept up the golf balls with a butterfly net. He traded them for cash. On a good day, he could fish out twenty to thirty golf balls. I sold a few to my boss, who was an avid golfer. When we reached the house, we lugged the canoe on the shore and then carried it to safety, stumbling through ankle-deep mud and cow dung.

The double-pane windows buzzed with hundreds of flies feeding on their dead family and friends. Heap of black dried corpses piled on the windowsills and between each windowpane. We couldn't get rid of the dead ones trapped between the two panes without taking out the window, so they stayed there. When I vacuumed the floors, I also sucked up the live and dead flies.

The scratching and scurrying from mice and rats fighting in the walls competed with the television sound in the living room. The rats squealed so loud, I feared they would pop out through the old drywall. Oso set up a bear trap in the basement. The basement floor was a mix of dirt and rocks, and the walls had extensive crevasses that led outside. Oso got me another cat to replace Sam, and she chased the mice, but she never dared confront the huge, hideous rats.

In my parents' home, after my brothers left, I finally had my own bedroom. I was twelve years old. One night, while my parents were out, I heard a soft scratching in my closet. I ran to Camilla's room and pleaded with her. "Please sleep with me. There's a mouse in my closet." I stuffed towels under the closet door so the mouse couldn't get out. Camilla sighed, shook her head, and spent the rest of the night with me. Gilles caught the mouse the next day and let it outside without harming it.

The kids were out with friends, and Oso and I were watching television one evening when we overheard a loud snap immediately followed by an even louder squeal. We sprinted to the cellar, where we discovered the tail of a rat sticking out from a hole in the dirt wall. The trap had disappeared with the rat, but Oso had nailed the other end deep into the ground. He carefully yanked the metal chain, and it appeared; the biggest damn rodent I'd ever seen. Monstrous bulging eyes, one limb caught in the trap, he was one wiggling, shrieking, furious son of a bitch. "Get me a knife!" Oso said.

I darted upstairs and came back, bringing Oso a small cutting knife. "No! Get me a knife!" he said, showing me the size of the blade by spreading his hands a foot apart. I ran back up and grabbed his machete from the summer kitchen. I held my breath as Oso tugged on the chain, dragging the beast closer to him. Before he brought down the blade on the poor creature, I hightailed out of there.

I couldn't bear to see the rat being gutted to death with the machete, even if I had myself killed a rat once. My fiancé's father raised foxes and sold the furs. They supported the cages from the ground on beams three feet high. During feeding, pieces of meat dropped under the cages, and out came the rats. My boyfriend and I once lay on top of a cage, carrying a 22-gauge shotgun. I remember being very nervous and excited when I wiped out one of those pesky rodents. I hate rats.

Unfortunately, rats were not the only animals crawling in through the basement walls. Oso and I were playing cards in the dining room one evening when we suddenly detected the unmistaken odour of a skunk. Ah, there must be a skunk lurking outside. We stepped outside on the porch, but the potent scent dissipated. "Oh no, the skunk is in the house," Oso said. We found it in the basement. It had fallen into a vast cement barrel used to hold water before the house was hooked to a well. The poor skunk was circling in its prison, trying to figure a way out. The barrel measured one metre by one metre with cement walls. "What are we supposed to do?" I asked Oso, scratching my head.

We called the SPCA and various other wildlife organizations, but nobody offered any help. I dialed the landlord. He said, "If you pick them up by the tail, I've been told they cannot pee."

"Well, can you come and try it?" I replied.

"No way!" he snickered.

Oso had an idea. "Let's put a plank in the barrel. It might climb out, leaving the same way it came in." Carefully, Oso lowered the plank on the side of one wall. We left the skunk alone to figure it out. Thank God, it worked, and the skunk left, taking its stench with him. The next day, Oso filled the holes in the walls with dirt.

Still, the critters invaded the house. One morning, I got up before dawn to find a live bat clinging to the wall of the dining room. I secured it with a bucket and dragged the bucket to the floor. I wrote a note on the bucket, "Caution, live bat inside," and left for work. Blackbirds often got stuck in the kitchen woodstove, coming down the chimney. We released them outside.

Several friends and family members visited us from New Brunswick during our five-year stay at the farmhouse. While working on my book, I asked a few of them what they remembered most from their visits. Their answer was unanimous: the flies!

We decorated the cracked walls with canvases Oso had accumulated over the years. He nailed two fox skins, one red and one white, on the panel wall in the living room. Behind the couch, he hung a heavy wall carpet portrait of a aboriginal on a horse, scouting for bison. Again, my sole contribution to the décor was my small wooden cross. I hung it in the dining room.

Every day, the kids marched the long driveway to catch the school bus. I'd often find their lunches in the ditch beside the road. I never told Oso about it, and I wondered what they ate when they got to school. Even if I bought what they chose for their sandwiches, they hated brown bread, which Oso insisted was the only bread we buy. We were on a strict budget; we spent one hundred dollars per week on groceries for two adults, two growing teenagers, a large dog, and a young cat.

I remember putting items in my grocery cart and adding the prices on a piece of paper, stopping when the numbers reached one hundred. Sometimes, I had to remove a roast from the basket before I made it to the cashier. I've always loved challenges, so I pretended it was a competition, dropping as many food items in the basket as I could without blowing the budget.

Ottawa Weather Office

The weather office was on the second floor of the main Ottawa Airport terminal building. Monitors showing various weather data from instruments installed outside completely covered one wall. We worked on a large table in the centre of the room, analyzing various weather maps. The office comprised a wide-open space with several telephones and computers; we received hundreds of calls per day.

A closed radio room accommodated the various weather radios and automated weather telephone lines. We had access to a small but well-equipped kitchen near the boss' office. Wide windows allowed us to track the weather outside, and every time it changed, I updated my weather observations.

Roughly fifteen people worked around the clock to notify the Ottawa population of the weather. Meteorologists in Montreal prepared the weather forecasts, and it was our job to disseminate it. I was pleasantly surprised to find two other women were part of the staff. They eventually moved on, and for a long time, I was the only girl in the office. Just one of the guys, they'd say, although some of them held their farts until I vacated the room.

The weather takes no time off, so we worked through weekends, nights, and holidays. Three people covered a shift. One person, the junior employee, hence me, measured and reported the various weather elements. Another individual answered the telephone, briefed pilots and anyone else who required weather-related information. The calls ranged from engineers needing detailed wind data to people calling for a precipitation forecast to decide whether to hang clothes on the line. A third person dealt with the media and conducted live weather radio broadcasts. We analyzed the weather maps because while we were not responsible for drafting the forecast, we needed to explain it to the population. After I gained more experience, a colleague and I revised the forecast for Ottawa, without informing the Montreal office. A journalist hailed them to inquire why there were two different forecasts for Ottawa, one on the official network from Montreal and one related to CBC on the radio. I received a call from a furious meteorologist that day.

My primary task was to observe and report the various weather elements. Rain or shine, I trotted outside on the roof of the terminal building every hour and often between the hours if the weather turned. I estimated the names and heights of the clouds. Sometimes it was obvious, a textbook cloud. Other times, my training officer would say, "Your guess is as good as mine."

Working twelve hours on night shifts and weekends can bring people together in a profound friendship or create mortal enemies. Luckily, I made more of the first.

In 1989, the office moved from the airport to downtown Ottawa. The government contracted weather observing to a private company. By then, I had gained two years' experience, and they expanded my tasks to other work in the office.

I loved my job. One day, I picked up the telephone. Weather office, météo bonjour. A stunned male voice responded, "Oh, it's a pretty young female voice. If it had been someone like Nick Nickerson, I would've told him to take his goddam forecast and shove it up his ass." Without missing a beat, I replied, "Thank God I'm not Nick Nickerson." After the guy finished laughing, he said it was the best answer he'd ever received, and from that moment on, he was always nice to me when he called.

After a while, they let me do live radio broadcasts. I came back to shift work after a six-month assignment in client services. During those six months, the office had begun to do live French CBC radio broadcasts for the Prairies. I drew up the information for Alberta, and I put on my headphones, waiting for my cue to go live. The reporter introduced me and asked, "So, Liette, what will the weather be like in our beautiful Manitoba province to-day?" Shit! I'd prepared for the wrong province. I peered at the weather maps on the wall, and I concocted a forecast. An hour later, I was on the air again with the corrected information.

"Excuse me?" the announcer said. The forecast temperature for the upcoming night suddenly switched by a difference of five degrees from my previous broadcast. I blabbered on about the cold front advancing quicker than expected.

Two years after I started working in Ottawa, I received a letter that stated my job was terminated. Unbeknownst to me, my official post was at the Toronto airport, but I was on loan to Ottawa. The letter explained I was still a full-time employee of the government, but the post I was occupying had been cut be-cause Environment Canada contracted the weather observation work in Toronto. The news arrived at the same time the govern-ment debated cutting employment benefits for anyone accepting a package after losing their jobs. I worked a Friday night when my

Union representative called me. He asked me if I would engage in an interview with the *Ottawa Citizens Newspaper* regarding my situation. After confirming with him I would not get in trouble, I agreed. The journalist came to the office and interviewed me, taking a few pictures. The next morning, I went home. When I returned to the office Saturday night, the security guard at the door grinned, "Wow, you're famous." What? He handed me the newspaper, and there I was, on the front page, my bold face in colour, occupying half the page. The title read: *UI changes threaten job buyout packages*. My heart skipped a few beats. I was expecting an insignificant article on page twenty-five of the newspaper. I drove home Sunday morning after my shift, petrified of my boss' reaction. I had four days off before I had to go back to work.

Four stressful days later, I was back in the office on dayshift when Tony walked in. They had sent the big boss from Toronto, and I assumed I was screwed. He glared at me. "Do you know how many times I've seen your face come across my fax machine?" I smiled sheepishly and raised my shoulders. "Sorry." Turns out, they received several requests from local citizens rooting for me, and within a couple of weeks, I had a permanent position in Ottawa.

I worked twenty-three years for Environment Canada, first in the weather office and then in climate change. I finished my career with Transport Canada, but I occasionally saw Tony at friends' retirement parties. He was a great boss who became a friend. Sadly, Tony died from cancer in 2019. He was sixty-seven.

Mother's Day

I dislike Mother's Day.

Maybe I expect too much. It just seems that no matter where I am on Mother's Day, someone is missing. My mom lives on the Canadian east coast. If I visit her for Mother's Day, then I'm not with the kids. If I stay with the children, my mom is not there.

I remember Mother's Day growing up. My parents rarely treated themselves to a restaurant. My dad worked hard for limited money, and my mom stayed home raising six kids. But on Mother's Day, my dad would say, "Children, make your own dinner tonight. This is your mom's day, and I'm taking her out." They would dress up; my dad wore his black suit and my mom slipped on her favourite dress. My parents barely surpassed five feet, but they looked grand, all dressed up for their tête-à-tête.

Kids' loyalties are often torn between their biological parent and the person acting as their parent. It had been years since Jessi and Chris had seen their biological mom. Chris did not even remember what she looked like.

Absence makes the heart do strange things. It seemed each year that passed, she climbed another step on the ladder, propelling her high on a pedestal. A queen on her throne.

Did I feel a pang of jealousy? You bet I did. She was not here when they were sick or when they got in trouble. Yet the kids ached for her, and I didn't understand why. Today, I know most children yearn to have a relationship with their biological parent. At the time, I didn't appreciate it.

So how do stepchildren handle Mother's Day? How to deal with the conflicting loyalties?

The kids crafted a card for their biological mom and we mailed it to her. They addressed the card: To Mom with love for Mother's Day.

I woke up on Sunday, hearing noises in the kitchen. Their father came in and winked, asking me to wait in bed. It was my first Mother's Day in the old farmhouse, and Jessi had turned fourteen in January. Chris was twelve.

Still wearing their pyjamas, the kids knocked on the door and carried their precious cargo to our bed. Their faces beamed, and my heart melted. I noticed coffee stains on Chris' yellow top, but of course, I didn't say a word about it. Jessi tied her long hair in a bun, to avoid getting a few strands in my food.

They had scrambled a couple of eggs, browned two pieces of toast, and stirred coffee. On the tray, beside the coffee cup, a card. Handmade, of course. On the card cover, Jessi wrote in large blue letters, Happy Liette's Day! She drew a picture of a happy but thoughtful face, with a large question mark on its head. Inside the question mark, she scribbled "Happy Liette's Day," followed by a few more question marks. She drew a red heart and colourful flowers. A small smiling wiggly worm was coloured in the bottom right corner of the page. I suspected it was Chris' contribution.

I opened the card and read her words:

"This card is for all the LIETTEs I know! The same Liette who talks to me as a friend and helps me out when I'm down. So now I've made a new holiday just for you, so I can tell you WE ALL LOVE YOU!!! Love Jessi. AFA.

My heart exploded with love, and I knew no matter how hard life with their dad could become, I would never abandon these kids. From that day on, Mother's Day became Liette's Day.

That all changed, however, when Jessi turned nineteen and her biological mom came to town.

A Bent Steering Wheel

1988

Have you ever wondered how much force is needed to bend a steering wheel? I admit, I'd never asked myself that question either. We survived our first winter in the old farmhouse. The ice of the Jock River melted, and the water rushed downstream. The scent from the thawing cow poop filled the yard and the house. We planted our own vegetables. Lacking experience, I planted the complete package of seeds. My dad had quite the laugh when I told him I transplanted eighty tomato plants in the garden. The soil was rich with cow manure, so the plants thrived. By September, we were hauling two full laundry baskets of red tomatoes out of the garden every day. I brought some to work; I boiled and froze some, and, in the end, I threw them whole in the freezer.

The kids had adapted to their new schools. Jessi, as usual, had made several friends. She was not interested in helping me with the garden. Her social life was way more important. Chris asked more questions and tailed me while I planted the seeds.

He wanted to help water the plants and he loved to watch them grow. I didn't pressure the kids to weed because it is something I love to do. Weeding is meditating for me. It's also a way for me to feel connected to my dad.

The kids were not fussy eaters; except for whole wheat bread, they devoured almost anything we cooked. They succeeded in their school year and proceeded on to the next grade.

Late one evening, Oso and I drove home from the movies. He slammed on the brakes, stopping in the middle of the driveway. I jerked my head up just in time to glimpse the dark wings of an enormous owl floating in the car's headlights. I gripped Oso's arm. "Turn off the lights!" We were plunged into darkness. "Look," I whispered.

In the black night, he couldn't see where I was pointing, but he responded, "Whoa..." Our landlord plowed the meadow, and the tall hay swayed in the wind. But tonight, the entire field was alive with bioluminescent bugs fluttering in the warm spring night. We stared in awe at the thousands of fireflies twirling over the field. Horny male bugs, strutting their lights, luring the females to their faith. The fireflies danced a foot above the grass, creating a dense carpet of tiny lights so bright, we could see the hay's seed heads.

We lit up a joint and gaped at the incredible sight of these shimmering insects twinkling in the soft night breeze. Holding hands, we admired the glowing field for half the night. We murmured to each other as if speaking louder would break the spell. Both of us hypnotized by the live spectacle.

"Sing to me, Oso."

Oso had taught me a song by a well-known Quebec singer, Felix Leclerc, Le P'tit Bonheur, and it soothed me. I marvelled at the tiny lights hovering in the field, and I pleaded, "Sing, Oso."

And he softly sang to me.

Toward the middle of summer, Oso suggested the two of us go camping. Our neighbours, who owned the farmhouse, agreed to supervise the kids, and we drove to a scenic campground along the Rideau River south of Ottawa. We arrived late Friday evening and in the light of a flashlight, we set up the tent. We dragged our sleeping bags and clothes into the tent and settled for the night. The following day, we biked the trails and splashed in the water. The sun was shining, and we had an awesome day together.

That evening, after putting out the bonfire, Oso wanted to have sex, but I was exhausted. I loved working shift work, but it took a toll on my body. I yawned in my sleeping bag and suggested we wait until the next morning.

Oso stormed out of the tent, dragging his sleeping bag behind him. He flung open the trunk of the car and yelled. "Get the fuck out." I scrambled out as he tore the tent down. He hurled the tent with the pegs and poles into the trunk. As he slammed the trunk, he roared, "Frigid bitch! Get in the fucken car." His eyes were black. I saw raw hate in them, and I crumbled.

I quickly slid into the passenger seat. Oso got behind the wheel and floored the gas pedal. Cursing and shouting, he banged his fist on the steering wheel so hard, it bent. I grabbed the door handle and held on. The half-hour ride back to the house was pure hell. With each word Oso spit out, I sunk deeper into the seat, terror spiking through my spine. I cowered, paralyzed with fear. The thump of my heart matched the roar of the engine. I clasped my hands together, but I couldn't stop them from shaking. I resisted the urge to clamp them over my ears. My head was buzzing. Where was the man who serenaded me with sweet songs? Who was this monster?

When we got home, he was no longer talking to me. He stormed up to bed. The kids' doors were closed. I was still in my pyjamas, so I slipped into bed beside him. His back was turned. I mumbled, "Good night."

He hissed, "Fuck. You. Bitch." I lay quietly. The tears wet my pillow.

The next morning, I couldn't move my body out of bed. I spent most of the day curled up under the blankets. I told Oso and the kids that I had caught the flu and, except to bring me a bit of food, they left me alone. The intense fear left my body traumatized as if a truck had plowed through me. I got up a few times to puke in the bathroom. Oso had uttered unpleasant words to me before and more often to the kids, but never anything like this. Every time I closed my eyes, I saw his angry fist punch the steering wheel, and the nausea crept into my stomach.

I didn't understand his rage. I knew I'd done nothing wrong. This was not my fault. Yet I was willing to do anything to prevent it from reoccurring. Oso served me my dinner in bed. He apologized profusely and swore to never lose his temper with me again.

It was Father's Day, so I forced myself out of bed to call my dad. I prayed he wouldn't notice the quivering in my voice as I reassured him I was fine. My sweet, gentle father, who loved and cherished me. If he knew, oh god, he couldn't know; it would crush his heart.

The next time Oso initiated sex, I shut my mouth and opened my legs.

Sex Containers

They say communication is the key to a good relationship. Oso and I had talked about sex at the start of our courtship. The conversation had been:

Him: "I like sex."

Me: "Well, I like sex too; I mean, who doesn't?"

And that was it.

Looking back, the conversation should've been:

Him: "I really really like sex."

Me: "Well, I like sex too; I mean, who doesn't? But, huh, what do you mean by really really?"

Him: "I have a powerful sex drive. To be content, I need it every day and sometimes twice a day. Otherwise, I'll make your life miserable."

Me: "See you later, dude."

After the camping incident, I labelled our sex life into four different containers. But before I describe them, you must be wondering why the hell did I not pack my bags and leave? It's a valid question and I'm afraid I don't have a definite answer. One thing was certain, I could not imagine abandoning the kids.

There was the indifferent sex container. Every time I touched Oso, he wanted sex. So, I tried to avoid any physical contact with him, which was hard for me because I'm a touchy-feely person. If I cuddled into his arms for a hug, the first thing he'd do was lift my shirt to squeeze my boobs. I dressed conservatively, trying to go unnoticed. I wore big flannel pyjamas to bed. Nothing worked; Oso still demanded sex. I'd go to my happy place, and I'd pretend I was elsewhere. It was easier to say yes than to endure two or three days of berating. I'd feign enjoying it, but my mind was elsewhere.

There was the forced sex container. No, he never physically forced me. But, once in a while, I put my foot down and said no. He never reacted well. It was okay for a day, maybe two, but then I'd sense the anger build up, and he'd explode. He claimed that sex was the most important part of a relationship and he felt rejected whenever I refused. He accused me of not loving him. Not the type to brood long, his voice grew louder, along with the profanity. He called me hideous names, frigid, cold bitch, and he threatened to go elsewhere. He took out his anger on the kids. Knowing I had no defence against his rage, he controlled me with his voice. So, I would lie there and let him fuck me. The bent steering wheel was a powerful reminder of the extent of his temper.

There was the painful sex container. I suffered my first yeast infection when I was sixteen years old. It became chronic. My ovulation every month provoked a new infection. The doctor prescribed medications for six months at a time to break the cycle. My friend describes it well when she says she begs her husband to scratch her in there with a metal hanger (not that he does). Needless to say, I didn't feel very sexy when clumpy cottage- cheese-type yeast oozed out of my sore, itchy, red vagina. Oso asked, "Hey, honey, are you in the mood?"

I said, "I can't; I have an infection."

He smiled. "We can use lubricant."

"It still hurts," I said.

"I'll be quick." I looked at his face and figured it was easier to endure the pain for a few minutes than to go through a rage episode. I turned around; I couldn't face him, my face defeated. Each thrust felt like a hot curling iron jammed into me. I grasped the sheets, and I pulled hard, my knuckles turning white. I closed my eyes and bit my lips, sometimes drawing blood. If the pain became unbearable, I couldn't help it. I whimpered. He would pull out then and finish by masturbating against me.

Believe it or not, there was the consensual sex container. Oso amazed me with a delightful meal, including candles and wine. We had a romantic dinner, and he inquired about my day. Then he offered to give me a massage, no strings attached. He vowed I was the most beautiful woman in the world. My body reacted to the massage, and I got turned on. We had sex, good sex. I even gave myself permission to reach an orgasm. As soon as we were done, I raced to the bathroom to take a shower. Oso wondered why I was unlike most women who wanted to cuddle after sex. I questioned my sanity. I was becoming an expert at pretending. I began to seriously doubt my ability to make the right decisions. When I dared mention his brutality, he reminded me his colleagues at work stated he was a real sweet guy. "You're the only one that sees me that way." He kept telling me my family was not normal, my dad was an exception, and he would never be like him. "I'm not your father," he often repeated. After the consensual sex, I hated myself. I not only betrayed my body; I betrayed my soul.

Occasionally, I would be the one to instigate sex. It gave me power over him. I would pose naked and watch him turn into jelly. He would tremble. And for a few minutes, I was in control of the situation. In control of my life. It seemed to be the only way to assert myself. I took the lead, and I felt strong. A twisted sense of power. It wouldn't last, but for a short while, I could pretend to be in charge of my life.

There were no linear lines or patterns in our sex life. Depending on what was going on, I jumped from one container to another. Most of the time, I tried to stay in the indifferent container. I made sure he wouldn't go three days without sex.

My mother had her suspicions because one day she told me, "If a woman says yes to sex because she's afraid, even if it's with her husband, it's a rape."

I shook my head. Oh, Mom, if only you knew.

Insomnia

I consider myself an eternal optimist who constantly worries about the worst that can happen. I know that's an oxymoron, but it's the best way I can describe myself. My dad used to tell us that happiness was not in external things but is something we nurture inside of us. I find happiness in little things, the flutter of a butterfly, the geese honking high in the sky, the aroma of coffee. A cheerful person with an uncontrolled imagination.

Oso's family shared a camp with friends near a small village called Chénéville. Chénéville is a small Quebec municipality, one hundred kilometres from Ottawa. The camp rested on a one-hundred-acre maple farm. We'd often spend weekends there, visiting with the in-laws. I loved going to Chénéville. We would ride the four-wheeler in the summer and plow through the snow with the snowmobile in the winter. We hunted, fished, snowshoed, and boiled the maple water into exquisite maple syrup. I enjoyed long walks in the woods.

When I worked on weekends, Oso would occasionally take the kids and go to Montreal or, more often, to the camp.

My fear of sleeping alone at night began at an early age. While my parents were out, my brother let me watch a scary movie. All I remember is a man's shadow lurking on the walls and dead women in chimneys. I was six years old. My imagination took over, and I saw shadows in my bedroom for months.

I'd often enter my parents' bedroom late in the evening, "I can't sleep." My dad said, "Close your eyes and sleep." My mom told me to pray, and sometimes it helped. As a teenager, I remember playing solitaire in my bed late at night. I played with actual cards, as we did not have video games or cell phones back then. I didn't know that my insomnia was related to anxiety. Heck, I don't even think I'd even heard the term anxiety. Various psychiatric associations only recognized anxiety as a disorder in the early 1980s. My mom used to talk about her mom, describing her as a very generous person but with poor nerves.

An event in my early teens dramatically reinforced my fear of sleeping alone. I was babysitting at my cousin's house, and I fell asleep on the couch. I woke up around midnight, sensing something was wrong. A giant, strange man sat on the chair next to me. He smirked. "You know you should lock the door." I stared at him. He added, "Please tell my brother I dropped by." He got up and left. I ran behind him and bolted the door. Breathing heavily, I leaned my back against the door and then quickly pushed myself away from it.

I'm not afraid of the dark, and I'm not scared of being alone. I am terrified of sleeping alone in the dark. Even today, if I spend a night alone, I check the locks three times. I lean a chair on the basement door, and I switch on the house alarm. I think about my aunt, whose husband died, and how she spends so much time alone in their camp in the woods. "Aren't you afraid?" my mom asked her. She replied, "I've been afraid so long that I'm no longer afraid." I repeat my aunt's words when I lie awake at night, listening for the door to open. It's a constant struggle to persuade myself that I'm safe.

I've often discussed my insomnia with my doctor. At certain rough times in my life, she prescribed me some sleeping pills, but I never liked taking medication, so I would only accept them for a few weeks. During one such visit, she said, "Could it be anxiety?" "Excuse me?" Liette does not have any mental issues such as anxiety. Liette is a very well-rounded individual. Of course, I worry a lot, but I never figured I had anxiety issues. My cousin Ruth told me she comes from a long line of nervous women (her mother is my mom's sister), and I couldn't agree more. It wasn't until in my late forties that I finally admitted I suffer from anxiety. I didn't think I was perfect, far from it, but I had grown up in a loving home. I was convinced my upbringing protected me from mental health issues. A few of my friends told me they got anxious when I visited them because they knew how much I liked a clean, orderly house. I asked too many questions. I'm nosy. But I did not suffer from anxiety, or at least, I refused to believe it. I blamed my overacting imagination. I worry too much, I said, like my mom.

Except for bouts of insomnia, the anxiety didn't play too much havoc with my mind. I kept myself entertained, playing sports and enjoying friends.

But now, the constant stress of living with Oso and the kids was exacerbating my anxiety. My body protested. The skin on my fingers became hard, ugly-looking. Then it turned into itchy and flaky sores before cracking open. The welts looked like paper cuts at first, deep and painful, and then they opened wider and bled. The doctor diagnosed eczema and prescribed cream, but it didn't seem to help much.

One late winter Friday evening, Oso left with the kids to go to Chénéville, and I did not feel safe in the old, isolated farmhouse. The owner saw me on Friday afternoon and joked, "Your husband is going away this weekend. I just might come over for some fun." Although I knew he was kidding, I was frightened. I brought the big husky dog into the house. He was not house trained, but I could deal with any incident the next morning. Oso had showed me how to load the twelve-gauge shotgun, and we practiced target shooting at the camp. He left the gun behind, so I loaded it and leaned it between the bed and the orange crates. I pulled a heavy chest in front of my bedroom door and lay down to sleep. My plan was simple. If someone tried to open my bedroom door, I'd give them one warning: I have a gun and I'm not afraid to use it! I fully intended to do so. I left a night light on and tried to sleep.

Oso's voice woke me up. I abruptly sat in bed and stared at his empty side. The voice sounded again, "Why are you not sleeping?" My chest tightened and I had trouble breathing.

"Where are you? I can't see you?"

I groped his pillow, and he yelped, "Stop poking me."

"You're not here, I can't see you, you're not here." Terror crawled up my spine, and my breathing became laboured. "I can't see you; I can't see you," I screamed, and I punched his pillow with both hands.

"Stop hitting me," he yelled. Suffocating, I swallowed big gulps of air, trying to push it down my constricted chest. I woke up on my hands and knees, my heart racing. Breathe, Breathe, Breathe. The next day, I went to work exhausted, but I didn't reveal my panic attack to anyone. Somehow, I made it through a twelve-hour shift and drove home for another night alone.

I again placed the heavy chest in front of the door and some-how fell asleep. Early on Sunday, I tried to unload the shotgun. As much as I struggled, I couldn't remember how to pop those stubborn bullets out. I left the gun loaded in the bedroom with a note on the kitchen table.

Caution, loaded shotgun on the bed.

Catherine's Visit

Summer 1988

The phone rang, and by Oso's reaction, I knew it was Susan, the biological mom. Summer was almost upon us, and I expected her to invite the kids like she always did, though the visit never happened. But no, this time, she offered to send Catherine to us for the summer. It was 1988, and Catherine was turning ten in early July.

Oso glanced at me. I nodded yes, of course. Jessi was fourteen years old, and Chris would turn thirteen in November. Since it was unlikely they would ever get to see their mom in British Columbia, we were excited to bring Catherine to us.

Both kids cleaned their rooms, and we put an air mattress on the floor next to Jessi's mattress. The kids wandered around the house. *Is it time yet? Is it time yet?*

We arrived at the airport well ahead of the flight's landing. The kids giggled, not sure what to expect. How will this little girl feel about us? Adding one more child to the family didn't bother me. Jessi and Chris were beyond thrilled to see their little sister.

We paced the second floor of the Ottawa International Airport. The flight was on time. The airline had assured us they took good care of kids flying alone. She took a direct flight from Vancouver, five hours.

Oso had not laid eyes on his daughter in seven years. The last time he held her, she had been three years old. Of course, they chatted on the phone and exchanged letters and pictures. Skype or Facebook did not exist yet, so we had limited communications to birthdays and Christmases. A ten-minute long-distance call could cost up to thirty bucks.

"Do you think she will recognize me?" Chris asked. "Will she be scared?" Jessi added. I couldn't help but feel the frenzy of their anticipation. I wondered what she was like. Was she like Jessi, strong and outgoing? Or like Chris, shy and introverted?

Oso stared at the gate, hardly able to contain his excitement at being reunited with his little girl. Again, I wondered why he left her so many years before.

We had sent Catherine a photo of Oso so the airline staff knew they were handing her over to the right people. I'm not sure if she showed them the picture. She didn't need to. She pulled her hand from the flight attendant's hand and sprinted toward her dad. Oso dropped to his knees and opened his arms. She jumped into her father's arms, almost knocking him over. We stood still as they desperately held on to each other. Father and daughter reunited after seven years. She let go, her face wet with tears, and turned to her brother and sister. They kept touching her to make sure she was real, to confirm it was her. They talked and giggled, giddy with excitement. She turned to me, and I opened my arms. Without hesitation, she threw herself into my arms.

If she was tired, she didn't show it. She was ready to take on the world. She was adorable with her elfin face, short brown hair, greenish/brownish eyes, and mischievous smile.

We did many activities with her that summer. We visited the in-laws in Montreal, where she got to know and spend time with her family. She couldn't speak a word of French, and Oso's family struggled with the English language, but they understood each other.

The kids' maternal grandmother lived in Vancouver, and she visited us for a couple of weeks that summer. She stayed in a hotel, and we spent every day with her. I suspect she wanted to make sure Catherine was okay. She was a lovely woman, and the kids and I adored her. A bit on the plump side, she wore glasses, and her grey hair was straight and cut short. I questioned her about Susan. She didn't want to talk much about her. They didn't get along, and she said Susan struggled through life. She came to visit again a few years later. We received birthday and Christmas cards until she passed away.

Catherine fit right in as if she had always lived with us. I had wondered whether she was going to be like Jessi or Chris. She turned out to be a bit of both but developed a special affinity for her brother. She spoke her mind like Jessi, but she was sneaky like Chris. Jessi was more of a city girl, and at fourteen, she worried about her body and image. Chris and Catherine were earthy types. She shared the bedroom with Jessi. Their whispers echoed late in the evening, reminding me of myself and Camilla growing up.

We did not tell the kids to shut up and sleep. Two months was too brief a time to spend together. How do you cram seven years into two months? We took them to the Canada Day celebrations in Ottawa. It warmed my heart to see Catherine and Chris becoming so close. They couldn't get enough of each other.

They raced after the various mascots and wanted to have their pictures taken together.

Catherine was a delight to have around, spunky and daring, yet respectful. Her exuberance was catchy; she was a child easy to love. She and Chris found an old video cassette tape in Montreal. Someone had pulled out the ribbon, and it was completely twisted. Chris was determined to find out what was on it. He spent hours putting it back together. Unfortunately, the damage was beyond repair. I guess he wanted to impress his little sister. He didn't have to try; she was totally absorbed by him.

Jessi still spent time with her friends, and most of the time, she didn't want her younger sister trailing along. However, I'd never seen Chris so happy. He and Catherine disappeared together for hours. Catherine later told me her brother taught her how to smoke cigarettes, hiding behind the house. I'd often find them giggling, and when I asked, they'd brush me off. They became a team, accomplices. Chris had a purpose. He was a big brother. We took them canoeing down the river, and she pointed and shrieked when she spotted a golf ball. She and Chris splashed each other in the canoe, and before we knew it, we were wet and laughing, almost tipping the canoe. She didn't seem to miss her mom much and she seemed to enjoy her stay with us. Susan called several times during the summer to talk to her and see how she was doing.

Oso was on his best behaviour, happy to have all his children with him. The summer whipped by, and soon we had to say goodbye.

Oso insisted on taking her to the airport by himself. He wanted to spend the last few hours alone with her, and I suspected that he especially needed to be alone after she'd gone. I hugged her tightly and I tried to console the other two as we watched the car leave. Chris was heartbroken. Both kids cried and waved as the car pulled away. Catherine, her nose crushed against the window, strained her neck to see us until the car disappeared.

The Pills

Fall 1988

The day began as any other routine twelve-hour shift. The sunny and warm Sunday fall weather promised a quiet workday. My task for the day was weather observing. I sighed. A long and boring day. Although I loved my job, I thrived under pressure, when the weather got crazy and the phone rang off the hook.

We worked twelve-hour shifts and got no time off for breaks or lunches. We'd cover each other, but sometimes if it was busy, we had to eat between phone calls.

I was in the kitchen warming up my leftovers from last night's dinner when the telephone rang. My colleague picked it up. "It's for you." He grinned. We were used to it. Oso called me two to three times during a twelve-hour shift.

I pleaded with him. "I don't have a private phone; we all share the same telephone, and my co-workers tease me about you calling all the time."

"But, honey," he said, "It's because I love you so much."

"I understand that, but –"

He cut me off. "Don't you love me as much; don't you miss me?"

"Yes, but I get reprimanded by my boss for having too many personal calls."

"Well, it's not my fault if they don't understand true love," he said. "And if you loved me as much as I do, you wouldn't care what they say."

"But, the other spouses, they don't –"

"You're lucky, someone loves you like I do. They're jealous, that's all."

A colleague, after such a call, said, "Wow, that man sure loves you." But I shook my head. Was this love? My mom loved my dad very much, yet she only called him at work if it was important. If Oso loved me, would he not respect my wishes? I groaned and let it go. I didn't want a full-blown meltdown.

I snatched the receiver. His voice was urgent. "Jessi swallowed some pills; I don't know how many. We're rushing to the hospital. Meet us there." I slammed down the phone, grabbed my purse, and hollered to my colleague as I bolted out the door.

Jessi had turned fourteen in January. She was getting tall, taller than me, which made her laugh. She'd lean on my shoulder and look down at me with affection. An extrovert, she loved partying with her friends. Kind and courageous, she possessed a strong sense of justice. She wasn't afraid to fight for what she thought was right, and she argued with her dad on his level. When she gained strength over the argument, he'd bellow, "Go to your room; you're grounded for a month."

She'd fold. Muttering under her breath, she'd storm upstairs and slam her door. Once he calmed down, I'd reason with him. I tried to be the peacekeeper, desperate to have the happy family life I grew up in. Eventually, he'd agree the punishment did not fit the crime, and he'd apologize to her. They'd hug, cry, and make up.

I raced to the hospital and sprinted to the emergency ward. I froze at the door. She sat on an examination table, a tube stuck inside her nose, reaching into her stomach. Through the open end of the tube, a doctor pumped black tar into her belly. Her father and a nurse held her while she gagged, puked, and sobbed. Did I just step into the middle of a television hospital drama show? This was not happening to my family.

I stared at her, and she raised her head to look at me. Fear and sadness filled her beautiful brown eyes. I approached the table and gripped her hand as they cleaned her up. I tried to talk, to say something, to reassure her, but the words caught in my throat. My tears flowed as I sought to console her. Oso moaned, his shoulders slumped, beaten.

They took her to a hospital room where she lay on the bed. The nurse said she hadn't swallowed enough pills to cause any definite harm, but we should not ignore this cry for help. Oso's voice was feeble. "We argued. I sent her to her room."

Immediately after swallowing the pills, she ran outside and screamed to her brother for help. He quickly alerted his dad.

We sat with her for a while. She kept saying she was sorry. We kept telling her we loved her. She stayed in the hospital for the night for observation. The three of us sat down for dinner, and her empty chair was a dark reminder of what had transpired. That evening, Oso and I sat by the river, watching the water gush downstream. He looked defeated. I fumed, but it was not a good time to bring up his discipline techniques. I wanted to scream at him, to tell him it was his fault. Maybe if I shook him? I envisioned throwing him into the cold, tumultuous waters of the river. Yet I held his hand as the moon shone across the water. I didn't understand. Why did he get so angry? Why the need to hurt the people he loved? I knew he loved his kids enormously. His eyes welled up when they made him proud.

They released her the next day after we all promised to go for family therapy with the Children's Aid Society of Ottawa. As teenagers, the kids rebelled against the world, but most of their frustration targeted their dad. Fights occurred more often and were becoming vicious. I took the kids' side, which infuriated their dad. I couldn't help it; it broke my heart the way he talked to them. Jessi had tried to hurt herself, and I hoped this desperate act scared him enough that he would mellow out. He'd almost lost his daughter. If that didn't change him, nothing would.

I knocked on her bedroom door. "Come in." I sat with her on the bed. I waited. She bowed her head in shame. I sensed her anguish. "What happened?" I asked her. I needed to know if I had to worry every day. She was strong, a fighter, so I doubt she wanted to die.

"I was so mad at Dad, I wanted to punish him." We talked about using other strategies to express her anger, her pain. She leaned her head on my shoulder. "I'm so glad you're here with us."

Jessi did not fear her dad, and she argued with him. Chris reacted differently. He sulked and then either ran away from home or hid in his room. They cleaned the dishes, but sometimes they'd put a dirty dish back into the cupboard. Their father would go ballistic when he found the dish. He'd scream and make them take out every dish in the cupboard and re-wash everything. One day, Oso stormed out of the kitchen, clutching a dirty plate he'd found hidden away. Seething, he shoved the plate in Jessi's face and hollered, "You're as worthless as a tit on the forehead! Go to your room. Now!"

She shouted, "I hate you," and stomped upstairs.

I stared at him. How could he say something so cruel to another human being? To his daughter? She slammed her bedroom door. My heart shattered, and I pleaded with him with my eyes.

I tried to protect the kids from the verbal abuse, but I failed miserably, getting myself in trouble. I never raised my voice at them. Later, Jessi told me that life got better after I moved in with them.

This pattern became the story of their lives. Even as adults, Jessi and her dad would get into huge fights and she would call me, crying. She swore she never wanted to see him again. I'd just listen and nod. Even after my divorce, I could never say one bad word about him; she would not tolerate it. She worshipped him, and she had an infinite well of loyalty. I still clench my teeth, remembering the unconditional love she had for him. I asked her about it one day, and she said she knew he was not the perfect dad, but she added, "He never abandoned us. Even when the going got tough, he never abandoned us. He raised us mostly by himself until you came along. He could've left us, but he didn't."

As promised, the four of us attended family counselling every two weeks for the next six months. Our assigned social worker's name was Marie. I felt comfortable with this plump woman and her no-nonsense attitude. Toys flowed out of boxes, and bright posters of flowers decorated the wall. A safe space for families where children feel protected. During the one-hour bi-weekly sessions, we each vented for ten minutes before it was time for someone else to speak. Then, with Marie's help, we discussed various strategies to handle differing incidents. For example, when Oso found one dirty plate, the kids had to re-wash that one plate and not everything in the cupboard. Marie recommended we hold family meetings where each of us talked. I grabbed on to Marie; she became my anchor, my lifeline. Oso and the kids liked her. They quoted her when the arguments started, "Hey, Marie said this, and Marie said that."

Sometimes, it worked, and it diffused the situation. Most times, it did not.

The Wrong Size Pot

The trees were bare, and a few snowflakes threatened the dreary November sky. It wouldn't be long before patchy ice formed on the Jock River. In the backyard, fog blew from the cow's nostrils.

Oso had been in a sour mood ever since Catherine's departure. To make things worse, the environment director from the New Brunswick Community College called and offered him a teaching job. He had to refuse because we now lived near Ottawa. Years later, he told me he blamed me for the lost opportunity – hence, why he lost his temper with me. It was a pitiful excuse. He had lost his temper many times before he received that offer.

I heard the commotion from upstairs. What now? Jessi and I both rushed downstairs. Oso had a firm grip on Chris's arm and he was pulling out his belt. Chris' face was contorted in sheer terror, his eyes bulging as his dad dragged him away. "Wait! What happened? What are you doing?" I shrieked.

Oso looked at us, his eyes dark. "He stole money from my wallet. I'm gonna teach him a lesson. Lock yourselves in the bedroom. You do not want to see what is going to happen to him." I pleaded with Oso to not hit him as I pulled Jessi to our bedroom. He winked at me and mouthed, *I only want to scare him.*

Jessi and I sat on the floor, holding on to each other. Horrified, we sobbed. I tried to reassure her. I'm not sure how long we stayed there; the house was quiet. I think Oso took Chris outside. When he told us we could come out, he assured me he didn't touch him. Jessi left for a walk. Chris' bedroom door was closed. He didn't come out until the next day. I wanted to go to him, but I was afraid of Oso's reaction, so I did nothing.

Shift work had advantages. I enjoyed a day alone. I love all our Canadian seasons, and the autumn is no different. A time to slow down and prepare for the winter ahead. The geese honked high in the sky, flying toward more clement weather.

Oso had recently signed a three-month contract for work. The kids were back in school, but we were getting regular calls about skipping classes and homework not being done.

I grabbed a shovel and dug the hard ground to pull out the last potatoes and carrots.

I chopped wood for kindling and built a fire in the old wood cooking stove. The logs sent a warmth and cozy perfume through the dining room.

Oso had wrapped the thermostat with masking tape and forbade us to touch it. He didn't want us to use the electric stove because of the high hydro bills. I struggled each month to balance the chequebook. "I do this for you," he'd say. "So you don't have to worry about the money."

I opened the blinds in the dining room and the faint light brightened the room. I kept a few herb plants growing on the windowsill, parsley and basil.

Today was a good day. Oso would come home from work to find a decent house, clean kids, and a sweet-smelling roast and potato dinner cooking in the wood stove oven. When the kids arrived home from school, I asked them to go pick up a few fall flowers. They helped me set the table, and I made sure it was the way Oso liked it. The knife on the right, the fork on the left, the glasses on the upper side of the plates. We laid the salad and dressing in the middle of the table. Jessi arranged the flowers in a vase and displayed them in the centre.

I asked Chris to empty the garbage can. I checked to make sure the kids' clothes were clean and they had washed their faces and hands. We worked together while the kids blabbed about school.

I smiled as I inspected our beautifully set table. We would have a nice family dinner, like in any normal household.

I noticed the compact brown Aspen car pull up the long driveway and watched as Oso stepped out of the vehicle. We stood near the table, smiling, and said hello to him as he came inside. Without uttering a word, he eyed the table. He glanced at the kids, then inside the garbage can. He walked to the woodstove from which originated a warm glow and a sweet smell that tickled the saliva. Opening the oven door, he peeked inside. Slipping on the oven mitts, he lifted the cover of the large clay pot, revealing a fine roast and root vegetables. I waited in anticipation.

He slammed the cover on the pot, turned and said, "What were you thinking? The pot is too big for the roast and vegetables. You're wasting space for nothing."

The Abyss

I sat in the car in the driveway.

I'd just gotten home after a busy twelve-hour day shift. I'd woken up at five-thirty to make it to work by seven. It had been a brief night since we fought late into the wee hours. Oso would not let me sleep until he decided the fight was over. At midnight, I told him, "I need some rest; we can finish this discussion tomorrow."

I went to bed. The sounds of his steps approaching had me grabbing the sheets, holding them tight to my chin. "Oh no," he said. He grabbed and yanked the blankets, tearing them off the bed. "You started this; we're gonna finish it."

I'm not sure how I started the fight. It took little to piss him off. We argued until three o'clock, ending with me apologizing and swearing my love to him. When the alarm blared, he turned to me, "Stay with me today."

I sighed. "I'm not sick. I have to go to work. If I call in sick at the last minute, someone will have to replace me, or the night person will be stuck working a double shift."

He insisted, "What is your priority? Is your family not your priority? What's wrong with you? Why do you prefer to work instead of staying here with me?" He didn't understand that calling in sick contradicted my values. My dad never called in sick unless he was ill, and even then, my mom had to force him to stay in bed. I pushed Oso away, and I got ready to leave. I could hardly put one foot in front of the other, but I needed to get away from him, and I wasn't sick. It had snowed overnight, and the car got stuck in the driveway. I asked him for help. He said, "You're too stupid to listen to me and stay home, go fuck yourself." Trying to control my trembling voice, I called the office and told them I'd be a bit late. I grabbed a shovel and began clearing the snow. The landlord noticed and came to pull me out with the tractor. Fortunately, they took care of the snow removal in the winter.

I had completed my shift and here I was, sitting in the driveway. I stared ahead without seeing. Dinner must be ready, yet I didn't know how to get out of the car. My legs seemed useless.

This life I was living. How did it get this crazy? I was not a victim. At least, not what I thought a victim looked like. Women who stayed in abusive situations came from violent homes. They didn't have a job and were uneducated. I had a career. I grew up in a home without violence. How did I find myself here, sitting in the car, scratching my bleeding fingers, not knowing how to open the car door? I didn't even recognize I was being abused, but I knew what was happening was not okay.

Did I think about leaving? Of course, I did, almost every day. So, why didn't I leave? Jessi and Chris. How could I leave them?

Anything could trigger a fight. That was the worst part, not knowing what would prompt the shouting. Always tiptoeing around the house. Constantly stressed.

Our arguments were always one-sided. Oso yelled while I tried to get a word in. The fights ended when he decided. I never had the chance to say my piece. I'd wait for him to calm down and then I'd bring it up again. "What!" he'd exclaim. "You're still stuck on that; we settled the matter." And that was the end. The frustration I felt was growing and gnawing at my insides.

Oso would eventually notice I was in the car and he would come get me. What kind of mood would he be in? Did the children behave today? Are the children home? Did the school call? Did they run away again?

My head was telling me to leave him, but I'd fallen in love with the kids. They were not mine; I couldn't take them with me. If I reported him to child services, I'd have to prove the abuse, and I'd never seen him hit the kids. Were the kids better with us than with strangers? If they lived with a foster family, would they allow me to visit them? Would they ever forgive me? Jessi adored her father. Chris loved him, of course, even if he feared him. Oso might kill me if he lost his kids because I snitched on him. Some days were not so bad; some days were even good. Spending a weekend at the cottage or Montreal or even occasionally roasting marshmallows on bonfires.

I sat in the car. I thought about my parents, my family, wondering if they suspected how unhappy I'd become. I was ashamed of the life I had chosen. Could I leave everything and go home? What about my job? And of course, I would never leave the kids. I could not abandon them. Unsure of my feelings toward for Oso, I still wished we could make the relationship work. If I tried harder, it might be okay. Leaving the family also meant admitting defeat. I'd never failed at anything before except my relationship with my fiancé. I didn't want another failed relationship.

Most things come easy for me. I'd always done well academically, and I love learning new things. Popular in school, I had wonderful friends whom I still keep in contact with. The teachers liked me. I finished first in my class in college, and I had an awesome career with the federal government. I was never an expert in any sports, but I did well in every sport I played. Yes, my heart was broken when my fiancé and I split up, but we were not married. We were not living together. I had my whole life ahead of me. I took care of my health. I didn't smoke anymore; I drank in moderation, and I was active. Failure was not in my vocabulary. When I was in my thirties, and my doctor told me I was suffering from high blood pressure, I was dumbfounded, and I bawled in her office. She shook her head. "You do everything right. You eat well; you are not overweight, and you exercise regularly," she said. "It's hereditary, not a failure." Still, I left her office in tears.

To stop the cycle of violence, sometimes I'd get desperate, and while he'd be screaming at me, I'd lift my shirt and bra. The result was instantaneous; his eyes lit up, and the fight was over. However, it also meant I had to carry through with it and have sex. We had what I called the indifferent sex.

I opened the car door and I forced myself to walk toward the house. I slid in the back door and Oso met me in the corridor. He opened his mouth. The words poured out: anger and complaints. Bla Bla Bla Bla.

I snapped. I jumped and I grabbed his neck. I didn't plan to strangle him, I simply needed him to shut up. Just please shut the fuck up! Shut up. Shut up. Shut up. I am a small person with small hands. Oso had wide shoulders and a muscular neck from working in the woods. I did not have the strength to kill him, but for a split second, maybe I wanted to. My action shocked me and I let go immediately. I bent over and giggled hysterically.

Oso stared at me and laughed. I told him we needed to go to marriage counselling, and he agreed. I was learning to fight back. But I was ashamed and scared of my behaviour. I was not a violent person; I'd hurt no one in all my life. Looking back, I understand why I reacted with violence. My desperate mind went for the fight instead of the flight.

Hitchhiker Bum

It was December 1988, but even with the white dusting of fresh snow on the ground, I found it difficult to be in the Christmas spirit. As discussed, Oso and I went to therapy together. The psychologist, a woman in her fifties, tied her grayish hair in a bun and smiled kindly as we walked in. She asked a few basic questions, then said, "How can I help you?"

Oso said, "I often want sex, and my wife repeatedly says no. It makes me feel unloved and rejected. I don't understand why she doesn't agree that sex is very important in a relationship."

She looked at me. "What about you? How do you feel about what he said and about sex?"

I said, "I don't think it has anything to do with love. We have very different sex drives. I used to like it, but now I feel pressured to have sex, and it becomes a chore. If I say no, he yells at me and calls me names, like frigid or bitch, and he tells me to fuck off."

Toward the end of the session, the therapist said to Oso, "Can you work on remaining calm and understanding when she is not in the mood?" He nodded. Then she looked at me. "Can you try to not take his words seriously when he's shouting? They are only words."

I stared at her, "So when he calls me a fuckin bitch, I should not let it bother me?"

She responded, "That's right. Try to let the words slide off your shoulders. Try to be less sensitive."

I left her office feeling confused and defeated. Was I overreacting? Was Oso right? Couples fight and anything is allowed? Was it just me? Did my parents shelter me to the extent I had a hard time fitting into the real world?

I refused to go back to therapy. What was the point?

A few days later, I drove home after a twelve-hour day shift. During the ride, my mind replayed our fight from the previous night. It was late, and I told him I needed to sleep. I curled up in bed, turning my back to him. I sensed him climbing into bed. He kicked me in the lower back, propelling me to the floor. I didn't fall hard since we slept on a mattress. I bolted downstairs, him on my tail. Desperate to get away from him, I crouched behind the big wood stove in the kitchen. Of course, he spotted me right away. When he saw me curled in a foetal position, he burst out laughing. "Look at you, acting like a battered woman. You're so pathetic." He turned around and went back to bed. His snickering echoed all the way up the stairs. I waited for a long time, sobbing. I didn't know what to do anymore. I didn't know how to stop the violence. I didn't know how to leave. I was messed up.

The holiday season felt bleak that year, but I wanted to brighten things up by buying a Christmas tree. The kids would have a nice holiday. I stopped at the local Richmond tree nursery, and for thirty bucks, I bought a bushy balsam fir tree. The lady helped me put it in the box of our pickup truck. We had bought a truck to haul the timber that fed the wood stove in the kitchen. It was our primary source of heat. The frost drew pretty pictures in the house windows in the winter while the breeze whistled through the cracks. Winters can be fierce in Ottawa, with the average temperature around minus eight degrees Celsius. The nighttime temperature can often go down between minus twenty to minus thirty-five degrees Celsius. Once we bought the truck, Oso needed a new chainsaw to cut the wood. We also bought a four-wheeler to drag the wood from the forest. Then, of course, we needed a trailer to carry the four-wheeler. We were heavily in debt.

I didn't have the money for a Christmas tree, but I smiled as I left the nursery. We had purchased a few presents for the kids. I worked for the government full time with a salary of twenty thousand dollars per year. I was often the only one working to feed a family of four. Oso's contract was ending at the end of December, and we didn't know if he'd find work quickly.

Oso and I called him the hitchhiker bum. I recognize now that it was not a very flattering name, but we meant it nicely. Of course, we never mentioned it in his presence. He always wore a long brown trench coat, regardless of the weather, winter or summer, rain or shine. I often wondered where he went every day or what he hid in the brown paper bag tugged under his arm. He'd stand on the main Richmond Road and put his thumb out, and we'd often pick him up. He seemed harmless, and he was always polite but evasive when I asked him questions. We'd drop him off at the intersection of a side road on the way to our house. He'd never let us drive him to his house. We respected that.

As I pulled out of the nursery, I saw him, the hitchhiker bum. I picked him up and we were chitchatting when I glanced in my rear-view mirror. The tree was gone! Vanished! The box was empty! We turned around and we looked and searched, but our Christmas tree was lost. The hitchhiker bum said he needed to get home, but he suggested I go back and tell them what happened. He patted the door. "Who knows, in the Christmas spirit, they might just give you another one." I dropped him off at his usual road crossing and I drove back to the nursery. I couldn't afford another thirty dollars, but I had to try.

I parked the truck in the middle of what seemed like hundreds of Christmas trees, flashing colourful lights. Joyful music blared on the outside speakers. A few families were attaching their tree on their car roofs, and I couldn't help but smile at the wide grins on the kids' face.

I rested my forehead on the steering wheel and closed my eyes. These families seemed so happy. Were they also pretending? My mom often said that if we could look behind every closed door, we'd know there is no such thing as the perfect family.

The same young lady who sold me the tree seemed surprised to see me when I approached her. "I was driving and I looked back and the tree was gone. I searched everywhere. Someone must've seen it fall and picked it up." I stared deep into her eyes, mine pleading. *Please believe me. Please help me.* Hopefully, she won't think I brought the tree home, and I am lying to get another one.

The kindness in her eyes matched the anguish in mine. "Lady, just go get yourself another tree. Merry Christmas." Hope. I felt hope.

Pregnant

Summer 1989

"We should bring some pickles," Chris said, a twinkle in his eyes. "You know, in case of an emergency."

I was twenty-seven years old when I began drooling over pregnant women's bellies. Each time I witnessed a mother cradling her baby, I couldn't help but stare, and my eyes teared up. To say I wanted a baby is an understatement; I wanted six babies. You must wonder why on earth would I want a baby with Oso? I'd like to say that I seriously assessed our situation and knew he would change his parenting style once we had our own baby. After all, he would not be a single dad this time. I had a steady income, and we would be a happy, well-adjusted family. And I'd like to think that if he didn't, I would take off with my child. The reality was simpler; my hormones consumed my body and squeezed every ounce of reasoning out the door. I didn't want a baby; I craved a baby.

I consider myself an easy-going person. I've never liked conflict, and I get along with most people. But when I want something, I get impatient. I must have it now. I hate waiting. So, when my body decided it must have a baby, I told Oso it was time. He agreed.

Did I think a baby would improve our relationship? Of course not. There was nothing wrong with our relationship. I mean, yes, there was something really amiss with it. And yet. We had some rough patches, but overall, I'd convinced myself we were doing pretty good. I choose to ignore the bad parts. I'd made a promise to stay, and I would keep my promise. Regardless of our situation, I needed a baby like I needed my next breath.

In June, my boss sent me back to Cornwall on a three-month weather presentation course. This time, I had my room and free access to the cafeteria. The distance from Ottawa to Cornwall allowed me to come home every weekend. Jessi called me, "I have good news, and I have bad news."

"Okay, give me the good news first."

"I found a job!" She was very excited; it was her first job. She worked at the Richmond bakery. She was fifteen years old.

"I'm so proud of you," I said. "And the bad news?"

"I flunked math, and I have to attend summer school." I knew her social life had priority over her studies. Life at home was not always easy for her either.

I went home for a night during the week, and Oso and I had sex. In the morning, he smiled and said, "You're pregnant."

Two weeks later, I peed in a tiny bottle and handed it to the nurse. She called the next day and said, "Congratulations, you're going to have a baby."

I sat down and then I jumped up and danced. I laughed and I cried. I stared at my stomach, laid my hand on it. Somewhere in there, a tiny, wonderful egg was growing. I was no longer just me. I was me and a baby. I was already in love.

I couldn't wait for Oso to come home. I called him immediately. He broke down on the phone. "I knew it, I told you."

Jessi whooped and hugged us when we told her I was pregnant. Chris grinned and congratulated us. I kept a journal during my pregnancy, but I was not very consistent at writing in it. As a teenager, I kept detailed personal diaries. I was thirteen years old when I forgot it in the bathroom. During dinner, my brother casually asked me how Daniel was. Lesson learned. I protected my personal thoughts.

I savoured every minute of being pregnant. A bliss in the middle of a blizzard. Oso was gentler with me now that I was pregnant, but the fights with the kids continued. Jessi disappeared for long stretches. In my journal, on August 19th, 1989, I wrote: *Jessi ran away from home today.* Nothing else, no explanations. Then, over the following few days, I noted random stuff about my pregnancy, my course in Cornwall, and taekwon-do classes. Ten days later, on August 29th, I scribbled: *Jessi came back home today.* Although she was only fifteen, we worried less about her because we knew most of her friends. By the time our baby was born, she had turned sixteen and had permanently left home.

I wanted to announce this incredible news to my family in person. The doctor shook her head. She'd only approve of the long drive on the condition that I stop halfway and take breaks at least every two hours. After all, it was a twelve-hundred-kilometre drive from Richmond, Ontario, to Memramcook, New Brunswick. Oso had just started a new work contract, and Jessi worked at the local bakery. I winked at Chris. "Want to come to New Brunswick with me?" His grin said it all. We packed the car and hit the road. It was nice to spend time together, just the two of us. I was relieved Oso was not coming. Although my parents tolerated our relationship, I felt they still didn't approve. Oso said I acted differently when I was with my family. He didn't like to share me with them. He accused me of neglecting him. It was easier when he wasn't there.

We couldn't afford a hotel, so we packed our tent and camped halfway. That evening, we lit up a bonfire and roasted marshmallows.

Chris clutched the flashlight and held it under his chin. "Time for horror stories," he said.

"Are you sure?"

"Of course; otherwise, it won't be real camping."

I chuckled. "Okay, you start." And he did. He made up stories of gore and monsters, his imagination running wild. We giggled while our marshmallows sizzled in the flames.

We curled up in our individual sleeping bags. Chris whispered. "Liette, do you want a boy or a girl?"

"I think it's a boy, just a feeling I have, but I am fine with either. How about you? Would you prefer a little brother or a little sister?"

"It would be fun to have a younger brother since I already have two sisters."

We played games and invented stories to pass the time. We brought a cooler, and we ate a picnic on the side of the road, tuna sandwiches with pickles. Chris kept the last one for the one-thousand-kilometre mark. He solemnly raised it in the air, and we thanked it for its ultimate sacrifice. We shared the juicy cucumber in the middle of the forest on the old Renous highway in New Brunswick. To reward ourselves, we stopped for ice cream at the edge of the road. We rested on a picnic table, savouring our special treat. Normally, I was elated to go home, but the closer we got, the more nervous I became.

Chris was excited to announce the good news to my family. "They're going to be so happy." I smiled, but I had a lump in my throat. How would they react? I was not married, and my parents were devout Catholics. They were not fond of Oso either.

I drove in silence for a while, deliberating how I would tell them I was expecting a baby. "Chris, please don't say anything. I prefer to announce it myself."

The day after we arrived, I helped my mom with dinner. Trying to work up the nerve to tell her. "I have news." You cannot hide the truth from my mom.

"You're pregnant," she said. I nodded. She also nodded. When my dad got home, she said, "Liette has some news."

"Oh?" His eyebrows lifted.

"She's pregnant."

My dad peered at me. His little girl. "I guess they live together; it was to be expected."

I mumbled under my breath, "My baby was conceived in love."

During our one-week visit, we spoke little about the baby. I wanted to shout the joyous news to the world, and yet I stayed quiet. I had known they would not be thrilled. Would they cherish my baby as much as they cared for their other grandchildren? My dad loved to cuddle them when they were young. My mom got on her hands and knees and played with them. She pulled them on sleighs and went gliding in the snow. My brother once remarked that she didn't play with us as much when we were kids. She explained, "I had six kids to take care of and a house to keep. I didn't have time."

My family – brothers, sisters, nieces, and nephews – got together to have a picnic at the Centennial Park in Moncton. I have fond memories of Sunday picnics at that park during the summer when we skipped the beach or my uncle and aunt's cottage. We never dined in restaurants, but one day, my parents bought a bucket of Kentucky Fried Chicken. We had a picnic on a blanket surrounded by tall trees. I licked my fingers. I thought the chicken must've come directly from the heavens.

Chris ran with my cousins. They pushed each other on the swings and shot down the slides. They splashed water in the enormous pool. Chris asked my dad for the car keys to get his towel. I knew something was wrong the instant he returned. His eyes lowered to the ground, he said. "I locked the keys in the trunk."

The park was twenty kilometres from my parents' house. My dad and brothers tried in vain to open the trunk. I cringed when my dad, his voice sharp, told Chris that he should've been more careful. I was not used to seeing my dad angry, especially when it was clearly an accident. Chris's lips trembled, and it broke my heart. It wasn't fair. Chris was being berated because he was Oso's son. After an hour of trying to force the trunk open, my brother drove to my parents' house to get the spare key.

We stayed in New Brunswick for a week. Every place we visited, someone recognized us, and we'd have a lively conversation. Chris had never lived long in one place, and he shook his head in wonder. "Do you know everyone?" We took him to the famous Parley Beach in Shediac where he swam in the salty ocean. We had a picnic at the edge of the village, where the river dumps into the Bay of Fundy. My mother noticed him walking alone along the shore and wandered over to talk to him. Years later, she told me his eyes were sullen and when she asked him about it, he replied, "I'm not even baptized."

I wonder now why it bothered him. Jessi had been baptized, but the family never attended church, and I'd never seen them pray. I went to mass every Sunday, but the kids showed no interest in joining me. Maybe it was the beginning of his lengthy quest to find his place in the world.

It was a pleasant but tough week. I wanted to scream my happiness at being pregnant, and yet I didn't feel like I could freely discuss it. When we said our goodbyes, my dad held on to my shoulders and stared into my eyes. In his eyes, I saw concern, sadness, hope, but most of all, love. My mom hugged me and said she would come help me when my baby was born.

Relieved, Chris and I had a pleasant drive back home. I understood my parents would embrace and love my child because he would be a part of me.

Cravings

I did not crave pickles throughout my pregnancy. I craved chocolate, but then again, I don't need to be pregnant to crave chocolate.

I embraced being pregnant. I savoured every single minute of my growing belly. From the moment the nurse said positive, I glowed with baby thoughts. Oso was being extra nice. He kissed my belly and whispered to our little baby boy. We didn't do a test to find out if it was going to be a girl or a boy. Gender parties were not a thing back then. But one night, I awoke to a male voice calling my name, and Oso said it was my baby boy reaching out. Jessi and Chris teased me about my growing bump.

Somehow, I knew this would be my only pregnancy. Although I wanted six kids, my gut warned me this would be it. A week before giving birth, I sat in a salon, getting my hair done. The hairdresser said, "You must be so relieved that this is almost over."

I smiled and caressed my belly. "No, I love being pregnant. He can take his time coming out."

In November 1989, four months into my pregnancy, Oso and I prepared for bed. "Oh my God, listen to that wind. It sounds like a pack of wolves gutting a sheep," I said as I buttoned my flannel pyjamas. "Any leaves left on the trees will be gone by morning."

Oso replied, "Never mind the leaves. Hopefully, the trees survived this mess. Mother Nature is having a bad tantrum."

I placed my hand on the window. "Do you think they will break?" The rain and sleet flogged the windows with such ferocity that I fretted the storm would erupt into our bedroom. The cold air filtered through the surrounding cracks. I sat on the bed. "Do we have any chocolate?" I asked.

"I don't think so," Oso said.

I sighed, and I slipped under the warm covers. "I guess this craving will have to wait."

Oso pulled up his pants and tied his shoes. "Where are you going?"

He grinned. "My pregnant wife wants chocolate, so I'm gonna get some chocolate."

"Have you gone insane? You'll get blown away." He shrugged and left the room.

I rushed to the spare bedroom to watch him leave. Both hands clutching his coat, he leaned his body forward, fighting his way through the fury threatening to blow him away. The car's rear lights quickly disappeared in the dark and violent storm.

Not a sound came out from behind the kids' closed doors. I envied the ease with which they fell and stayed asleep.

Oso drove ten kilometres through perilous conditions to a Richmond convenience store and then ten kilometres back to bring me two Hershey bars. His clothes dripped on the floor, and his face beamed proudly as he handed me my treat.

I ate the chocolate with as much passion as the skies whipped the storm across the land.

We kissed goodnight, and I lay in bed awake for another hour. How could I ever doubt his love for me? Losing his temper once in a while, I could live with that, no? Nobody's perfect, right? Who could resist a man willing to brave the raging weather to satisfy the craving of a pregnant woman?

Weddings and Birth

I wanted our child to be born to married parents. My Catholic upbringing still had a powerful hold on me. But getting married in a Catholic church meant Oso had to seek an annulment from his first marriage. He never wed the kids' biological mother, but when he first moved to the Yukon, he married a can-can dancer. The marriage lasted one winter. After freezing her boobs hauling wood from outside, she flew back to her hometown in California. Oso applied for the annulment, but we knew it would take a long time to get it, if it was even approved. It had to come from the Pope! In the meantime, we got married at the justice of the peace. My friend Chantal and her husband acted as witnesses, and they even took the kids for the weekend while we enjoyed a brief honeymoon at the camp in Chénéville. Chantal's husband worked with Oso, and we'd become close friends. The ceremony occurred two months before Ben was born. Of course, Jessi and Chris attended the wedding.

I bought a gorgeous cream-coloured maternity dress, and Oso wore a blue suit and tie with a white shirt. It was a simple ceremony. I felt a tinge of sadness as we stepped out of the chamber with no one to share the moment with. Suddenly, I heard loud cheers and a gang of Oso's colleagues appeared and applauded, hurling rice at us. Oso worked for the municipality, and he had told them we were getting married. If they liked him this much, he must be a good man. Maybe the therapist was right, and I made too big a deal of our fights. I needed to learn to let the words slide.

The first contraction woke me up at one-thirty in the morning. It was a weird sensation, not painful, but I knew this was it. During the birthing classes, they instructed us to go back to sleep if labour began during the night. Tired from shift work, I snoozed until the cramps became stronger. I let Oso sleep until five and then tapped his shoulder. "Time to go." On our way to the hospital, he stopped in Richmond to get a coffee.

I had an easy pregnancy, and I loved every minute of being pregnant. I gained nineteen pounds. Oso and I had enrolled in taekwon-do classes a few months before I got pregnant. I continued punching and kicking until my eighth month. I'd always been active in sports, and I was in good physical shape.

Labour progressed and we paced the hospital halls. Lassie played on TV in the waiting room. I called the office, "Take me off the schedule; I'm having a baby." My due date was one week away, and they expected me to work that evening. I did not want to take time off before my child was born. I'd rather maximize my time with my baby after the birth. The government paid us three months of maternity leave.

By late afternoon, they confined me to a bed. I had prepared for a normal childbirth, no drugs. The doctor became worried about the baby. His heartbeat lowered with each contraction. They plunged their hands into my vagina and screwed a tiny wire on the baby's head. They attached the wire to an electrode so they could monitor the heartbeat more effectively. The doctor shook her head while she looked at me. She gave me a choice. "If the heartbeat stays low, we will need to do a caesarean. You can be awake for the procedure if you take an epidural now. If you don't, and we have to do an emergency c-section, we will not have time for the epidural and we will have to sedate you."

I took the epidural. The nurse stayed by my side, monitoring the baby's heartbeat. Suddenly, she bolted out of the room and raced back with the doctor. They rushed me into the operating room. While they tied my arms extended like Jesus on the cross, I tried to get reassurance from Oso. He sat by my head, curious about what was happening. I prayed with all my heart. *Please let my baby be okay, please let my baby be okay.*

My perfect baby boy was born at six-fifteen pm on Sunday, March 4th, 1990. A beautiful, healthy little boy. I couldn't hold him right away since they still had me wired. They checked him over and handed him to Oso. He was perfect; everything was perfect. We called him Ben after Oso's godparent. I stayed in the hospital for one week. Ben (or likely me) had a hard time nursing. I was recovering from the surgery and weak from not sleeping. A local radio station called me to do a live broadcast. It was a local French station, and they had followed my pregnancy every time I'd done a weather broadcast with them. *He is so small; he is so small,* I kept repeating.

Oso wanted our baby to be circumcised. Since I do not have a penis, I respected his decision. That evening, desperately needing to sleep, I accepted a sleeping pill. The newborns spent the nights in the nursery. Still, I couldn't sleep. Worried about the surgery,

I got up and dragged my drugged, tired body to the nursery. I leaned down toward a peaceful sleeping baby. My heart exploded with love. The nurse tapped me on the shoulder. "Madame, that is not your baby. Your baby is over here." So much for mothers being able to recognize their baby's cry.

The following evening, minutes after I dozed off, a nurse gently tapped my shoulder. "You have an emergency phone call from home." Oh no! What now?

I wobbled to the nurses' station and picked up the receiver. Oso was crying. "Chris is gone to British Columbia," he said. "He called his mom and told her I tried to choke him. She panicked and sent her brother to come get him. He's gone." Chris was fourteen years old.

"Did you?" I asked.

"Did I what?"

"Did you try to choke him?"

He seemed pissed now. "Of course not."

After I handed her the phone, the nurse asked me if everything was okay. I sighed and shook my head. I dragged my feet back to my room. My mood flicked with each step I took. Right step, anger. Left step, sadness. Right step, anger. Left step, sadness. Anger. Sadness.

By the time I crawled under the blankets, I was an emotionally messed up, conflicted mortal. For the first time since becoming a stepmom, I felt resentment toward one of the kids. I was in the hospital with my new baby. This was my moment. Couldn't I get this one time without a family crisis? Was I being selfish? A desperate fourteen-year-old boy called his mother and told her his dad tried to kill him. A grown-up man was bawling because he gained a new son but had also lost one. Still, the tears washed my face. Could I please have one moment of peace?

Six days after he was born, we took Ben home. I became paranoid that Chris or his biological mom would tell the Social Services Oso had tried to strangle him. Would they deem us unfit parents and take our baby away? I couldn't sleep, I couldn't eat, I could hardly function. My family was twelve hundred kilometres away, both kids had left home, and I was no longer in love with my husband. All my affection, all my love was completely devoted to my baby. My life began and stopped with him. When Oso held him, I felt a ping of tenderness toward him. We could make this work. However, the fear that they might take Ben away was rotting me from the inside. I called Marie's office. I begged the receptionist to schedule time with her as soon as possible. "Hang on," she said. "Marie can see you tomorrow at ten am."

I stepped into Marie's office carrying my sleeping baby in his car seat. She smiled and pointed to a chair. "Congratulations, he's beautiful! Now, please sit down and tell me what's wrong."

I blurted out my fears, telling her what Chris said. When I stopped talking, she said, "Chris is an asshole; nobody is going to take your baby." Wait, what? I stared at her.

She repeated, "Chris is an asshole; nobody is going to take your baby."

While I'd been driving to Marie's office, I'd imagined many scenarios, what I was going to say, what she might say, how I would respond, trying to prove we were good parents. Her saying Chris was an asshole was nothing I had imagined. She didn't believe Oso had tried to choke his son but that Chris had invented that story because he was desperate to go live with Susan. Marie promised me nobody would take Ben away. I left her office weighing fifty thousand kilograms lighter. I did not want to consider that Oso tried to hurt his son, but I was at a point where I didn't know what to trust anymore. Their relationship had become toxic, and I knew Oso had a temper. Marie, not believing it, did more than ease my fear of losing my baby; she reinforced my belief that Chris was lying and that we could still be a happy family.

I wonder now if Ben's birth triggered Chris's desperate attempt to go see his mom. She had called again and promised him he could visit her in June. None of us believed her anymore.

Jessi was ecstatic about having a little sister or brother, but while Chris said he was happy, he had not shown it. I loved both kids, but Ben became the highlight of my life. My little person whom I had carried and loved for nine months.

Three months later, Chris called us. His voice trembled. "Can I please come home?" We paid for his flight, and Oso picked him up at the airport. Chris' balloon did not deflate; it completely blew to hell. When we questioned him, all he volunteered was, "She's crazy." He sadly shook his head and repeated, "She's crazy." Afterward, he gave up on being good or caring about being good.

Ben loved his older brother; his face lit up whenever Chris played with him. Once in a while, Chris babysat while Oso and I went for a quiet dinner. When Ben was six months old, he sat on the floor while we played games with him. Chris approached Ben, who suddenly screamed, eyes wide. Chris stopped, startled, and backed away. Ben calmed down immediately, but kept his eyes on his older brother. Chris approached him again, and again Ben howled, his eyes full of fear.

"What happened? What did you do?" I questioned him. He strongly denied having done anything wrong. A part of me refused to believe Chris would hurt his brother on purpose. I checked him all over and I did not see any marks. Maybe he had a moment of impatience. I made Oso swear to never leave Ben alone with Chris. A barrier wrapped itself around my heart. Although I loved Chris, I would never trust him again with Ben.

Shortly afterwards, I carried Ben in my arms while I fetched meat from the freezer. As I leaned to reach for the meat, Ben panicked and wailed. I calmed him, but it made me wonder: did Chris put Ben in a box? The other girlfriend used to lock him in a closet; did he do the same with Ben?

As promised, my mom flew out for a couple of weeks to help me with the baby.

It was early March and still cold, with lots of snow covering the ground. Oso picked her up at the airport. I worried. He'd been gone for over two hours. Was the flight delayed? We didn't have Internet or a cell phone for me to check. The car stalled on the way back, the gas tank empty. He left my poor mom in the car on the side of the road while he jogged to the nearest station to get gas.

I loved having my mom, not only to help me with the baby, but to keep me company. She took Ben in her arms, and I saw the love in her touch, her eyes. I was breastfeeding, but she helped with meals and chores and showed me how to take care of a baby. We washed him in a basin in the kitchen near the warmth of the woodstove. My mom never liked to cook, and on the flight, she had stressed about what she'd prepare for the kids. To her surprise, both kids were gone when she arrived. Jessi was renting a room above the bakery in Richmond, and Chris was in British Columbia. I didn't tell my mom how Chris got there. I told her he was lonely for his mom, and she paid for his ticket to go visit.

My C-section wound turned red and swollen, so my mom rocked Ben while I visited the doctor. She examined my lesion and shook her head. "What have you been doing?" "Nothing I wasn't supposed to," I lied. I did not tell her I had chopped wood for kindling to warm the kitchen so we could give Ben a cozy bath.

I had asked Oso to do it, but he laughed and said women had been giving birth since early mankind. It was the most natural thing in the world. "You're not sick. Women in other countries give birth in the morning and work in the fields in the afternoon." I chopped the wood.

I certainly did not tell the doctor that ten days after my C-section, Oso lowered my bottom pyjamas. She had warned me, "Wait six weeks before intercourse." I reminded Oso the doctor had recommended we wait.

He said, "From the back, it will be okay." Worried my mom would hear us fighting, I didn't insist. Pretend at all costs that life was great, that we were a happy, loving family. What would the doctor say if I told her the truth? I lied to her, I lied to my mom, I lied to everyone, including myself. I was ashamed.

Years later, my mom told me she heard us fighting, but the argument was about the cat. Our cat did not appreciate having a baby in the house, and she hissed whenever she went near him. It scared me and I decided it was best if we gave her away. Oso was furious and said, "When you take a pet, he/she becomes part of the family, and you can't abandon them." I briefly wondered why he'd abandoned Catherine. The stressed cat peed on the couch each night. Oso threatened to hurt her, so I put her outside every evening. She hated spending the night outdoors. One evening, as I grabbed her on the stairs, she spat at me. I was exhausted, frustrated, and at the end of my rope. Before I could stop myself, I kicked her. She gasped when my foot connected to her ribs, and she darted down the stairs.

I love animals. A friend and I had made a pact during high school. When I reached fifty, if I didn't own a horse, she promised to kill me because my life would've been in vain. (I never got that horse, but my friend agreed to not send a hitman). I flopped on the step, horrified at myself, and that's when I noticed the blood on my shoe. The air left my lungs. I found Sam hiding behind the couch and I cuddled her, humming the songs my mom used to sing to me when I was sick. She seemed okay and I couldn't even tell where she was bleeding. Soon after, I put up posters, hoping for a suitable home, but nobody wanted her, so I took her to the SPCA. I left her there and drove home in tears.

As much as I pretended that life was good, my mom knew me better. She stayed with us for two weeks, and when I drove her to the airport, she struggled to contain her emotions. My dad was the emotional one. I could make him shed tears simply by writing mushy love stuff in his birthday card or on Father's Day. I'd never seen my mom cry. Standing there, waiting for her flight, she had tears in her eyes. I misread her dilemma and reassured her we would visit soon.

Years later, she told me she wanted to grab me and Ben and take us home with her. She'd always felt bad that she hadn't said it. I told her it would not have mattered; I would not have gone. I was determined to make this relationship work. We could fix this. With both kids gone, Oso would have no reason to get upset.

It broke my mom's heart to see that we only had a mattress on the floor and an old orange crate for our night table. I didn't care about the furniture; it was what was happening on that mattress she should've been worried about.

Later that summer, the annulment came through, and we got re-married in an old Micmac church in Beaumont, Memramcook, in New Brunswick. We invited our two families. I visited the cozy white church with the bright red roof when I was a kid, and I thought it was the most beautiful church I'd ever seen. I remember thinking, *this is where I will get married one day.*

When the Acadians came from France in the 1700s, they shared the New Brunswick land with the Micmac people. They built the church with the Micmac in 1842. Beside the church, you can still visit the remnants of the old Micmac cemetery. They buried almost eighty people in the ground, many of them dying very young. The name "Memramcook" comes from the Micmac, meaning crooked river.

The modest church sits on the Petitcodiac River, affectionately called the chocolate river because of its muddy brown waters. The Petitcodiac River had the highest tidal bore tide in North America at over two meters in height. But the construction of a causeway between Moncton and Riverview in the 1960s led to extensive sedimentation, which significantly reduced the tide. After a considerable push from the public, the city opened the causeway gates in 2010, and the tidal bore grew again. The restoration was successful. In July 2013, professional surfers rode a one-meter-high wave twenty-nine kilometres up the river to establish a new North American record for continuous surfing.

Next to the church, locals can rent and live in the old presbytery house with a matching red roof. Gilles and his wife stayed there for a few months.

Jessi couldn't make it to our second wedding since she still worked in the bakery, but Chris came. Oso's parents and his youngest sister also attended.

My mom talked to the local priest, and he agreed to marry us in the old Beaumont church. The church has no central aisle, so we walked up the side aisle, Oso and I, holding hands. Camilla, my maid of honour, walked up with my father-in-law, our two witnesses.

My mother-in-law was an excellent seamstress. She altered my cream maternity dress, so I wore the same dress at both weddings. Our son, Ben, had been born in early March; he was three months old.

I stood in the front of the church with Oso. We watched our family march up the side aisle, one of my cousins singing in the background. I wondered how many brides stand still and smile while praying for an earthquake to stop the wedding. I suppose in countries where arranged marriages are still the norm. My only thought was: *run, run while you still can*. But I did not run. I pretended it was the happiest day of my life. We were legally married, so why would I run now? This was even my idea. Oso didn't care if we got married or not. I forced my lips into a grin, and I got married a second time to the same man. A man I no longer loved. Why was I here? Why was I doing this? Honestly, I wasn't sure. Wasn't it the plan? Grow up, get married, have kids. I was twenty-eight years old, and I convinced myself that this was what I was supposed to do. Not all days were bad. We could go weeks without fights. I'd invested so much of myself in this family, I would not quit now.

Jessi had turned sixteen that January. She rented a room upstairs from the bakery where she worked. We now had a baby boy. I could not imagine Oso yelling at this beautiful little person. Life was going to be perfect from now on.

The priest who married us had started in our parish the same year I began grade one. When the teacher announced Father Brian's visit, all the girls in the class giggled. I think most of us were in love with his brown curly hair and strikingly beautiful brown eyes. He sat with us on the floor and played his guitar and sang while we watched him, mesmerized. After the wedding, he told my mom that he could sense God's presence in the lovely Micmac church during our ceremony. If God was there, was he holding my hand or shaking me, trying to make me come to my senses? Maybe God was thinking, what the heck are you doing?

My sister-in-law held Ben during the ceremony.

After the wedding, we slipped into the backseat of my father-in-law's fancy car.

We held a modest gathering in my parents' garage. Louis-Marie cooked steaks and chicken on the barbecue, and we shared a potluck meal with wine. Bert and his wife had decorated the garage with tissue flowers; it was beautiful. My parents paid for the food, so our wedding cost us twenty bucks for the priest.

Second Escape Attempt

1990

It was a Friday evening, and Chris asked to go out. The previous weekend, he had gone out Friday and not come back until Sunday night. He was supposed to be in by midnight on Friday. Oso grounded him for a month.

Ben cooed in his room, so I headed up to nurse him. I picked him up, and he smiled at me. My heart melted every time I looked at his perfect, handsome little face. He inherited my bluish/greenish eyes. I sat in the rocking chair in his recently renovated room. Two weeks before Ben was due, Oso found me sitting in the hall crying. The landlord had promised to fix the baby's room, but he had been busy and had not finished it. Oso completed the renovations while I was in the hospital, and the room was beautiful, the prettiest one in the house. He painted the walls a light grey, except for one surface where we wallpapered colourful monster trucks. I painted the used furniture white, and I glued a Mickey Mouse picture on the drawers, the toy box and the garbage can. We bought a used crib and, of course, a rocking chair.

I love cuddling and rocking a baby. When I was sick, my mom rocked and sang to me. I got comfortable in the chair and lifted my shirt to offer Ben my nipple. He eagerly sucked my milk. I can't imagine a stronger bond between mother and child. Once in a while, he paused, peeped up at me and smiled. I never knew a heart could hold so much love.

I heard the eruption happening in the stairwell. Chris raced upstairs with Oso behind him. He was fourteen years old, and he was learning to fight back. He yelled, "I'm gonna leave this house and never come back."

"Yeah, well, where the fuck will you go?" Oso's voice was louder.

I spotted Chris in front of Ben's room, and I said, "I will go with you." Chris nodded and slammed his bedroom door.

I didn't notice Oso come into the room, but his words were vehement. "You! Fuckin! Bitch!" My eyes shot up. His were raw and black. I swallowed. He towered over me. Ben stopped feeding and howled. I wrapped my arms around him, and I covered him with my body.

I put my hands to his ears, trying to shield him from the hateful words coming out of his father. *Hush, little baby, hush-hush, it's okay.* I rocked him and kept my eyes down. The intense, vulgar words hitting me made no sense: *Fuck, Stupid, Crazy, Traitor, Bitch.*

I rocked Ben back and forth. "Please, please, please," I begged Oso. I whispered, "It's okay, little baby, it's okay." I lost sense of time, and then suddenly, it was over. Oso stormed downstairs. I struggled to breathe. It took me thirty minutes to soothe Ben and finish nursing him. I rocked him until he fell asleep and then laid him gently in his crib. The house was quiet now. I crunched on our bedroom floor and grabbed the phone. My hands shook while I dialed zero. "Hello, this is the operator. How can I help you?" I kept my voice low, and I tried to appear calm. I felt so much shame. "Hello, operator…. Can you please… give me the number for a battered women's shelter?" Her voice was gentle. After she gave me the number, I dialed and squeezed my hands together, trying to settle my trembling fingers. "Hello," a soft female voice said. "How can I help you?"

I hesitated for a few seconds. Then the words poured out. "Please, please, I need to leave. He swears and yells at me while I'm breastfeeding our baby. Please, I have no family around. I have nowhere to go. Please help me. I need to run; I can't do this anymore."

In a rush, she asked, "Are you in physical danger?"

"No, he doesn't hit me, but please, I have to leave. He screams at me while I'm breastfeeding, please. Please." My shoulders shook from sobbing, and I kept repeating my plea. Sweat ran down my forearm from gripping the handle.

She sighed. "I'm so so sorry; all our shelters are full. It's the weekend, and some men drink and get violent. The women leave their house on Fridays, they come here with their kids. They go home on Mondays. We will have room then. You shouldn't stay there. Do you have anyone you can call, friends?"

I shook my head. "It's okay," I said. "Thank you."

Before I hung up, she made me promise to call the police if Oso became physically violent. She also made me swear to reach out to the shelter on Monday. I promised, but I never called back. Oso did not beat me, so I didn't think I was being abused. I didn't want to take space from women who were in real danger. Women whose lives were threatened. I never feared for my life. But I lived in fear.

A friend I met in Cornwall called me from British Columbia a few minutes later. I don't remember what I told him, but a week later, I received a letter from him with a cheque for one thousand dollars. He said to keep it hidden in case I needed to quickly get out of the house with Ben. I never cashed it.

I called my friend Chantal. They were expecting a baby, and they had a crib, so Ben had a safe place to sleep. I ignored Oso's pleas for me to stay. Chris remained in his room. I grabbed Ben and a few personal items, and I left. Chantal opened the door and took one look at me. "Oh my God, you're shaking. Give me Ben before you drop him." After I put Ben to bed, I sat with her and told her a bit of what had happened. I didn't want to tell her everything because Oso worked with her husband and we were friends.

The next day, Oso called. "We're a family. We need to work this out. Come home. You're putting our friends in a difficult situation. I work with the guy, remember? It's not fair to involve them in our private family matters." I went back. Where else would I go? I was a shift worker with no family around. I was still shaking when I hugged Chantal and thanked her for being such a good friend.

Jessi loved her dad ferociously, and when she wasn't at war with him, she was ready to go to war for him. She longed for her biological mom, but it was not a visceral need like her brother had. Even after she moved out, they still fought. But he couldn't ground her anymore. Now she slammed the door on her way out.

Before she left the house, her bedroom was a total disaster. Clothes strewn all over the floor, some clean, some dirty. It was a hazardous journey to get to her bed because of all the books and magazines sprawled everywhere. Makeup and hair accessories covered her dresser. She left every drawer in the dresser open. Crumbs on half-emptied plates attracted ants for their dinner. I did what my mom used to do with my sister; I closed the door.

After I found a used tampon in Jessi's drawers (the smell drew me in), her dad locked both bedrooms and put a sign on the doors: *Danger! Contaminated areas, do not go in.* Both kids slept on the hall floor that night. He wouldn't let them in to get their pillows or pyjamas. The technique worked for a short time as they both tried to keep their bedrooms cleaner afterward.

I wanted Ben to be baptized. I still attended church every Sunday. Oso had stopped believing in the Catholic church a long time ago, but he still believed in a greater force watching over us. He agreed and fully took part in the baptism. We had to choose godparents. For me, the choice was obvious, Jessi and Chris. The official role of godparents is to witness the christening and to help bring up the child in the Catholic religion. In that respect, the kids were not the right choice because neither of them was raised to believe in religion. However, in my mind, godparents are special people chosen to hold a sacred place in a child's life. Jessi and Chris were those special people for me.

It turned out that godparents had to be sixteen years old, so Jessi could be the godmother, but Chris couldn't. I asked my dad to be my son's godparent, and touched, he happily agreed. My father fell in love with Ben the first time I took him home for a visit. Since he couldn't make it to the baptism, Chris replaced him. Father Kennedy conducted the baptism in Richmond. I liked him because he accepted everyone in the church. Someone asked him if unmarried couples could attend mass and he said, "The Catholic religion does not approve of people living in sin, and although the Church welcomes them to mass, they are not allowed to take part in the communion. But if Christ himself was up here instead of me, he would welcome everyone with open arms, so who am I to judge?" I attended communion against the church's directives. Father Kennedy made me feel welcome.

Jessi and I wore dresses for the baptism. Mine was white with blue polka dots, while hers was navy blue. Chris wore blue dress trousers and a white shirt. Oso had a tee-shirt and jeans. Ben, being the wonderful baby that he was, smiled at the priest and never cried nor made a fuss, not even when Father Kennedy poured the blessed water on his head.

A Friendly Cop

I couldn't sleep. I glanced at the alarm clock. The red numbers displayed two-thirty in the morning. I heard a noise, and I hoped it was Chris coming home. Then again. Knock. Knock. Knock. Someone was banging at the door.

Who knocks on the door in the middle of the night? I pulled myself from the warm covers and tiptoed to Jessi's room to look out the window. Her bedroom was empty because, although barely sixteen, she had already fled the coop. In my zombie state, I believed if I stayed quiet, the person at the front door might go away. Before I reached the window, I saw the reflection of the flashing red and blue lights dancing on the bedroom walls. I groaned. "Oso, please wake up. The cops are here."

Grumbling, Oso grabbed his robe, and we dragged our feet downstairs to open the old wooden front door.

A tall, friendly looking cop stood on the porch. He apologized, explaining that he had tried to call us first. "Your telephone must be out of order; I kept getting a busy signal." We lived in an old farmhouse outside of town, away from the road, amid a vast field, so it was plausible. Oso and I glanced at each other and mentally agreed we would not tell the friendly cop we unplugged the telephone so he wouldn't be able to call us in the middle of the night.

Honestly, only cruel and uncaring parents disconnect their telephone at night because their fifteen-year-old son has a habit of running away and getting in trouble. Is that what we were? I didn't think so. We were parents at the end of their rope. We were parents who had attended bi-weekly social services family therapy sessions for months. Desperate parents who had no clue how to handle our two teenagers. Hence, for one night, we took the receiver off the hook, hoping to get a good night's sleep. I pretended we were a normal happy family, not one who gets a visit from a friendly cop in the middle of the night.

The cop explained, "We caught Chris stealing a radio in a parked car and we brought him to the police station. You'll have to pick him up in the morning, and then you need to sit with the social services and come up with a plan to address his behaviour." Even the friendly cop was tired of calling us in the middle of the night. We agreed.

After the cop left, Oso and I chatted for a while, trying to figure out how we would deal with the situation. I checked on Ben. Sleeping blissfully in his crib, he was completely unaware of the drama unfolding outside his small bedroom.

After breakfast the next morning, Oso picked up Chris at the police station and brought him home. He scurried to his room, where he hid until noon. I called Marie at the social services in Ottawa, and we agreed to meet later that week. A team of well-intentioned social services staff, led by Marie, welcomed us warmly in a cozy meeting room.

Chris had run away from home when he was ten years old. The situation did not improve as he grew older.

He began cutting school until he finally stopped going, no matter how much we encouraged or threatened him. Oso worked in the woods, and I was often off during the day, so I'd go meet the teachers. We tried in vain to find strategies to get both kids to stay in school. They promised to behave better, but they kept messing up. The law changed in Ontario in 2007 to require children to remain in school until they turn eighteen years old. Before that, kids could quit school at sixteen, which Jessi had done.

Chris disappeared almost every weekend. He'd go out on Friday night with our permission. We expected him home by midnight, but he showed up Sunday afternoon. Richmond was not a big town, and most of the time, he did not make it to Ottawa. The cops called us in the middle of the night when they grabbed him. I lay awake at night, waiting for the door to open or the phone to ring. I watched with envy as Oso fell asleep in less than five seconds. Chris was a kid. Oso called the cops and reported him missing. One of us picked him up in the morning, and Oso grounded him for a month. Grounded or not, he sneaked out of the house. The same scenario happened every weekend.

Chris graduated from middle school, and they held a graduation. It surprised me he wished to attend the ceremony. He hated school, but he was excited about going to high school. Chris seemed to think that any change would be better. He had figured that if he lived with his mom, he'd lose weight and make friends. That plan had failed. When he talked about high school, he had hope in his eyes. I took him shopping for new clothes for the special day. I let him pick what he wanted to wear. He bought black pants and a white shirt. He was already a big guy and could wear his dad's jacket and tie. His choice of shoes blew me away. He grabbed a pair of greenish/blueish big heel, pointy shoes, and as he tried them on, I hoped he'd change his mind. They must have been the ugliest shoes I'd ever seen, but I kept my mouth shut. This was his day. He walked around the store in these long pointy shoes, and he said, "I love them." I hoped Oso would not laugh at him when Chris put on the entire outfit. Oso looked at him.

"You sure are a handsome dude." Chris cracked an enormous grin, and we drove to the graduation. The girls dressed in pretty outfits, and most of the guys wore suits. I did not see any other boys with such ugly shoes. Chris strutted to get his diploma in his ugly greenish/blueish pointy shoes. He would go to high school in September.

After the ceremony, they served a lunch outside. I noticed most of the kids were chatting and laughing except Chris. He sat alone on a bench, looking sad and out of place. A boy, about his age, walked by and offered him the rest of his bag of chips. A kind gesture. Chris grinned and said thank you as he grabbed the bag. The boy smiled and walked away. I felt infinite gratefulness for the boy who had showed such kindness and immense sadness for Chris, who seemed to have no friends.

Oso was always the disciplinary parent, which usually consisted of yelling, swearing, insulting, and then grounding the kids for a month. When grounded, they'd go to their room right after dinner and couldn't come out until the next morning. Of course, they had no television, cell phone, or computers. Most of the time, I smoothed things with Oso and negotiated a reduced punishment for them.

The kids and I did not fight. I took their sides against their father, which sometimes helped but mostly made it worse. I tried to show a united parental front, wondering how I could be part of such calamities. Two of my behaviours that infuriated Oso: me siding against him in front of the kids or ignoring him when he was enraged.

The social services suggested we send Chris to a place for troubled teenagers in Texas. I didn't understand; we lived near Ottawa, Canada. Wasn't there anything closer? We couldn't afford to send him to the United States. Texas? It seemed very far and very extreme. Yes, Chris was a troubled teenager, and he was constantly running away from home. He skipped school all the time; he experimented with drugs, and he spent a few nights in jail. But he hadn't hurt nor killed anyone; he never got violent. Marie knew us well, and she knew Chris, so we put our faith in her.

When parents have no clue what to do anymore, and professionals tell them Texas is the best place for their son, what are parents to do? The Ontario health care system agreed to cover the costs because there were no boot camps in Canada for troubled youth. The alternative was a youth detention center in Ottawa. They counselled us, advised us to think about it, and we drove home in silence. Of course, Chris wanted nothing to do with it, promising again to behave. But we knew these were empty promises; we'd heard them many times before. Desperate parents do desperate things, and so Oso and Chris packed their bags and flew to the United States. A part of me was relieved. Oso would be cool now. No need to get angry anymore. Both kids would be out of the house.

I hugged Chris and told him I loved him. "Stay safe, it's just temporary." Oso and Chris flew to Texas after a brief stay in Florida. While Oso registered him in the camp, Chris asked for the washroom. He was not coming back. They knocked on the door to realize he had climbed out the window. They found him hitchhiking on the road, trying to get away. He stayed in that place for almost six months. We'd get monthly reports. He seemed to do well. The comments were mostly positive. They said he didn't take part fully in the activities, but he didn't get in trouble either. Then he caught pneumonia and had to be hospitalized for a few days. I opened the mail to find a bill for $96,000. My lungs suddenly couldn't get enough air. We sent the bills to Ontario Medicare, but in the beginning, they refused to pay. It was not part of the deal. The bills kept coming, and I kept sending them to the provincial government. After a while, they stopped coming. I didn't know if the province paid for them or if the US doctors gave up. I consulted a lawyer. He explained to me that since I never officially adopted the kids, I was not responsible for any debts they accumulated.

Oso flew back to Texas a few days before Christmas to bring Chris home. He wouldn't talk about what happened there except to say he hated it. He spent Christmas with us, and since he had turned sixteen in November, he left the house permanently shortly after the holidays.

Catherine and the Social Services

Fall 1990

Ben was seven months old when Marie called us for a meeting at the Children's Aid Services. Chris was still in Texas, and Jessi lived in Richmond. We drove to her building and sat across from her desk. Although she had reassured me they would not take Ben away, I was terrified they'd changed their minds. I gripped Ben on my lap while Marie explained that the kids' biological mom could no longer take care of Catherine. "Vancouver's social services contacted us, and they said Catherine's mom is sick and can no longer care for her daughter."

Catherine was now twelve years old. Marie asked if we would take her. Without any hesitation, we agreed. Marie looked at us, and I saw kindness and sadness in her eyes behind her glasses. She asked Oso to leave the room; she wanted to talk to me alone.

"You've been through hell with Jessi and Chris," she said. "Catherine is no longer the sweet ten-year-old girl who stayed with you a few summers ago. She is now an angry, rebellious teenager, and even her own biological mom cannot handle her.

I should not do this, but I strongly suggest you say no. Go home and take care of your little family. Think of your baby and provide a calm home for him. The social services in Vancouver will make sure she goes to a suitable home."

I was not afraid to take Catherine. I cared deeply for her. I knew I had enough love in my heart to take her in. However, Marie was also right. More yelling and screaming, more cops, more drama was too much for me. I was underwater in the deep end of a pool, breathing through a straw, and they wanted to put a brick on my head. I would drown, I knew it.

Oso came back into the room. Marie asked again, "Will you take Catherine?"

"No, we can't," the words choked in my throat. Oso glanced at me, his eyes sad. He did not say a word. We left the office, our hearts in turmoil. Saying no to Catherine is the third hardest thing I've ever had to do.

The next time we saw Catherine, she was eighteen years old, and she came with her baby girl to visit us. She spent two weeks with us in our new house during Christmas. Her daughter was a couple of years younger than Ben. She was a young mother, but she seemed to take good care of her baby. The innocence in her eyes was gone, but there was still a mischievous twinkle in them. She remained vague about her child's father.

Several years later, Catherine stopped talking to me. When I pressed my granddaughter to tell me why, she revealed Catherine had been raped while in foster care. Her dad told her I was the one who decided not to take her. A twelve-year-old girl was raped, and I could've prevented it. I wept all weekend. How could she ever forgive me? How could I ever forgive myself?

A Vagabond

Spring 1991

I invited a homeless person to dinner. He'd been living on the streets for three months. He called me yesterday and since I worked in Ottawa, I suggested we meet in a downtown restaurant. It was early spring, but there was a warm breeze coming from the south. The restaurants opened their patios for the weekend. The buds on the trees were eager to burst after being dormant through our long Canadian winter. I waited on the Royal Oak terrace near the Ottawa market.

It was a Sunday, and I'd just finished a twelve-hour shift at the Ottawa Weather Office. The office had moved downtown after the government contracted out the weather observing.

I fidgeted in my seat as I waited for him to show up. "I'm waiting for someone, but I will have a beer, please," I told the waitress. She smiled and brought me a light beer.

I waved to him as he approached the restaurant. I was happy and relieved to see him. He was still alive. He had dark circles underneath his eyes and his checkered shirt was hanging loosely over his ragged jeans. Since he left home, he'd lost weight.

He was sixteen years old. My stepson. He slept under a bridge in Ottawa. During the day, he mostly sat in front of the Rideau Centre and begged passersby for money to buy food, cigarettes, and maybe drugs. His hair was messy, matted, and too long. I greeted him with a hug. He emitted a strong unpleasant smell, but I pretended not to notice. The waitress came back, and I hoped she couldn't smell him.

I peered at him while he stared at the menu. I wasn't sure what to say. How do you greet someone who makes the streets their home? At first, we chitchatted about the nice weather we'd been having.

"How's Dad?" he asked.

"He's okay. He misses you."

"I'll come by soon," he replied.

I said, "Tell me what it's like to live on the street."

He looked around furtively, checking over his shoulders. He admitted he was frightened most of the time. Not feeling safe in the shelters, he tried to sleep under bridges, protected from the cold and other itinerants. Another homeless man attacked him in the shelters, yet he wanted nothing to do with coming home. He still wouldn't talk about his stay in Texas, other than to say he hated it there. Maybe he hated us for agreeing to such a plan. We'd hoped it would fix him, as if he was broken.

I watched him eat. He hardly chewed the food, gulping down his salad, then a full dinner plate. "Do you mind if I have a beer?" he asked. We both knew he had no money to pay for his meal. I would cover it.

He asked about Jessi and Ben.

Some people say it's a choice to live on the streets. I don't know. I guess Chris had a choice; he could come home. But what if home was a toxic place? The relationship between Chris and his dad had become venomous. I blamed his dad. Chris was just a kid. A messed-up kid. Yes, he stole from us; he broke into locked cars and stole radios. He ran away from home, quit school, but he was just a boy. A sixteen-year-old teenager who'd rather risk his life in the streets of Ottawa than live with us.

It was easier to blame his dad than to look at myself. The kids' biological mom lived across the country, so I was the closest he had to a mother. Yet I'd not been able to protect him. If he was my blood, would I have done things differently? I could afford to buy him dinner, but I couldn't afford to rent him an apartment. I knew I wouldn't hesitate to throw myself in front of a bus for Ben. Did I do all that I could to help Chris?

He applied to get welfare from the government. They called the house to ask if he had a place to stay. His dad said yes, so they denied his application. "Saying no means I'm abandoning him; I will never do that."

Before we parted, he smiled sheepishly. "Can I borrow a bit of money?" I'd expected it. I pulled out a few twenties from my purse. "I will reimburse you as soon as I get a job," he said.

"Don't worry about it," I smiled. He thanked me and gave me a kiss on the cheek.

"I love you."

"I love you too. Please stay in touch."

I watched him walk away. He dragged his feet. I guess he had nowhere to go. I wanted to howl.

He turned around to wave one last time, and then he was gone. I didn't know when or if I'd see him again. We had no way to reach him. Sometimes after a shift, I strolled in the streets near the Rideau Centre where I knew lots of homeless people gathered, but I never saw him.

I remained for a long time on the patio, slowly sipping my beer. I remembered the little boy who danced with the waves. My heart shattered. I resisted the urge to run and grab him and beg him to come home. I silently screamed...*I'm so sorry. Please be safe. Please forgive me. I'm so sorry. Please, please be safe. Please.*

Weeks later, I picked up the phone and when the social services asked me if Chris had a place to stay, I hesitated. "I can't do this anymore. No, he can't come home." They approved his demand, and he finally collected a welfare cheque and rented a room in a rundown Ottawa neighbourhood. I convinced myself that I said no so he would get some money. But I was relieved he wouldn't be coming back home. Life was easier with both teenagers out of the house. I looked forward to a peaceful, happy life with my small family.

Seventeen and Pregnant

Jessi called and asked if they could come over for a visit. I could tell by her voice something was not right. She sounded measured, as if she was trying too hard. She definitely was not her usual cheery self.

We greeted them at the door and invited them in. It was February 1991, and they brushed the snow off their coats before hanging them on the hooks by the door. "It sure is cold out there," Jo said.

Jessi had been dating Jo for only a few months. He seemed like a nice guy, tall and handsome with an Italian look. They shared a cramped apartment south of Ottawa. She'd turned seventeen in January and Jo was a couple of years older than she.

They held hands as they sat on the couch. When Jessi's eyes teared up, Jo put his arm around her shoulders. "What's up?" Oso asked.

She took a deep breath and blurted out, "I'm pregnant."

Oso slowly got up and paced the living room. I stopped breathing. His hands formed into fists. He stopped in front of her and hissed, "You fuckin whore."

Jessi's eyes opened wide, and they dried up quickly. Flashes of anger replaced the tears. She stormed up from the couch and confronted her dad, her face a few inches from his. "I'm not a whore," she shrieked. Jo and I remained quiet as we watched the father/daughter showdown. She slowly repeated, "I'm not a whore." Then she turned around. "Jo, let's go."

Oso and I stayed in the living room as they grabbed their boots and coats. The door slammed shut.

I didn't know what to do, nor what to feel. A tornado of emotions ran through my veins. I was furious with Oso. Jessi was still a child, barely seventeen and pregnant. Her train was heading into a brick wall. She had limited education and a part-time waitressing job. Jo worked odd jobs. They were going to be parents. Of course, she could decide to give her baby away or have an abortion. But since they came over to announce the news, I doubted she would choose those options. What kind of future would she have? What kind of life would this baby have?

Once Oso calmed down, we talked. We sat on the couch, and he shook his head. "Call her and apologize; she must be so scared." I told him.

"Tomorrow," he said. "I'll call her tomorrow."

And he did. The next morning, he called her, and they both cried on the phone. "Invite them over," I said.

We discussed various options with them. Abortion. Adoption. Parenthood. Did they consider all their choices? We tried hard not to push her in any direction.

My son was not yet one-year-old. I knew how rewarding parenting could be. But I had a steady job, a steady, even if volatile, relationship. I thought I was better prepared to be a parent. She was seventeen years old with so much to learn and her whole life ahead of her. We told her we would support them with whatever decision they made. She went through with her pregnancy.

Marianne's sister-in-law lived in Ottawa, where she worked at the Ottawa Regional Cancer Centre for a Gynecological Oncologist. During a visit to New Brunswick, she casually said to my sister, "The doctor came in last week, and he seemed upset. He said he had an interesting but heartbreaking case. A pregnant seventeen-year-old teenager with ovarian cancer."

"Oh my God," my sister said. "That is Liette's stepdaughter, Jessi."

Seventeen, Pregnant and Cancer

I don't remember. I honestly do not remember the precise moment when I learned she had cancer. You'd think it was something I would never forget. I've racked my brains, I've tried hypnosis, I've tried cannabis (I'd stopped using cannabis when I got pregnant and hadn't tried it since). I parked in front and stared at the old farmhouse. But it's hopeless. I don't remember.

I remember how they found the ovarian cancer. She was five months pregnant. And I remember being terrified.

She complained of stomach cramps. At one point, the pain was so intense, Jo called an ambulance. The hospital staff ran a few tests and told her she was constipated. They prescribed her laxatives and sent her home. Jo told me she fell off the bed and lay on the floor in pain. He called the ambulance a second time, and again, the doctor treated her for constipation.

She had morning sickness for the first three months, but she quit smoking and drinking and tried to take good care of herself. She and I had long chats about being pregnant, giving birth, and raising a baby. She was scared, but she was also excited. I was not too worried about her pain. She could be such a drama queen.

It reminded me of a stomach flu she had at fourteen. The entire family caught it and she was the last one to suffer. I had an early shift in the morning. All night, she dragged herself to the bathroom to throw up. I remember the screeching noise the bucket made as she pushed it in front of her, all the way across the hall. I felt bad for her, but I knew it would pass. I'd comforted her as best I could, and I'd given her medication. Her loud moaning and groaning, combined with the screeching sound of the sliding bucket, kept me awake. She sounded like a hyena being eaten by lions. One long wail to the bathroom and back. Finally, I could not take it anymore, and I got up. "I know you are sick, and I feel bad, but please suffer in silence so I can sleep." I did not hear another peep all night.

However, this time, it was serious. During the routine five-month pregnancy ultrasound, the doctor discovered a mass on her left ovary. The growing fetus hid the bulge, but the ultrasound showed an enormous lump on her ovary. The doctor performed a biopsy, and we anxiously waited for the results... Cancer.

My stepdaughter was seventeen years old, pregnant, and now they told us she had ovarian cancer.

The oncologist held a family meeting. Jessi had not yet reached the legal adult age in Ontario, so we were required to attend. She wanted us with her, and of course, we needed to be there. We sat around his desk, and I watched him as he described the various options.

I was pissed at the doctors; how did they miss this? I was pissed at the hospital; constipated, they said. I was pissed at Oso. Somehow, I blamed him for this. I was pissed at Jessi; why did she put herself in this mess? I was pissed at God; why did he let this happen? I was pissed at the Universe. Where is my six kids' happy, stable family home? As pissed as I was, my anger paled in front of my fear. The doctor listened patiently as we interrogated him. He tried his best to answer all of our questions. He ran his hand through his greying hair as he tried to reassure us.

He recommended surgery to remove the tumour and ovary. He was confident he could do it without harming the baby. After the surgery, they would begin mild chemotherapy. He said they had been giving chemo to pregnant women, and in the short term, the treatment showed no harm to the baby. "What about long term?"

"We do not have enough data, but we don't think it will have any permanent effect on the child."

"What if she doesn't get the chemo?"

He shook his head. "The cancer could spread, and she may not survive long after her pregnancy."

"Think about it," he said. "Take a few days to discuss, but don't take too much time."

We stayed up. We talked and cried most of the night. What do you want to do? We asked her. She was shocked. I felt helpless. "I want that thing out of my body. They have to take it out. I want the chemo." She caressed her belly. "I love my baby, but I don't want to die." She sobbed quietly.

We more than agreed. In fact, we were adamant about it. The surgery was a success. The doctor removed her ovary along with a tumour the size of a football. Her best friend took her back to their apartment to recover. Jo took their car to work, so either Oso or her friends drove her to her chemo appointments. I worked full time, and I took care of Ben.

Her hair thinned at the same time her waist grew. She'd get sick with the chemo, but she bravely faced the world. They reduced the chemo treatment because of the baby, so she kept most of her hair.

With the help of her friends, we organized a baby shower. It was a surprise. One cousin came down from Montreal. We had the shower at Jessi's best friend's house. She shrieked with delight when she walked in the door and we all yelled, "Surprise!"

Meagan

In November 1991, we got a call that Jessi was in labour. We rushed to the hospital. She was excited, though in a lot of pain. Jo held her hand. We stayed as long as we could. They kicked us out to the waiting room when the time came for her to push. After two hours, we welcomed our beautiful baby granddaughter, Meagan.

Jessi couldn't breastfeed because she was receiving chemotherapy. After Meagan was born, the doctors increased her chemo dosage.

Mother and baby were fine, so after a couple of days, they took Meagan home.

They came for a visit a few weeks later. When we opened the door, we noticed that she only had one strand of hair left on her almost bald head. It was long and hung on the side, partly hiding her face. Her dad laughed. "Why don't you cut that off?"

She caressed it. "But it's all I have left," she replied, her voice broken. My heart cracked.

Thankfully, the surgery and chemo beat the cancer, and although she needed to be checked regularly, the awful disease did not come back. Her hair grew back, long and wavy, and she was stronger from having fought and won this battle.

Jessi was barely an adult herself, and she loved to party. So, for the next few years, we babysat Meagan almost every weekend. I didn't mind at all. Having Ben and Meagan with us was easy. They played well together for the first few years. Then they became typical big brother, younger sister. He made her cry. It was easy; she was a sensitive little girl. She would often say, "You're my uncle; you have to be nice to me." He was not mean, but he did like to push her buttons.

I made her upside-down pancake for breakfast. It became our thing. She did not want her mom to get the recipe; it was a treat she only wanted at Grandma's house. Her mom told me she envied my relationship with her daughter. It was fun to take both kids to the park. They held on to my hands and one said, "Maman," while the other one called me Grandma. People gave us strange looks, and I smiled. I loved it.

Jessi called me when Meagan was not yet two years old. She was crying. The power company had cut their hydro since they had not paid their bills. It broke my heart to think of them with a baby and no electricity. "Pack your belongings; I'm coming to pick you up." Jo was at work.

She sobbed in the car as she told me about the hydro being cut. She said they barely had enough money for groceries. I reached out and gently touched her arm.

Her mood then switched. "Wow, it's so expensive to go out," she said. "Jo and I went out last weekend, and we paid for a babysitter (I must've been working). The bar had a fifty-dollar cover charge, plus our drinks and a cab. The evening cost over one hundred dollars."

I glared at her. I could open the car door and kick her out. Then I realized she was a kid, raising a kid. I remembered what I was like when I was eighteen. She was barely an adult; she had a young baby, and she had survived cancer. My frustration quickly evaporated, and I told her it was gonna be okay.

She called Jo and he picked up a few things from the apartment on his way from work.

Jessi worked hard to take care of her baby and help us around the house. I noticed Jo was not always very nice to her. After dinner, Jessi helped with the dishes. Jo did little else than sit and watch television. I asked him to help her, but he got upset and took it out on her. He insulted her in the kitchen while they were doing dishes. She silently wept. He needed to leave.

After one month, and with Oso's blessing, I asked them to sit down on the couch. Jessi and Meagan were welcome to stay as long as they wanted, but Jo had to leave. I would not tolerate his behaviour in my home. Ironic that I accepted it from my husband. I was really hoping he would go and she would stay.

Unfortunately, she followed him to Toronto, where his parents lived. My parents had bought us a heavy-duty stroller when Ben was born. We gave it to them, and they used it for a while until he sold it for drugs.

They came back to the Ottawa region after several months, but the cops picked him up during a fight when he kicked a chair from under her. I never saw him again. Many years later, he died alone in Toronto from an overdose.

When Jo left with the cops, Meagan was not quite three years old. Afterwards, Jessi had lots of different men in her life. They moved often during those years but always stayed close to Ottawa.

When Meagan was six years old, I picked her up from school one afternoon. The next morning, her friends asked her who I was. She replied I was her grandma. They said, "No way, she looks way too young to be your grandma." She sighed and explained that I was her grandma because I had married her grandpa. Her friend responded, "Ha, so she is your step-grandma!"

Indignantly, she shook her head and replied, "No she's not; she's my grandma."

Haute Couture

Fall 1991

It was late October when Chris called us at three o'clock in the morning. He was stoned or drunk or both and he was bawling. "I need to speak to Dad," he said when I picked up the phone. His dad took the receiver. "I'm gay," he sobbed. His dad replied it didn't matter, that he would always love him.

"You're my son, and I will love you no matter what."

I never understood how Oso got so angry at what I thought were insignificant incidents yet remained so calm in other instances. I didn't think Oso was homophobic, but I also didn't think he would appreciate his son being gay. He later reassured Chris that he loved him but warned him to never bring a boyfriend to the house. He never did.

A few days after Chris called, Jessi told me he had gotten a job as a cook in a vegetarian restaurant in Ottawa. She and I ate there when we knew he was working. He came out of the kitchen, proud of his chef hat. Unfortunately, although he was a wonderful cook, he was not very reliable, and sometimes he didn't show up for work, so he lost that job. He borrowed money from us to attend a high couture school in Ottawa. Very artistic, he always had a talent for drawing. But he was not assiduous, and he had a hard time with discipline, so he quit the school not long afterwards. Of course, the money we loaned him was gone.

Oso and I drove to the apartment Chris shared with other kids in a dire situation in a rundown neighbourhood in Ottawa. I sat in the car while Oso barged out and banged on the front door. He was furious. "You no good lying fuckin thief." The shouts echoed clearly through the screen door. Chris yelled also, defending himself. Oso's voice was loud and hard. Chris' voice was apologetic and clearly in distress. He kept promising he would pay us back. The screaming seemed to go on forever. I knew I should go in and try to stop it, but I couldn't move. I wanted to flee. I covered my ears with my hands. I stayed in the car, too scared to go in, too scared to leave. The key was in the ignition. It tempted me to drive away and leave them both there. *Leave, leave.* But I didn't. I just sat there, twisting my hands, breathing deeply. When Oso came back to the car, we drove home in silence.

The Biological Mom

1992

Susan, the kids' biological mom, called Jessi and asked if she could come for a two-week visit. Jessi vaguely remembered her, not having seen her since she was seven years old. Susan now lived in Vancouver. Jessi was on edge, ecstatic and scared. A single twenty-year-old mom, she lived in a lowly apartment with her baby girl. She cleaned her place, anticipating her mother's arrival, scrubbing the floors twice. Chris, of course, had seen her mother when he ran away while I was giving birth to Ben. He had been living off and on in British Columbia with his sister Catherine, so he'd met his biological mom from time to time. I'm not sure which continent he explored that year, but he was not around when Susan came.

"What should I say to her?" Jessi asked me countless times. I was happy for her; I knew how much her mom meant to her. But yes, I admit I also felt a slight pang of jealousy.

Three days. That's how long her mom stayed before Jessi told her to pack and go back home. It's easy to tumble down from a pedestal when you stand so high. Nobody is that good. Nobody can measure up to such expectations. She fell down. Hard.

Jessi called me, bawling, "You're my mother, she's not my mother, you're my mother, she's not my mother." It's difficult to explain the twists and turns my heart experienced in this instant. I was shattered by the sound of her sobs yet overjoyed to be called her mother. It crushed me to see her in such pain yet I was so grateful to be the first person she turned to.

She composed herself and told me what happened. Jessi desperately needed her mom to be the mother she had longed for all those years. Her mom, however, tried to defend her absence, blaming her health, her own mom, blaming Oso. She was unstable. She talked about suicide. She did not play by the mother/daughter rules.

"She told me Dad had pushed her down the stairs. I don't want to know anything about that. It's between them."

Jessi had to be a mom to her mom. It was too much. She kicked her out and told her not to come back.

PART THREE

A New Home

In 1992, after five years of living in the old farmhouse, we scrimped and saved five thousand dollars toward a deposit for a modest bungalow in Val-des-Monts, Quebec. The two-bedroom house sat on roughly 743 square metres of land. A majestic mixed forest bordered the house on both sides and in the back, offering tons of privacy. Working shifts allowed me to avoid most of the traffic, giving me a commute time of fewer than forty-five minutes to the office. The day we moved into our home, I danced in the living room. The start of a new chapter. Ben was two years old, and Jessi and Chris lived in Ottawa. Oso's family drove from Montreal to help us move.

Ben grew into a healthy and delightful toddler. He was the perfect little human person. He raced everywhere. It seemed he had two speeds, sleeping or running. He was a happy child. His laugh was contagious, and he adored playing outside. I took him swimming at the YMCA, and he shrieked with delight while splashing in the water. We visited New Brunswick in the summer as a family. In the winter, I flew there with him on my laps. My parents fell in love with him.

Ben was in awe of Meagan, his niece, and he cuddled with her on the large living room chair. Oso and I still had the occasional fights, but with both teenagers out of the house, life was tolerable.

The old school bus had rusted during the five years we stayed at the farmhouse. I convinced Oso to sell it, and to my surprise, it sold quickly. Oso drove it to its new owner, and I trailed behind with the car. He grimaced as he grabbed the steering wheel. The bus had been his companion for twelve years. I couldn't help it; I cracked a smile.

On the right side of the house, we had plenty of room for a vegetable garden. Oso attached himself to a hoe and cleared out the land so I could plant vegetables. He built me a charming greenhouse using six-foot-long wood logs and old patio doors his sister had given us. He added a used wood stove and even a water tap, which flowed through a buried hose from the house to the greenhouse. It became my sanctuary.

We held annual Méchouis in the backyard. We roasted a pig on an outside pit, taking turns, rotating it by hand all night. Several friends came and pitched a few tents on the lawn, crashing for the weekend. Oso's family drove from Montreal and, of course, Jessi and Jo brought Meagan and joined us. Chris showed up when he was in town. Oso built the pit, and we feasted on a few improvised picnic tables. Lots of good food and plenty of booze. Every year, Ben grabbed a small pail and collected water from his toddler swimming pool. His aunt shrieked as he drenched her back with the cool water. We jumped in, and by the time the pool was empty, everybody was soaked.

Oso and I had enrolled in taekwon-do classes in Ottawa in the fall of 1988. I'd visited a few martial arts dojangs, and Mr. Lu's teaching impressed me. We joined a beginner class with forty other black belt hopefuls. I tested for my green belt while five months pregnant with Ben. The instructor used to laugh at me, but he was proud of me. "Careful, careful, she's pregnant," he'd warn the other students. Oso and I were the only two of the forty students to reach the eminent black belt. Chris enrolled, but he quit shortly after attaining his yellow belt.

Taekwon-do is an intense martial art sport, and we sustained a few injuries along the way, but we embraced it. After we obtained our first-degree black belts, Oso and I opened our own taekwon-do dojang in the Val-des-Monts school gym.

Mr Lu held the second-degree black belt test over three weekends and it included a physical and technical test, and a written essay. The technical test comprised self-defence skits, patterns, sparring, and breaking boards. I waited my turn while Mr. Lu assessed other students, and then it was finally my turn to slip my gloves on. I boldly looked up at my opponent as he towered over me by at least a foot. The adrenaline ran through my veins, and I felt no fear. I relied on my training and speed and besides, these combats were controlled. Testing each other, we threw a few punches and kicks. I lifted my left leg toward the sky, and I brought it down on my opponent's shoulder. This strike is called a hammer kick. The lanky guy grabbed my ankle with both hands and shoved my leg up toward the roof. Oso cheered from the side. He heard a loud snap. I felt nothing. For a few seconds, I wondered why I had collapsed. Oso and a friend dragged me to the wall where I tried to figure out what the hell had just happened. Once everyone completed their sparring match, Mr. Lu came to see me. Not much taller than me, he'd come to Canada as a child, on a boat from Vietnam. Now in his late twenties, when he strode into the dojang, everybody bowed their heads.

He said, "You've passed all the tests so far; if you can break just one board, I'll give you your second-degree black belt."

Normally, I would've had to break several boards using various parts of my body while standing or jumping. I would die before letting a 12 x 10 x ½ inch pine board prevent me from getting my second degree.

I raised my arms. "Lift me," I ordered Oso and our friend. They pulled me up and, using them as human crutches, I hopped to the front of the dojang. Mr. Lu instructed his assistants to lay a board between two bricks. I stood on one leg, each man holding me under the arm. "Let go," I yelled. I smashed the board with the side of my hand, and as it shattered, I dropped to the ground again. They hauled me to the side, and I whispered to Oso, "I'm gonna be sick. Please take me outside." He carried and sat me on the curb, where I passed out.

A doctor, who had been observing the event, took one look at me. "She's going in shock." They flung me in the car and Oso rushed to the nearest clinic a few blocks away. He grabbed a wheel-chair and wheeled me into the clinic, explaining my predicament to the receptionist. She ushered me in to see the doctor. The nausea and dizziness had passed, and I hardly felt any pain. However, when I tried to stand, my leg was like cooked spaghetti. I'd torn my hamstring. A few days later, my leg showed the destruction. From the middle of my buttock to my calf, an impressive mixture of blue, red, purple, black and yellow colours adorned the entire width of my limb. I boasted and showed it to my colleagues, my trophy. I was a badass second-degree black belt taekwon-do holder.

After an evening of teaching a taekwon-do class, Oso encouraged me to go out with another female student. We hung out at a local bar, and I got home around ten-thirty, excited to tell Oso about our evening. He sat waiting on the couch, his look grim. I smiled, "Hi there."

"Where the hell were you?"

I stared at him and raised my shoulders. I don't know what got into me. I said, "Oh, relax and take a Valium."

Ouf, was that ever the wrong thing to say. He shot up and screamed at me. He raised his left fist in the air with his arm bent and slapped his bicep with his right hand,

"Fuck you, bitch. Eat a fuckin bucket of shit."

I pleaded, "I don't understand why you're mad. You knew where I was and with whom. It's not late. Why are you so angry?"

He glared at me. "You understand nothing, do you? You're so stupid! You went into a bar with your taekwon-do uniform. I was worried sick that someone would challenge you into a fight and that you'd get hurt."

I shook my head, "But you said I should go."

We met a couple of friends through taekwon-do and soared down rivers with them. We canoe/camped for three days, always taking Ben with us. He relaxed in the centre of the canoe, staring at the shore, scouting for wildlife, as we whipped down the river. He screamed with excitement when he spotted an otter or a deer.

We'd been in our new home for two years, and life had been tolerable.

Early one morning, Ben, now four, strolled into our bedroom. I woke up to his beaming face inches from my nose. "Mommy, Mommy, I had a wonderful dream. I flew like a bird over the trees." His smile lit up the room as he babbled beside the bed. My heart swelled up with love for this little person standing in front of me, tugging at his Batman pyjamas. Oso lay next to me on the other side.

As Ben chattered away, Oso pulled down my pyjama bottom. *No, no, please, not now. Please no.*

I smiled at Ben. "It's Saturday morning, the cartoons are playing on TV."

"But, Mommy, I want to tell you about my dream." I felt Oso pushing inside me from behind. *Oh God, please not now. Please.* I looked at Ben's beautiful, radiant face.

"Go watch the cartoons, and I will be up in a few minutes. You can tell me all about your dream." I hated to interrupt his babbling, but I could not let his dad fuck me while my toddler stood there. I knew if I stopped Oso, it would turn into a fight, and I didn't have the heart to upset my son. He raced out of the room while I lay without moving. I'd rather stay still for a few minutes than wreck my son's happiness.

When Oso turned on his back, I pulled up my pyjama bottoms. I headed to the bathroom, my head high, my chin trembling. I couldn't look at him. If I looked at his smug face, I would disintegrate. The hot shower flowed freely over my head as I collapsed on the floor. I stuffed the facecloth in my mouth to muffle my screams. When Ben knocked on the door, I cleaned myself up, wiped my tears, and prepared breakfast.

That evening, encouraged by what my mom had told me about rape, I said to Oso, "When I let you have sex with me because I'm afraid to say no, you're raping me." He smirked and shook his head.

"Talk to a woman who's been violently pinned down and raped, then you'll know what a rape is."

I guessed he was right. Nobody ever held me down and forcefully penetrated me. And if I was being raped, I'd never stay with my rapist, right? How could I admit to being raped if I sometimes enjoyed the sex?

Our Dogs

A cousin's dog in Montreal had a litter of golden retrievers, and we adopted one. We named her Tess. She was a dominant puppy, cute, all golden yellow. She followed me everywhere.

Tess was our second pup from the in-laws. We had previously adopted a small mixed-breed cute doggy called Zoe. A small pooch with long black and white hair. We knew little about raising a puppy, so we skipped many important steps when we trained her. Hyperactive, she'd bark, jump up and down, and run around in a circle, chasing her tail. She loved to cuddle with us, and she would lick us to death if we let her. We succeeded in house training her, but when she got nervous, she couldn't help it and peed on the floor. She was Ben's best friend. He used to stroke her fur while cuddling his dodo blanket and sucking two of his fingers.

One day, my pope-blessed wood cross fell on the floor, and before I could retrieve it, Zoe chewed Jesus' arms off. I threw it in the garbage, and I stopped attending church. It's not that I didn't believe in God anymore. I still prayed every night with Ben when I tucked him to sleep. I simply figured that God had better things to do than to interfere in my marriage. I was on my own. Oso had forbidden me to give the church a single penny. It was easier to not attend.

Sometimes, when I'd get up in the morning to go to work, Zoe would yap excitedly all the way to the door. Oso tied her outside the next evening, but she yelped most of the night. He told me that if I didn't shut her up, he'd silence her with a baseball bat. I kept her in the basement for the night and in the morning, I'd rushed downstairs to carry her outside. One evening, I let her out without tying her up. She got hit by a car and killed on the spot. Oso's parents visited that weekend and we spent half the night crying, knowing that in the morning, we would have to break Ben's heart. His best friend had died. He shed a few tears, then he asked to see her. We half-opened the bag, and he caressed her ear, whispering, "Poor little doggy."

Two years later, Tess became part of our family. Oso had been back at work for about a month. He'd stayed home for almost three years to care for Ben while I worked, although Ben still spent several days per week at daycare. He was an extrovert and social so he preferred to play with his buddies.

I was relieved Oso had found a job. Not only would it help us financially, it allowed me to spend time alone with Ben. Life was peaceful when Oso was not around. I could relax without the constant fear of him getting angry. Occasionally, after witnessing a fight, I'd put Ben to bed and he'd tell me we should leave his father, that we could live together, just the two of us. I silently agreed, and yet I didn't know how to leave. Other times, despite all the fighting, Ben didn't want his family to break apart. Before he started school, I always kept him at home when I wasn't working. I was lucky to have a flexible babysitter. Once a month, I'd give myself a Me day and send Ben to the babysitter. A day with no pressures, no expectations. A day when I was not a mother and not a wife, but simply a woman listening to the birds sing. It was a day to recover, to find strength. It was my day. Periodically, I'd go for massages; other times, I stayed home.

On such a day, Tess joyfully trotted around me while I rode the lawn tractor. The radiant sun brightened my morale, and I hummed with the chickadees. The sudden screeching sound of tires burning the pavement made my head spin. A green pickup truck desperately veered to avoid Tess. I heard a sickening thump, and I saw Tess fly into the ditch when the truck's bumper hit her. The truck swayed from left to right and then rolled on its side. I jumped off the tractor, and I darted to the road. The driver came out the passenger door. "Damn dog, damn dog." He swore as he struggled on his feet to get to the sidewalk.

"Are you okay? Should I call 911?"

He bellowed, "No cops." I approached him and I understood. His body reeked of alcohol. He took out his cell phone, so I turned my attention to Tess. Her belly rubbed the concrete as she crawled toward me, using her two front legs. Her back legs trailed behind, without life. She whimpered, her bloodshot eyes begging me for help. I picked up her sixty-pound body, and I gently laid her in the backseat. *I'm so sorry, I'm so sorry, please hang on.* She moaned softly, and I knew she was seriously hurt, although there was no visible injury, no blood. I rushed her to the vet.

They put her on a stretcher, and after an excruciating hour, he told me the impact had broken her spine. She needed immediate surgery. "I will call you tomorrow to let you know how she is doing."

Shaken and upset, I drove home. When Oso finally arrived from work, I hugged him tightly. "What's wrong?" he asked. We sat in the kitchen and he listened as I told him what had happened. He glared at me. He shot up and slammed both fists on the table. "Do you think I work to pay for your fuckin stupidity?" he roared. He raised his fists again and before they came down, I bolted out the back door. I ran wildly into the woods until my legs give out on me. I knelt down, and I puked.

The Internet had become prevalent, and we had purchased a computer. We both enjoyed the various chat rooms and I vented with strangers. It felt safe to unleash my frustrations about my marriage and Oso. I logged in with a nickname and connected with others who also were incognito. That evening, I poured out my anger at Oso. A guy, whom I chatted with often, defended Oso. "He was upset about losing Tess," he said. "When people are upset, they say things they don't mean." In bed that night, I thought about what the chat room guy had said, and I tried to forgive Oso. Still, I felt what resembled hate for him. But then, I had to admit, it was my fault for letting both dogs out.

Tess didn't recover, and a week later, we had to put her down. I grieved for days. My pain reached deeper than the loss of our dog. I cried for my son, for myself, and for what my life had become.

I prayed for this man to die. I couldn't leave him. Even after I'd admitted to him that I didn't love him anymore, he wouldn't go. He warned me, "If you leave me, you will never see your son again." And I believed him. After all, he had taken Jessi and Chris away from their mom. She always knew where we were. She sent birthday cards, and she called them. So maybe he was bluffing, but I couldn't take that chance. I convinced myself that he had not taken them without her consent, but deep down, I knew better. Even if she knew where we were, what could she do about it? She had no money to pursue him through legal venues. If Oso had pushed her down the stairs as she claimed, she was likely afraid of him also.

When I told Oso I wasn't happy, he stuck his face a few centimetres from mine and pointed his finger at me. "If you leave me, if you break up this family, you will fuck your son's life forever."

During my annual visit to my doctor, she asked how life was at home. I shook my head. I confided to her I was thinking of leaving my husband. She stared at me. "Every teenager with mental health issues I see in my office comes from a broken home. If you can make it work, stay for your son." I stayed.

If Oso died, I would receive people's sympathy; it would not be my failure. I prayed to God, *if you won't take him, can you please make me fall in love with him again? I'm sure it's easier for you to understand why I wished him dead than trying to fall in love again.* I figured if I loved him, I'd want more sex, and if he was satisfied, he'd be nicer. It wasn't always bad. We had good days. My life was not miserable all the time. So, I prayed. *Please, God, let me fall in love with him or, if not, take him away.* I knew he was rough even in the beginning, when I loved him. But I made excuses for him. The stress of being a single dad. The kids did not act up to his expectations. But they were gone now, and we had a beautiful little boy. We had our own house, and we shared many common interests. If only I loved him, life would be perfect, or so I believed. Was I being naïve or simply the eternal optimist?

It's Complicated

Summer 1994

Our boss informed the entire staff we were to become weather forecasters, or we'd need to find other jobs. The department was shifting the office's vocation. I enjoyed my work, so I heartily agreed to go back to school. The government sent us away for three months on a condensed meteorological training. I attended the course in Montreal with two other colleagues. Andre and I worked together at the Ottawa weather office. We'd been colleagues for seventeen years. He seemed happily married with two sons.

Every second week, we drove together from Ottawa to Montreal, a two-hour drive. I opened up to him. He was a good listener. The government rented cheap apartments for us in downtown Montreal. Ben was four years old, and I hated to leave him. Every other week, I brought him with me and we stayed at my in-laws. My mother-in-law was excited to have us there, and I always came home to a pleasant dinner. Ben loved getting spoiled by his grandparents.

Being in Montreal every week for three months gave me a break from Oso, although he insisted on having sex three to four times on the weekends to make up for the lost time. It was our last day on the course, and I headed out of the city with Ben in his car seat. I was going back to prison. My contact lenses burned my eyes, and I squinted against the brutal sun glaring through the windshield. The cars honked as I struggled to keep my eyes on the road. My chest contracted as if someone had grabbed it and was squeezing it. Is this how it feels before a panic attack? I concentrated on breathing deeply. I was stuck in rush hour traffic in a city of now over three and a half million people, and I could barely see ahead. Ben glanced around, oblivious to my struggle. I peeked at him in my mirror. "Ben, you enjoy screaming, right?"

He grinned, "Of course, Mom."

"Let's have a yelling contest, okay?" He nodded, excited, his eyes wide. "Ok, you start," I said." He let out a roar, but I could tell he was holding back, unsure of my intentions. "Okay, my turn." My scream was desperate, primal, the pressure cooker letting out steam before it blew up. Ben whooped and then he roared at the top of his lungs. Taking turns, we howled as if our lives depended on it. I couldn't tell if the cars jammed against us heard us or not. I didn't care. If I didn't release some pressure, I wouldn't trust myself to make it home.

After Montreal, we worked in Toronto for three weeks of on-the-job training. Andre told our boss I didn't like to drive in a big city and suggested we go at the same time. Not knowing he'd said that, I requested the same thing.

We drove together, and we shared a beer after our shifts in the evenings. On the last day, he came to my room to help me with my luggage. I sat on the bed. How could I tell him I'd fallen in love with him? I couldn't imagine going back to my old life, to Oso. "You ready?" He asked. I nodded, and I grabbed my things.

We usually chatted non-stop, but this time it was quiet in the car. It's a five-hour drive from Toronto to Ottawa. Could I tell him? Maybe he felt the same way, but I could be totally wrong. Halfway through the drive, I said, "Andre, if you have something to tell me, now is the time."

He looked at me, his eyes shining. "I've fallen in love with you." I gulped, and I seized his hand.

He drove me home, and he dropped me off at my place. It was early morning, and Oso had gone to work. Ben was at daycare. I needed to sleep, but I lay in bed, bawling all day. We were both married. I could tolerate my life before, even if it was hard, but how could I now have sex with Oso while being in love with someone else? We hid our love affair, seeing each other occasionally but never having sex. It was a line neither of us would cross. We held hands, and we talked. We wept. I couldn't leave my husband for another man. It was not acceptable. I didn't want to destroy a family. Andre and his wife had two sons together; they had been married for over twenty years.

It was unfair to Oso. I hated him for not being Andre. I prayed harder. *Please, let this man die.* I imagined cutting the brake lines on his truck. I didn't even know what brake lines looked like and, of course, I would never do it, but thinking about it soothed me.

I pretended in front of everyone that I was living a happy family life. I pretended in front of my co-workers, my family, my friends, the entire world. Only Andre knew the truth. The guilt was slowly killing me. "Oso, we need to talk." He sat down. "I am so, so sorry, but I'm in love with another man."

His face fell. He got up and he paced the floor. "Who is he?"

"It's not important. I want to save our marriage."

"Who?" he bellowed. So, I told him. He grabbed the phone and dialed Andre's number.

He cried. "You already have a wife. Leave mine alone."

I heard Andre's voice, "She's not happy with you. She doesn't love you anymore."

"Leave my wife alone, you already have a wife." Oso hung up, and now we were both sobbing. "Are you going to leave me?" he asked.

"No, but I don't know how to save our marriage anymore. I'm so unhappy." Oso grabbed the phonebook again and found a number for a help line. A kind lady answered, and he broke down again.

"Help! My family is falling apart, and I don't know what to do." He could hardly talk, so he handed me the receiver.

The lady seemed annoyed to talk to me. "Where is the man I was talking to?" Oso shook his head. I told her he didn't want to talk anymore.

We tried couples therapy again. The psychologist asked us about our family background. Oso told her that his mom used to tie him to a metal pipe in the basement so she could do her sewing without being disturbed.

When we stopped talking, she gave me a puzzled look. "What were you thinking?" She asked me why I stayed since I didn't love him anymore. I shrugged and raised my shoulders. Oso snickered. She turned toward him. "Why do you stay with someone who doesn't love you?" He looked defeated and shook his head. He'd told me once that if he ever lived through another breakup, he'd disappear.

A few weeks later, I was driving to work early one morning. A pale glow lit the distant horizon as the sun peeked over the city. The streets were deserted. The Ottawa River runs between the provinces of Ontario and Quebec. Several bridges connect the two provinces. People drive through every day to live or work on either side of the river. We lived on the Quebec side, and the weather office was in Ontario. I approached the

Macdonald-Cartier bridge. The bridge is almost one kilometre long. It wouldn't take much, a little pull on the wheel, and I'd hop over the rail, into the water. I didn't want to die, but I was totally exhausted. If only I could go to a hospital. Someone would take care of me, and I wouldn't have to think or feel anymore. I had the same image every morning as I drove across the river. But I wouldn't leave Ben.

We continued couples therapy for a while and it helped a bit. Finally, I went by myself, and I told her about Andre. I didn't tell her about the fights with Oso. What was the point? I didn't need her telling me to not make a big deal about it.

One day, I caught a glimpse of myself in the mirror. I was on all fours, Oso on my back. In that instant, I knew I'd somehow find the strength to leave before I turned forty. It was a calm realization, knowing that one day I'd be strong enough to take off. You must wonder why I didn't leave then. I honestly can't say.

Five years after our Toronto trip, Andre's marriage crumbled. We had not pursued our relationship. I agreed to meet him in downtown Ottawa for coffee. The breakup devastated him. Although it pained me deeply to watch his suffering, I still wouldn't leave my husband. I had revealed to Oso I was in love with another man, but I still preferred to save our marriage. I was not a quitter. When I worked on my university degree part-time while working full time, I almost abandoned it many times, but I did not. It took me twelve years to complete it. When I began taekwon-do, I didn't stop until I had my second-degree black belt. I would not quit my marriage. I told André I was sorry about his separation, but I couldn't help him. He nodded, said he understood. As I watched him walk away, his shoulders slumped, I had to stop myself from screaming.

Third Attempt

May 1999

Seven years after we moved into our new house, I finally had the courage to walk away. Well, I didn't walk away; it was more like a sprint toward survival. It was inevitable.

Ben had turned nine in March. I was thirty-eight. I often disliked the way Oso spoke to Ben, but he was never as vicious with him as he was with the other two. I believed there were several reasons for this. Ben was my biological son, and I could leave and take him with me. He had not reached puberty yet and did not rebel against his parents, as many teenagers do. Oso was not raising him alone, and we were not struggling as much for money since I made a decent salary.

During dinner, Ben chatted about an anecdote that happened at school. Oso didn't believe him and called him a liar. Ben cried. "It's true, I'm not lying." Ben's honesty was one of the qualities I admired most about him. His dad got upset and raised his voice. I took Ben's side.

"If he said it happened, then it happened. He's not a liar." Oso glared at me.

After Ben was in bed, I hid in my greenhouse. Oso had grumbled all the while we did the dishes. He knocked open the greenhouse door. When he realized I was crying, he flew into one of his rages. He blared, "You have no reason to cry, you fuckin bitch. I'm the one who should be upset. You didn't show a united front in front of our son... again." Maybe he was right, but I could not let him call Ben a liar. I got up and stormed out of the greenhouse. He ran after me, yelling, brandishing his fist. "Tu es folle! You have bugs in your brain! Fuckin crazy woman." I raced until I was far from him and then fell to my knees on the ground. I held my head with my shaking hands.

I slept in the basement that night. I couldn't bear to be near him. The next day, he left to go to taekwon-do, and Ben took the bus to school. I called Marianne, needing approval to leave him. "I'm miserable. I can't do this anymore." Sobs escaped from my body. Marianne was raised the same way I was, by a mom who repeatedly told us not to provide any advice, but simply to lend an ear. I told her again I was unhappy.

She said, "A friend told me that if you have sex even once when you don't feel like it, you should leave."

I sighed. "I'm having sex three to four times per week without wanting it."

She briefly paused. "Leave him." I had visited Marianne in Kamloops a few days prior during a business trip. We spent almost a week together, and I had never mentioned a word of what I was going through.

It was the push I needed. That afternoon, I drove to the medical clinic. I worked shifts, so I hoped the doctor could give me a few days off to allow me to search for a place to live. I needed to figure out how I'd take care of Ben while working nights and weekends. On my way to the clinic, I practiced my speech. My family doctor was not there, so a different female doctor welcomed me into her office. She asked, "How can I help you today?"

The bubble burst. My speech, completely forgotten. I couldn't talk fast enough. Bawling, I blurted out my grief. She listened, not saying a word, simply nodding, encouraging me to continue. When I stopped, she said, "Wait here a minute." She stepped out and quickly returned, handing me a piece of paper. She'd written the telephone number for a women's shelter. I shook my head; I was not an abused woman. I simply needed a few days off work to organize myself and my son. She wrote me a prescription for a month off work and said if I needed more, to come back to see her.

Someone had finally heard me. Marianne had given me the push I needed to take the leap, and the doctor had validated my decision. I was not wrong; the way I was treated was not okay. The next time I visited my family doctor, she read my file. "You left your husband?"

"You advised me to stay," I said.

She shook her head. "I did not know how bad it was."

I sadly stared at her. "You didn't ask."

My hands shook when I called my parents. When I was young and did well on an exam, I would ask my dad to sign my paper so I could see the pride in his eye. If my mark was lower, I'd ask my mom for fear of disappointing my father. My mother picked up on the third ring. She was alone; my dad had gone golfing. "Hello."

"Mom, are you sitting down?" I blurted, "I left Oso. I can't take it anymore. I've had enough. I just can't do this anymore." Through her sighs, I felt her pain, but not because I'd left my husband.

"Liette, we love you, and we will support you with whatever you need. How can we help? Do you want to come home?" She wanted to be with me, to hold me as I wept. When my dad got home, they both reached out. I finally understood their love for me surpassed all their Catholic upbringing and what they needed was for me to be happy and safe. While writing my story, I called my mom many times to ask her questions. She has such an excellent memory. It did not surprise them I'd left Oso. They knew my situation was not healthy. They had prayed I would leave him sooner. My mom regretted not having brought it up when she came to help me with Ben. I was ashamed to tell them, and yet they never judged me. They never said we told you so. Would I have left him sooner if I'd known what their reaction would be? I'm not sure. I think I needed to work it out on my own. Who knows? If my doctor had questioned me instead of instructing me to try harder, for my son's sake? If the psychologist had cautioned me that being yelled and cursed at to force me to do things I didn't want to was abusive, instead of instructing me to suck it up? I can't blame others for my decisions, but I wished I'd found the professional support I needed.

I drove aimlessly all day, waiting for the afternoon to end, gauging my next move. I prayed I could find a gentle way to announce to my son I'd left his dad. After school, I picked him up. He sat in the backseat, and I couldn't hold it any longer. I pulled over on the side of the road and I told him, "I've left your dad. It's over."

He shed a few tears. Two months prior, he had turned nine years old, and now his world was crumbling. He bravely swallowed and said, "It's going to be okay, Mom; we're going to be okay." As I peered at his sad face in the mirror, my heart ached for him. Was I fucking my son's life for the rest of his life? Would he understand? Did I make the right decision?

I drove to the office to inform my boss I wouldn't be at work for a month. I parked the car and looked at Ben. "Are you okay to come in with me?" He put on such a brave face; I was proud of him. Months later, I found a day job and quit my position at the weather office. Ben came with me to empty my locker and deliver my goodbyes. I bawled as we hauled my possessions to the car. I loved my job, but a single mom on shift work with no family or friends to help became too difficult.

"Why are you crying?" Ben asked. "Wasn't it your decision?"

"Even when a decision is the right one, it doesn't make it easy," I said.

After we left the weather office, Ben and I drove around until darkness settled. I had nowhere to go. I didn't plan my separation. I had left a note on the kitchen table for Oso. A colleague had confided in me she had saved her overtime cheques in a private account while she planned her escape. I never intended to leave. I had no plan. Ben repeatedly asked me, "Where are we going to sleep, Mom?"

I forced my voice to sound reassuring. "Don't worry; we'll find a place. We're having an adventure." Finally, I stopped at a charming hotel in Gatineau and asked if they had any available rooms. I preferred a hotel with a pool so Ben could play in the water while I considered my next move. The guy at the reception desk smiled, and I caught the pity in his eyes. I'm sure he understood we were not on vacation. A woman with a light suitcase, failing to appear brave, a young boy holding her hand.

"Ma'am," he said, "we have another hotel down a few blocks. It's cheaper, and you'll be comfortable there. You are welcome to come here anytime for the pool." I nodded with gratitude. If I opened my mouth, only wails would slip out. He didn't need a drama episode from a strange woman. After we settled and had dinner, Ben splashed in the water while I calculated my budget and how much I could afford for an apartment. I had a one-thousand-dollar bond I could cash out. I thanked God I'd always kept my personal bank account.

We ended up sleeping in that hotel for three days, but my money was quickly running scarce. I called a family resource center where Oso and I had taken a few courses in parenting. For twenty dollars per day, Ben and I had a bed and food, plus access to social workers. I'd been a canvasser for the United Way campaign at work, and I used to tell my colleagues that one out of three people benefit from the campaign. When I asked the social worker how they functioned, she said they received most of their funding from United Way. It dismayed me to learn I'd become one of three. My son and I were now part of the statistics.

The isolated centre was located deep in a forest at the end of a lengthy road. It was an extensive building with approximately ten bedrooms and several larger rooms for various activities. A social worker stayed during the day, but at night, we were alone. I pretended to be brave for Ben. "Mommy, I'm scared." We held hands until he fell asleep. The doctor had wished to give me a prescription for sleeping pills, but I'd declined, afraid of getting addicted and trusting I was strong. She had insisted on giving me a sample, four little blue pills. Once Ben fell asleep, I swallowed half a pill, and I slept.

After a few days, Ben told me he was afraid and wanted to go home. I called Oso, and he said, "Of course, you can come back until you find a place to stay. No worries, I'll sleep in the basement." We went to the house, and it was okay for a day. The screaming started when I brought up my share of the house. Oso stated that if I tried to sell or take it, he would burn it to the ground.

I didn't know where to go anymore. I called Jessi. She rented a small apartment in Gatineau with Meagan, but she didn't hesitate. Ben and I moved in with her. After the kids were in bed, we sat on the couch with a bottle of wine. I told her I'd left her dad for good this time. She replied, "If you had not been there, I don't think we would've survived."

I didn't tell her everything. It wasn't necessary; she knew her father. But she also adored him, and I had to be careful. She wouldn't blame me; she understood, but she revered him. "This is between the two of you," she said.

We stayed with her for three days while I hunted for an apartment. She invited Chris for dinner. They argued. "Dad abused us," Chris said.

Jessi replied, "No way. He was strict, but he was not abusive."

Chris sadly smiled at me. "I will always admire you for staying so long."

Ben wanted to be near his dad, his school, and especially his friends. We visited a few apartments in town, but his shoulders slumped lower with each visit. We hunched on the curve, and he said, "If we move to the city, I will have to live with Dad." I lucked out; I found a comfortable apartment in the village, allowing Ben to be close to everything he loved. It was a modest building with four apartments. I rented a two-bedroom flat on the main floor. It was on a side street, a quiet place with a hot tub and an in-ground pool.

A young couple lived above me. It amazed me each time I arrived home to hear them giggling on their veranda. They must fake being happy and in love. I'd pretended for so long, I thought everyone was faking it. Yet I knew my parents still loved each other after a lifetime together. Fighting had become my normal. It wasn't my parents' normal, but it was mine. It's fascinating how our perception of reality changes with the events in our lives. I can only imagine how hard it must be for women to leave abusive partners if they've grown up in violence. It's always been their normal. I know men also suffer from domestic abuse, but the government of Canada website states that in 2018, in Canada, almost eighty percent of domestic violence victims were women. Professionals who should've been there to help me had encouraged me to stay in the relationship. *Let the words slide off your shoulders, they're just words. Stay for your son.*

The divorce procedures were long and painful. It takes a year to get a divorce in Quebec. I will spare you the nasty details of our mediation meetings. When children are involved, the provincial government pays for six free sessions. It took fifteen meetings to conclude our separation arrangement. Each morning I had to attend, I'd wake up from a restless night, nausea gnawing at me all day.

When Jessi told Meagan that her grandparents were getting a divorce, my seven-year-old granddaughter anxiously asked her mom, "Is she still going to be my grandma?"

Her mom reassured her, "She will always be your grandma."

When Oso caught her referring to me as Grandma, it surprised him. After preaching all his life that blood didn't matter, did he expect me to stop being a grandma because we got divorced?

I was thirty-eight years old. I was without a home. My family was twelve hundred kilometres away. My bank account was empty, and after working all my adult life, I owed almost forty thousand dollars to the bank. Oso didn't want the truck we'd just bought because it came with a twenty-two-thousand-dollar debt. I kept the pickup with the debt and the loaded line of credit. He planned to give me my share of the house later when he could. He estimated that at roughly seven thousand dollars. Of course, he refused to have the house appraised. He said, "If you send an evaluator, I will make sure the house is dirty and worth almost nothing, even if I have to destroy it." The divorce cost one thousand dollars, and Oso wouldn't cover any of it. "You want a damn divorce? You pay for it." After paying for half of the mediation sessions, I had no money left in my account. I sucked up my pride, and I hailed my parents. I sobbed when I asked them if I could borrow a thousand dollars.

"The cheque will be in the mail tomorrow," my mom said.

I was more than broke, but I was free. And I had my job, with a steady income. I was confident I'd get back on my feet quickly enough, financially, at least. I traded the truck for a compact Honda Civic. When I picked up Ben at school, he was all excited. "Can I open the sunroof?" he said.

My eyes darted up. "I have a sunroof?"

Why doesn't she leave? We shake our head when women stay in abusive relationships, even defending their partner. According to the statistics, a woman has to be beaten seven times before she flees. Oso didn't hit me. Of course, I was frightened, but I never feared for my life. I feared for my sanity. The reasons I stated through my story kept me with this man for thirteen years. I always expected the situation would get better. We had many wonderful times; it wasn't always bad. I'd like to say that I left because he called my son a liar. That was certainly the trigger for it. But as I ran away from his words that evening, something clicked, and I realized if I didn't stop the screaming in my mind, I would go crazy. The situation would not improve, and it was not okay.

The dynamics in abusive relationships are complicated. From an outside point of view, it seems so simple, just pack your bags and go. In reality, it is never that simple.

I fell in love with this enigmatic, charming, older man who promised me a roller coaster ride. We make our own decisions in life. I could stay or leave. Life is often similar to a playing card, two faces. On one side, a disastrous relationship. On the other side, a life without the kids. I chose the least painful. I would never abandon the kids. By the time they left home, Ben was born. The card changed. On one side, still the abusive relationship. On the other side, a life hiding Ben from his dad so he wouldn't steal him. Again, I adopted the least painful. What I didn't realize was the relationship was slowly killing me from the inside.

The therapist had encouraged me to not take his words seriously. Was I overreacting? I often questioned myself. Maybe my parents were not normal. I'd never seen them fight. Normal couples do quarrel. I remembered an argument Oso and I had the first summer we took Ben to New Brunswick. He was four months old, and I was elated to be home, showing off our beautiful baby boy. Oso and I headed to the city when I casually said, "Camilla asked me if we wanted to contribute to my parents' Christmas gift this year."

"How much?" he asked.

"Around sixty dollars," I said.

"And what did you tell her?"

"I replied sure, yes. That's a great idea."

The switch in his eyes was instantaneous. The madman was back. He banged his fist on the steering wheel and roared, "Mosus de peteuse de broue (you damn vain person)." He yelled at me all the way to the Canadian Tire parking lot. As soon as he parked the truck, I grabbed Ben and I scrambled out of the vehicle. He circled me, hollering, ordering me that under no circumstances was I to give any money to my siblings.

Suddenly, it was as if I was watching the scene sitting above the post lamp.

In the Canadian Tire parking lot, I detached from my body and viewed myself pacing around the truck, Ben in my arms. Oso pursued me, shouting, arms waving in the air. If I called my dad, I knew he'd come pick me up. I'd tell them everything, and Oso would return alone to Ottawa. My parents would help me and Ben. It would be over. I paced the parking lot. I did not want to be a burden to my parents. Maybe Oso witnessed the struggle on my face; he quickly calmed down. He apologized. "You worry every month about the bills. I simply want to help you. I hate seeing you stressed each month." Eventually, I'd gotten back in the pickup.

A month after I left Oso, and we had settled into our apartment, Ben and I packed our bags for a visit with my family in New Brunswick. Ben wanted to say goodbye to his dad. Oso sat on the porch, expecting us. Ben hugged him and stared, eyes wide, at the tears falling on his dad's cheeks. His strong, powerful, fearful dad was crying. In nine years, he'd never seen his father cry. We took two days to drive to New Brunswick, staying at a motel along the way. Ben kept asking me, "Mom, why did dad cry? Was it because he wanted to come with us? Was it because he is alone?"

He called his father every day and demanded to see him as soon as we returned. His dad became his hero, and I became the bad guy. Later, when he asked his father why he cried, Oso told him, "I love your mom, and I want our family back together. She left us and I'm heartbroken."

Final Cut

Ben and I enjoyed a wonderful two weeks in New Brunswick. My family surrounded me with love and support. One evening, after everyone had gone to bed, my mom and I relaxed in their sunroom and we chatted until two o'clock in the morning. I shared many things with her, but I said nothing about the sex. I wasn't ready to divulge that part of my life to anyone. "Mom, I can't tell you everything. It's too painful for me to talk about it and it would be too difficult for you." I confided in her about various issues and by the middle of the night, we were both crying.

I told my family it would be at least two years before I let another man touch me.

When we came back, I dropped Ben off at his dad's house. I drove to my apartment, and I hunched in the dark, alone, on the floor. I'd never felt so lonely in all my life. Since I'd left Oso in May, I'd been feeling free, almost euphoric, looking forward to going home. Now, I lay on the carpet with the lights out. I stared at the drab walls. I was alone. My best friend had moved away. Colleagues at work were simply comrades, and I wouldn't confide in any of them. I'd told one guy at work, whom I was closer to, that I'd left my husband. He'd said, "I didn't think you were that kind of woman." When I asked him what he meant, he said, "The kind who abandons the ship when the sailing gets rough." I shook my head, not bothering to explain the situation.

The only friend I had who lived near us was the one we used to go canoe/camping with. I sent her an email, and she replied they'd decided to not take sides and abandoned their friendship with both of us. I was on my own.

A week later, the telephone rang, and it was Oso. "How are you?" he asked, his voice tender. I broke down, and I invited him over. We began dating again. I know it sounds crazy, but the craving for another adult touch was so powerful that I was ready to go back to him. We took Ben and his friend to a movie and I grabbed Oso's hand as we walked to the theatre. I saw Ben's huge smile when he noticed. We even had sex, and it was good. Oso, of course, was on his best behaviour. He told me he was in therapy. "I finally understand what I did wrong."

I invited him for a swim at the pool at our apartment. Ben was playing with his friends, so I stepped inside to get snacks. Oso followed me into the kitchen and while I had my back turned, he walked up to me and grabbed my boobs. "Please don't do that," I said.

He opened his hands, shrugged, "Look at the way you're dressed." I was wearing my bathing suit. The exact words I needed to hear.

"I will dress however I want in my home, and anywhere else." I pointed at the door. "Leave." He grinned. He strolled toward the door. I watched his back. "Oso?" He turned around, his face hopeful.

I shook my head. "Don't come back."

PART FOUR

Coffee

1999

Free! I was free, absolutely free. Well, almost free. We had a son together and of course, Jessi and Chris, therefore our lives would always be linked.

Approximately three weeks later, Oso and I got into a fight on the telephone. When he raised his voice and cursed, I said, "I don't have to listen to you anymore." I hung up. He kept calling, and I ignored the ringing. He left nasty messages on the answering machine and the last message was: *I'm coming over and you're going to talk to me.* When the car pulled up in the driveway, I hid in my bedroom, sitting on the floor where he couldn't see me through the window. The door rattled when he banged on it. I held the phone in my hands, my shaking finger on the number nine, ready to dial 911 if he broke the door down. He screamed. "I know you're in there. I will knock this damn door if you don't open it!" He gave up and left when I remained hidden. I breathed an enormous sigh of relief, then I put my head on my knees and sobbed.

I'd fallen in love with Andre in 1994, but we were not seeing each other when I left Oso. I didn't even want him to know about my separation because I was fed up with men. Andre and I hadn't talked in over a year, and I had no idea of his feelings for me. For the first time in thirteen years, I could steer my path, and no way was I stepping into another relationship. The last five years had been agonizing, the two of us working together yet not able to be together.

Andre and his wife separated in February 1999, and I left Oso in May of the same year. Since we worked on a different schedule, I avoided Andre most of the summer. In September, our boss appointed me a day of overtime, and Andre was in the office. The Internet was still new for us, but he shared a few dating sites with me, saying he had gone on a few dates. As I lay in bed that evening, I realized not only did I still love him, but we were now both single. The next day at work, I typed him an email. Back then, we only had work emails. I wrote a single question: *Do you still love me?* I waited three days before returning to work. The anticipation almost drove me insane. We began each shift with a weather briefing, but I barely listened to my colleague as he spoke. As soon as I could, I opened my email.

One sentence, À la folie.

In September 1999, after five long years of yearning, Andre and I began our new life in a cozy, yet elegant restaurant set in an enchanting forest in Chelsea, Quebec. Shaking, we gawked at each other and made a vow: this date will be our anniversary. We knew that day was the first of our wonderful journey together.

In order to give Ben time to adjust to his parents' separation, Andre and I waited a year before moving in together. Oso warned me he never wanted to see my boyfriend at his house. He met a woman online, and she moved in with him in September, a few months after I moved out. Ben informed me his dad had a girlfriend, and he said I should get a boyfriend, so I introduced him to Andre. Ben asked me why his dad had drawn a picture of a skeleton head beside Andre's name in the phone book.

Oso's girlfriend had two sons who lived with their father near Montreal. The youngest one was a year younger than Ben, and he came to stay with his mom for a while. I hadn't met them yet. Early one Sunday morning in October, still half asleep, I picked up the phone. "Hello, Liette, how are you? My name is Sara, I'm Oso's girlfriend. Are you aware the kids do not have any school tomorrow?" I knew. "What are you doing with Ben?" she asked.

"I took a day off and I'll be home with him."

"Great," she said, "do you mind looking after my son also? I have to work."

"Hmm, I guess I could do that."

She and I never became friends, but we were polite with each other. She and Oso were together for twenty years before they split up.

It was Christmas, and I reassured Andre that it would be okay to go pick up Ben at his dad's house. "Oso has found someone, and he's happy with Sara. Everything will be fine. Just stay in the car." We pulled into the driveway. Oso was shoveling outside with Ben and Sara's son. From the snowbank where they were holding shovels, Oso lifted his hands above his head. He ran his right thumb across his throat from left to right and jerked his hand in the air.

"See," I said to Andre. "He wants us to turn the motor off and come in for coffee."

I smiled, and I lowered my window. The words were simple. "Get the fuck off my land or I will cut your fuckin throat."

My trembling hand clutched the window knob and rolled it up as quickly as it could. Ben got in the car and I said, "Quick, quick, go, go." I laughed hysterically. If I didn't laugh, I'd scream.

Ben was upset. "Why are you laughing at Dad?"

"No, no," I replied. "I'm laughing at something Andre said, unrelated to your dad."

Running

I invited Jessi and Meagan to breakfast at a restaurant in Ottawa so they could meet Andre. It felt awkward, introducing my new boyfriend to my ex's daughter, but the conversation flowed beautifully. When Andre left to go to the bathroom, Jessi whispered, "Liette, he's a very handsome man."

I replied, "You think so?"

"Oh yeah." Honestly, her words surprised me because although I agreed he looked swell, I'd fallen in love with his personality, not his looks. I beamed at him when he came back. I took a whole new look at him. True enough, he was and still is a very handsome man.

Since Oso and Andre couldn't be in the same room, Jessi always had two events for every special occasion: one event with her dad and Sara, and one event with us. At one point, she was in a steady relationship with a guy we really liked. He invited everyone to a surprise birthday party for her. Her dad was furious, and they had a huge fight about it, but he did not back down. Andre and I enjoyed the party and only learned of the drama afterwards. Of course, Oso and Sara did not attend.

Andre and I lived together in his house for four years before we built our own home in Cantley in 2004. Cantley is a charming village situated a fifteen minutes' drive north of Ottawa.

Shortly after we had our new house built, my parents came to visit us.

That same year, Jessi had a nasty breakup with the boyfriend we liked. While my parents were here, she called me two or three times per day. They were still sharing an apartment while both looked for another place to stay. The atmosphere was seriously tense, so he disappeared most evenings. She thought he was cheating on her, although I kept reminding her they were no longer a couple. Andre picked up the phone, and I knew right away it was her. I was torn. I did not see my parents often, so I wished to spend as much time as I could with them, yet I needed to be there for her.

My father shook his head. It was the first and only time I heard him say, "You don't owe them anything; they are not your blood." Even in his great wisdom, he never understood the strong bond and love I felt for them, my stepchildren.

Jessi, always trying to better herself, both mentally and physically, began a running program. She had muscular legs and an even stronger will, so she trained for a half marathon.

In 2005, in her early thirties, she registered for the Ottawa May weekend half marathon. The May run in Ottawa is the biggest race weekend in the country. Thousands of people take part each year and thousands more cheer the racers. The atmosphere is magic, bursting with energy. I found her and her new boyfriend, with Meagan, in the immense crowd. I hugged her tightly before the race began. "You've got this." We elbowed our way to the starting line and shouted when the runners bolted out the gate. We raced to her boyfriend's truck and drove to the halfway point.

Surely enough, we saw her coming, running strong. I jumped up and down, waved my hands in the air, cheering at the top of my lungs. Her face broke into a huge smile, and she waved at us as she whipped by. We ran to the truck to make our way back to the finish line, but we had to fight a horde of people. I panicked as I realized we could miss her finish. We finally made our way to the finish line and waited and waited. Did she complete the race in such an awesome time we missed her, or did she crash along the way? Either way, I had a lump in my throat. "If we missed her finish, she's gonna be so upset."

Her boyfriend replied. "If she's already finished, it means she did much better than she hoped. She'll be overjoyed."

We finally spotted her on the ground stretching beyond the finish line. She completed the half marathon in two hours and ten minutes. She was a tad disappointed we missed the finish, but she said she ran strong, thrilled with her results. We celebrated by going out to lunch at a nearby restaurant. She proudly displayed the medal around her neck. I had always hated running. Once, I had to run for a black belt taekwon-do competition, and I swore I would never run again. I had emailed Marianne, who was and still is a runner. *For a taekwon-do physical test, I need to run seven kilometres, and I hate running. I don't want to run. I have no choice, but after this, I will never run again. Where should I start?* The next day, the email came back: *Start by changing your attitude!*

Jessi inspired me to run together. I reached out to Marianne for advice. *Hey, I have been watching runners and they seem so happy. I want to try running. Where should I start?* The email came back: *Who are you and what have you done to my sister?*

I didn't work at it seriously, but I did train to get myself to a five-kilometre distance. Our first five-kilometre race together was a charitable cancer research run in Ottawa. It was September 2006, a beautiful, cool morning. We stood at the starting gate, grinning at each other, swaying, feeling the frenzy of the group. Both reflecting she had beaten cancer once. She was a stronger runner, but she said, "We are doing this together."

The starting bell rang, and I knew she wanted to bolt forward, so I encouraged her to do so. "Wait for me at the finish line."

"You sure?" she said. I waved her off. It was my first five-kilometre race. I ran and then I walked and then I ran again, huffing and puffing, finally crossing the finish line. She waited for me in the crowd, and I fell panting into her open arms. We sobbed as we held on to each other. We celebrated her conquering cancer as a pregnant teenager, and me not dying before reaching the finish line.

It's now been sixteen years since our first run together and I still run today. I registered to do a marathon for my sixtieth birthday. When I feel like quitting, I relive that finishing moment and how her energy and love pushed me to keep going.

We also took part in the twenty-four-hour cancer relay where Jessi walked the survivor walk and I bawled. We had yoga classes together and held Tupperware and Partylite parties at each other's home.

My friend Ann drove me home after a yoga class and asked me if I had any kids. "I gave birth to one, but my first husband had three and my second husband has two, so I guess that kinda makes six."

"How long have you been divorced?" she asked.

"It's been six years," I said.

"Do you still have any contacts with his kids?" She was curious.

"Of course," I replied. "I divorced the man, never the kids."

Jessi was a gorgeous woman; she had several friends and almost as many boyfriends. She was, however, very insecure, and she partied and drank a lot, which made matters worse. Her relationship with men never lasted long. Each time, she called me crying. "What is wrong with me?" she asked.

She also reached out to me when she got into a fight with her dad, which happened frequently.

The conversation went like this:

Her: "Hey, how are you?" I could sense the anguish in her voice.

Me: "I'm good, you?" *Uh-oh, boyfriend or Dad?*

Her: "I'm so angry at Dad; he's the most stubborn, obnoxious, mean person I know."

Me: "Oh why? What happened?" Nodding my head yes, smiling.

Usually, her dad said something that pissed her off. The two of them got into the worst fights, screaming insults at each other. She'd swear she never wanted to see him again. I'm done, she would say. Then, a few months later, they'd hug and become best friends.

Sharing a passion for life, they lived fiercely; they fought viciously, and they loved passionately. I never saw that side of her, the angry drunken outbursts that her daughter or partners shared with me. She aspired to be on her best behaviour whenever I was there. I saw her broken side and her insecurities, but I can't recall her ever being angry at me except for on one occasion, which I write about later.

The Bears

My body crawls in slow motion as I desperately kick my legs in the icy lake. I grapple with the waves, trying to avoid gulping the hostile water, although drowning might be better than being eaten alive. I'm not a strong swimmer, and the bear creeps up behind us. My son clings to my back. He hasn't learned how to swim yet. His arms grip at me, choking me. Every breath he takes is a whimper in my ear. Bears are excellent swimmers, and this one is easily gaining on us.

The nightmares began roughly three months after I left my husband. My eczema disappeared, but the horrifying dreams replaced my bleeding fingers. Each time, I woke up drenched in sweat and tears. The nightmares were similar: it was always a bear, an evil, huge, vicious, angry bear. They visited me in my sleep practically every two weeks. It was usually a black bear, but occasionally a grizzly bear, and once or twice, a polar bear. It was always a bear. I never dreamed of any other animals and I never dreamed about Oso. Most of the time, the bears didn't chase after me, but after someone I love. My parents, Ben or friends. My mom used to tell us not to eat heavy food before bedtime because we'd have nightmares about bears. *Vous rêverez aux ours,* she would say.

I'm in the forest with my family having a picnic. I sense him before anyone sees him. The energy in the air shifts. The hairs on my arms tingle as if someone has turned on a huge electrical breaker. A scream, BEAR! My entire body goes numb, and the sudden thumping of my heart drowns out any other sounds. My lungs constrict. I spot him, a black monster, foamy white drool coming out of his mouth, teeth baring as he charges. I abruptly grab my son and we run.

I sprint as fast as my legs can go, or as quick as Ben's legs can follow. He clutches my hand, his feet barely touching the ground as we race for our lives. I feel the bear more than I hear him. He's on our heels, and I taste the bile in my throat. My son climbs on my back as I jump in a lake. I swim toward the other shore. Surely, the bear will give up. Yet, he's closing on us. His sour breath on my neck.

Suddenly, everything goes quiet and nature stands still. Is he gone? A gut-wrenching noise breaks the silence. The bear sinks his teeth into my son's back. I hear the skin tearing and the bones snapping as the bear mauls him. A blood-curdling scream wakes me up, and it takes a few seconds for me to realize the howling is coming from my lungs. I'm in my bed, alone, on my knees, my chest heaving. *Breathe, breathe, breathe.* I repeat the words. My heart slowly attempts to return to a normal beat.

When I finally stop shaking and am able to stand, I hurry to my son's bedroom. He's sleeping soundly; my screams did not disturb him. I go back to bed, knowing that for me, there will be no more sleep tonight.

I confided to a friend, telling her about these dreadful re-occurring nightmares. She suggested the only way to stop these dreams was to kill the bear. Okay, but how could I kill a bear with my bare hands? I didn't have any weapons with me in my dreams. I googled for advice about these types of dreams, and a few sites suggested we portray people we fear as animals in our dreams. My son's father was the bear terrorizing me at night.

The nightmares occurred for more than a year, and they appeared every time I saw Oso. Because we shared custody of Ben, I often saw him when I picked up my son. Ben wanted to spend time with his dad and I'd read that it was better for the kids to share time with each parent. I needed a plan to stop these bears, or I would not survive. Every night, before falling asleep, I visualized myself getting bigger and bigger until finally I squashed the bear with my fist.

I closed my eyes and I drifted off. I'm playing kick the can with my siblings in my parents' backyard, a game we enjoyed with my brothers, sisters and neighbours when I was a kid. A variant of the hide and seek game, where we use a stick and a can to cover the base. My parents' house is in the countryside and beyond an extensive field stands a beautiful forest. My brother holds the stick, protecting the can, the home base. He closes his eyes and counts to fifty while we scramble to find the best hiding place.

I hide behind the garage, crouching down, waiting for my chance at the can. Suddenly, an enormous black bear shuffles out from the trees. My siblings yell and scatter in all directions. I scoot into the garage, but the bear comes after me, so I dash for the house. While I'm sprinting for my life, something amazing happens. I grow and grow until I'm bigger than the bear. I turn around to face it. I'm not big enough to kill it, but I'm certainly powerful enough to stop it. My hand goes out. "Stop! Enough! This ends now!"

He pauses, sits down, looks puzzled. I turn and I walk toward the house. He follows me. I challenge him again, my open hand on his snout. "Enough. You will not hurt me nor anyone in my family, never again." I'm no longer afraid; I'm in control. He squats down again, confused. But he doesn't pursue the attack.

I awoke with an immense sense of freedom, although the road to full recovery was just beginning. The bears continued their visits over the next two or three years, but they never attacked again. They lurked in a distance. I'd heard about post-traumatic stress disorder (PTSD), but I thought it only affected people who survived a war or had dreadful experiences happened to them. I didn't consider myself in either of those categories. A psychologist I briefly consulted after leaving Oso, had mentioned PTSD, but I'd shrugged her off.

In time, with more therapy and lots of support from Andre and my family, the bears showed up as teddy bears, resting on a shelf, watching, but not threatening. Today, I occasionally suffer from anxiety and insomnia, but I've not had a bear nightmare in over fifteen years.

Russian Roulette

Before I left his father, Ben and I shared a special bond. Sometimes, after a loud fight with his dad, I'd sneak into his bedroom where he lay, his eyes wide open, scared and confused. I'd snuggle with him. I wanted to reassure him, but mostly I needed his love. He owned my heart. He'd told me we should leave his dad and live together, the two of us. But, as he got older, he became worried we would split up. I made another promise. I swore to him we would always stay together, the three of us. His family.

After he'd seen his dad cry, he rebelled against me, blaming me for the divorce. Being dyslexic and having ADHD, he struggled in school. He spent more time at his dad's house, lashing out at me whenever he was with me. We took him to a child psychologist, alternating weeks between me and his dad. The therapist asked him, "When you're with your mom, how long is your elastic before you blow up?" He squinted his eyes, and he measured a tiny distance between his thumb and index. "And when you're with your dad?"

With a brash look, he said. "From here to McDonald's."

After yet another episode, when he screamed his frustration at me, I asked him, "What can I do to help you through this?"

He said, "You broke your promise."

"I know, and I'm sorry. What do I need to do for you to forgive me?"

"When I misbehave, you give me a consequence, so you need one. No tv and no chocolate (he knew me well) for a month." I solemnly swore to abide by this consequence, and I did, but it helped little.

When I mentioned moving with Andre, he said, "If you force me to move away from my friends, I will jump from a bridge, with no water underneath." To give him time to adapt, we stayed in our apartment for a year. He liked Andre, who had more patience with him than I did.

After the three of us had a pleasant picnic by a lake, Ben shook his head and said, "Mom, he's always nice to you, isn't he?" His father forbade him to mention the name Andre. It broke my heart to listen to him on the phone after we'd gone horseback riding. Dad, me and mom and um . . . we went horseback riding, and we had so much fun. And then mom and um . . . took me for ice cream.

Ben was ten years old when we moved with Andre. He hated living in the city, away from his village, his friends, and the house he grew up in. I drove him to school every day, so he was with his friends, but he couldn't see them as often. I didn't feel at home either. Andre had lived in that house with his wife, and although he tried hard to make me feel comfortable, it wasn't my home. We lived there together for four years before we had our home built in Cantley, where we still live.

We had some good days with Ben and some not-so-good days. I'd always been lenient with him, trying to compensate for his dad's sharp words. Needing to learn how to deal with his desperate tantrums, I enrolled in parenting workshops. It was a constant struggle to assert my parental authority. When he dipped his feet into the teenage years, he got angrier. One day, he snapped. "I don't like you anymore. I'm outta here." He called his dad to come pick him up, and he slammed the door on his way out. He was twelve years old.

My little boy. The person I loved most in the world. He would rather live with his dad than with me. I must be the worst mom on the planet. I was a total wreck. Each morning, I put myself in robot mode. I went to work, kept busy, pretended I was fine. But when I laid my head on my pillow, the agony was so intense, I could hardly breathe. Andre tried in vain to help me, to be there for me, but my body was shutting down. The pain was too deep. Andre later told me that witnessing my misery made him feel helpless and nauseous.

I couldn't sleep, I couldn't eat, I could hardly function. I needed help, so I begged my doctor for sleeping pills and a consultation with a psychologist.

I met the therapist in his basement office. A man approximately my age, he had kind eyes and soft manners. He patiently listened to me as I blubbered out my pain. He explained, "Oso had no respect for you, so your son thinks you don't deserve any respect. Teach him to respect you."

The therapist helped me set boundaries with Ben, and to this day, I feel he saved my life and my relationship with my son. After six months, during which Ben randomly visited us, we resumed shared custody. During those six months, Ben called me every evening at eight o'clock. His dad and his girlfriend retired to their room, and he was lonely. He wanted me to watch television with him. So, we did, every night.

The therapist insisted on talking about my past relationship with Oso. I was skeptical since it had been three years, and I had moved on. Andre and I were doing great, and other than the issues with Ben, I was happy. I quickly realized I needed to heal many traumas.

I told the therapist about the incident when we'd gone to pick up Ben at Christmas and Oso had made death threats to Andre. "Why am I so naïve? I've lived with this man for thirteen years; am I that dumb? I've always thought of myself as a smart woman, yet here I was, thinking Oso was inviting us in for coffee."

"No, you're not dumb," he said. "You had moved on; you were happy, and you're a good person. You assumed the same from him."

I also questioned him about the wild strawberries. Oso and I planted a rock bed, full of flowers, in front of the house. Every year, a bunch of wild strawberries would grow within the flowers. I'd wait in anticipation for the delicious sweet red fruits to ripen. But every year, Oso would pull the plants out and throw them away. When I'd cry and plead with him to leave them, he'd say, "The rock garden is for flowers, not for strawberries." A year after I left him, Oso brought Ben to my apartment. He smiled. "You should see all the beautiful strawberries in the rock garden; we're gonna have a feast this year. Probably enough to bake a pie."

I glared at him. I'm not sure if I wanted to punch him, kick him, or plainly kill him. I didn't understand. Was he toying with me, or did he simply not remember what he did the previous years?

I asked the therapist because, honestly, I was stunned.

"It's all about control," he said. "You loved the strawberries, so he destroyed the plants. Now that you're gone, he doesn't have to pull them out anymore. It's all about control, control over you." His words made sense to me, yet still.

"But he could be so loving, and we had months when all was good."

"Of course," the therapist said. "If he had been vicious all the time, you would not have stayed thirteen years. It's how he controlled you. After each cycle of violence, there's always a honeymoon cycle." We chatted about how hard it had been for me to leave this man. I had jumped in, and I didn't want to quit even if I was drowning. Yes, there was the fear he would disappear with my son; he had even said once he would kill me if I left. But it was more. What would people say? I felt immensely ashamed.

What you need to understand is that when Oso was good, he was very good. And during those days, I never doubted that he loved me. He could be so gentle and romantic, and I'd see the tenderness in his eyes.

I told the therapist about a technique that I'd hoped would allow me to leave without being judged. I'd provoke Oso. It was easy to get him upset. He told me ignoring him was the worse insult I could offer him. So, I'd pull his strings, make him mad, and then turn my back on him. While we lived in the old farmhouse, I tried walking away from a fight once. We argued in the kitchen, and I had enough, so I stepped out. "Oh no!" he said. He grabbed me as I tried to pull away. He yanked me back into the kitchen. My feet reared up, and I flew across the room, crashing into the wall. I fell to the floor. Oso rushed to me. "Oh my God, are you okay? I'm so sorry."

I screamed, "Don't touch me."

He let go of me and snickered. "So, now you're going to say I beat you up. What a sorry bitch you are." He snorted and walked away.

I was desperate. I provoked him, hoping one day he'd lose it completely and whack me a good one. People would see the bruises. Everybody would understand I had no choice but to leave him. Ben came home from school once with bruises on his arm. I asked him who grabbed him, and he said nobody had touched him. Oso asked me why I thought someone had physically hurt him. I looked him in the eyes. "Because I get the same bruises." His eyes welled up. Somehow, he knew what he was doing was not right. What I don't understand is if you know your behaviour is wrong and you are hurting the person you love, why not get help?

When I told the therapist what I'd done, he gasped. "You wouldn't have done that if you'd been in therapy with me." He shook his head. "Do you realize you played Russian Roulette?" Russian Roulette is a game where you put one bullet in a gun's chambers and you spin the cylinder. You put the gun to your head and pull the trigger, hoping that the single bullet is not in the cannon. I'm not sure I believed him. I've read that domestic violence has a pattern and that often, the violence increases over time. Contrary to a lot of the material I've read, Oso's violent behaviour did not escalate. Maybe the taekwon-do discipline helped, those thousands of kicks and punches into the bag helped relieve some of the tension. Oso was the chief instructor in our taekwon-do school since he attained his black belt before me. (I took a four-month break when giving birth).

In one of our subsequent sessions, I asked the therapist, "I don't understand. Oso always apologized and was very remorseful and sweet after he hurt me. I read that manipulators never admit they're wrong."

The therapist leaned toward me, his voice soft. "Liette, Oso was not a manipulator; he was an abuser."

I opened my mouth to protest, then I closed it again. I'd heard it before; hell, I'd even called a shelter for abused women once. The friend I'd talked to that same evening had mailed me a one-thousand-dollar cheque, so he believed it as well. When I'd spilled my guts to the doctor, she believed it and had provided me with a number for a shelter. It pissed off a colleague at work when I'd told her he did not abuse me. I only had the odd bruises on my arms. She'd blared, "When will women understand you don't need a black eye to suffer abuse?"

I'd never believed it. Until now.

When the therapist repeated the word "abuser," I'm not sure why, but this time, I knew. I'd been a victim; I'd let myself be a victim. How did I let this happen?

Thirteen years I lived with this man. Thirteen years of fear. Thirteen years of abuse. I sobbed all the way home. My entire body shuddered, my hands gripping the wheel so tight, my knuckles turned white. When I got home, Andre took one look at my face. "Tough session today?" He held me close until my sobs subsided.

A few months later, I drove around for hours, talking to myself, reliving each hurt. With each memory, I screamed at the top of my lungs. *You hurt me so bad.* It was raining; it was dark, and I drove and I hollered. *You hurt me so bad.* Suddenly, I knew I could forgive. Not for him. For me. And I did. I whispered, *I forgive you.*

A dark shadow lifted from my soul. I'd forgiven him. Now I had to learn to forgive myself.

HIV

My heart always skips a beat when the phone rings at a late hour. It is never good news. The phone rang at ten-thirty in the evening. It was a weekday, and Andre and I were already in bed.

"Pick up, pick up," I urged Andre, who slowly handed me the receiver. Jessi blubbered, and I could not make out what she was saying. "Calm down, slow down, breathe in, breathe out," I repeated.

After a few deep breaths and between sobs, I understood her brother Chris had tested positive for HIV. He lived in Europe and had married a German fellow. Apparently, he told his dad he cheated on his husband and had unprotected sex. He now tested positive for HIV.

The Government of Canada defines the disease as Human Immunodeficiency Virus (HIV), a virus that attacks the body's immune system. While HIV is a manageable chronic condition, if left untreated, it can cause a weakened immune system or Acquired Immune Deficiency Syndrome (AIDS).

I drew my breath. I tried to calm her, reassure her. "We have medications now. HIV is no longer a death sentence in Canada.

He can come home, get treatment. It does not mean that he will get AIDS. He can still live a long, healthy life."

Ben was barely a teenager, and he heard the commotion from his bed. He stood at our bedroom door, listening. After Jessi calmed down and we hung up, I explained the situation to him, reassuring him that Canada had effective medications for HIV. Shocked, he shook his head. "I don't know what upsets me the most, my brother testing positive for HIV or the fact he cheated on his husband."

I saw Chris roughly once a year after I learned he was HIV positive. He often lived in British Columbia near his sister Catherine.

When he was in town, he and I would go out to lunch or dinner. Sometimes, he came over to the house. It amazed me to see the transformations from year to year. When he first left home at sixteen, he was chubby, but he had quickly lost weight on the streets. The following year, he looked slim and lanky. He'd appear with new tattoos and new piercings each time. One year, he showed up looking very brawny. He took his medications and obviously spent a lot of time lifting weights. I later found out that those were his porn years.

Once, I had a hard time kissing him because he had sharp metal spikes coming out from his cheeks and chin. His body changed, his plans changed, but his eyes never did. He always had this sad, longing look. Even when he smiled or laughed, the happiness never quite made it to his eyes.

He dressed like a monk, wearing long bland robes and colourful beads. He travelled the world, doing whatever he could for money. Ben told me his dad had to get Chris out of an African country in the trunk of a car. Apparently, Sara's family had ties with important people in that country, and they sneaked him out. He'd lost his passport, and he was convinced that people wanted to inflict him harm. I'm not sure if it was true, or he was becoming paranoid.

During one of his visits to our house, he pulled out a large bag of jewellery, mostly large metal rings. "Please take one or two for yourself, Liette." He claimed he made them, so I believed him. I picked a couple of crude rings to keep.

His marriage did not survive the infidelity, and he spent a lot of time with a Canadian woman he met in India. They bought Indian clothes and jewellery, and she would sell them in the Ottawa Market. I met her a few times when Chris was in town.

He called from India to say he was going to be a father. I congratulated him. "Aren't you gay?" I asked.

"Love has no sex," he replied. The little girl was born in India, but tragically, she only lived for a day. They cremated her and spread her ashes in the desert.

When we'd meet, we'd have a pleasant visit, and he would tell me about his travels, his life. Then, as I expected, he would ask to borrow money, which I had ready in my purse. As always, he'd promise to reimburse me, but then he would disappear for another year. He either lived in British Columbia with his sister or travelled to some faraway country.

Wedding Invitations

Summer 2007

Jessi had always dreamed of a big wedding, with a fancy white dress and all the trimmings. After dating several men, she found her hubby. He proposed to her on her birthday. A bunch of us were there when he performed this cute riddle for her to figure out that it was a marriage proposal. Overjoyed, she bawled and hugged everyone. Tears ran down our cheeks when we tightly embraced. They went out for drinks to celebrate. Andre and I said we were too old for that crowd. We drove home.

That night, while in bed, I hoped she would not drink and do something stupid. She loved to party, and when she got drunk, she could get crazy. She told me the story the next day. They partied and drank, having fun until she didn't appreciate a look her future husband gave another woman. Upset, she accused him of flirting and screamed at him. They called a cab, and on the way home, she realized her diamond ring was no longer on her finger. They convinced the cab driver to stop on the highway and had him remove the backseat to search for the precious jewel.

When I was a child, my dad lost his wedding ring, and we searched everywhere for it. He was very upset about losing it. It was not an expensive ring; my parents were not wealthy, but we lacked for nothing. My dad loved gardening. Every year, he would fight the gophers and the deer to grow an extensive vegetable garden for his family. After dinner, he'd grab his boots and pull weeds between the tall rows of carrots and other plants. Weeding has always been a sort of meditation for me, so after school, I'd surprised my dad and removed a few unwanted grasses. As I tugged on a dandelion, I glimpsed a round, shiny, gold ring. It was stuck in the dandelion roots. My mom still says it's a miracle I found the ring. I grabbed it and ran to the house as fast as my legs would take me, my face beaming. I couldn't stand still, waiting for my sweet dad to come home from work. Years later, after he died, my mom offered me his wedding ring. "After all," she said, "you found it when we assumed it was lost forever." I humbly accepted it, and I keep it preciously close.

Jessi and Hubby searched and searched the cab until he remembered that during her angry fit, she had thrown the ring at him. He had caught it and put it in his pocket.

"Liette, will you be my maid of honour?" Touched that she asked me, of course I agreed. She'd planned her wedding since she was twelve years old and had decided I would be her maid of honour. I beamed and hugged her.

Since Andre liked to make wine, she asked him to prepare the wine for her wedding. They planned an outdoor wedding in Cantley, not too far from our house. The wedding planning was going well, and she invited Susan, Chris, and Catherine to come from British Columbia. She gave them at least a year's notice for the trip. She even offered to pay for their plane tickets. They swore they would be there. She was heartbroken when they told her a couple of weeks before the wedding that none of them were coming.

Three months before the big day, Jessi called me and invited me for lunch. After chit-chatting about details of her dress, her eyes watered. "Dad refuses to come to our wedding if Andre is there."

I gasped. I knew Oso despised Andre, but I never thought he would let his hatred prevent him from attending his daughter's wedding. After all, we'd been separated for eight years. "What did you tell him?" I asked her.

"I pleaded and pleaded, but he won't change his mind. I hope eventually he will, because I want both of you at my wedding." She told me she jumped across the table to strangle him during such a discussion. I guess he had that effect on people. We exchanged nasty emails: me, Jessi, Oso and Sara. I think Jessi wanted me to tell Andre not to come; she even told me, "You're my parents, fix this." Sara told me to step up and do the right thing. How could I tell Andre, who had welcomed her and her daughter in our home when they needed it, that he could not attend the wedding? How could I let Oso get away with this much hatred? Was this an attempt to control me? I told Jessi that it was her decision; she had to make a choice between love and hate. I didn't see it as choosing between her dad and Andre. To me, it was a choice about not letting bitterness dictate her wedding.

Jessi had gone back to school to get her high school diploma, and she had landed an assistant job with the federal government. She was very proud of herself; she'd come a long way from being a single mom on welfare.

I still worked for Environment Canada. My office was now in their Gatineau building. Several other businesses occupied the edifice. Jessi got a job for another department in the same building. I loved having her near me. We would meet for lunch or coffee and see each other regularly. Then, Sara landed a government job, and she worked in the same building. Jessi invited me for coffee, and I shared time with both of them. Sara was always nice to me whenever I saw her. One day, Ben said, "Mom, you know how she is always nice to you? Well, if you knew what she says about you when you are not there."

I grinned, "Life is too short for me to worry about what Sara thinks about me."

Jessi grew attached to her, and that was fine with me, although again, I sometimes felt a pang of jealousy. I laughed and said if Oso gets a government job in our building, I'd leave so fast, the revolving doors wouldn't stop turning for a week.

I usually took the bus back and forth to work. After several weeks of exchanging bitter emails, Jessi called me and offered to drive me home. I knew she had decided and I would not like it. She made idle chat in the car, and when we got home, she sobbed. "Liette, I cannot get married without my dad." I expected it, I understood it, and yet my heart sank. She pleaded, "Will you please come to my wedding even if Andre cannot attend?"

My heart shattered. I hugged her and said, "I'm sorry you made that decision, but yes, I'll be there for you."

Almost everyone I confided in told me, "If someone does not invite my partner to a wedding, my loyalty is to him, and I would not attend." But Andre agreed with me. When I told him he couldn't go, he responded, "Well, of course you have to go."

Over the next few days, I imagined myself as the maid of honour, sitting at the head table with Oso while Andre stayed home. I could not go through with it; it just wasn't right. Like my mother often says, we're only human.

I called Jessi and told her we needed to talk. I said, "I love you very much, and I will be there for you on your special day. However,

I'll attend as your stepmom and friend, not as your maid of honour. I will stay all day if you need me, but I will leave before the dinner. Andre and I will go out that evening and have a special meal on your behalf." It was the only compromise that made the entire situation okay for me. I would not let her down by not going to the wedding, but I also had to stand up for Andre and for myself. Truly, I hated to let Oso control my life again. "I'm really sorry, but it is the best I can do. I won't play a part in a wedding controlled by hate."

She cried. "You're no better than my dad; you're ruining my dream wedding."

Her words stung...badly. I swallowed hard. My anger surfaced. "I'm sorry you feel that way, but it's the best I can do."

She hurried away, and I heard her mumble, "I'll see you later."

We'd been chatting in an alcove between two staircases in the building where we worked. A few people passed by. I stared out the large round window at the raging waters of the Ottawa River. *You're no better than my dad.* Did she really mean those words, or was she simply hurt and lashed out? She'd witnessed her dad abusing me; she'd told me she would not have survived if I hadn't been there, and now she was saying I was no better than him?

Her words clawed at my brain all day, but regardless, I refused to sit at the head table with Oso.

A few days later, she calmed down, and she called me. "Will you come early the morning of the wedding?" She had, of course, arranged for a make-up artist and hairdresser. Oso's girlfriend and Jessi's closest friends were there to help her get ready. When it was time to put her veil on, she stopped everyone, lifted her hand, and said, "This is the bride's mom's job." Then she looked at me, her eyes shiny, and asked, "Liette, will you please put my veil on?" I choked. I reached for the veil and pinned it on her head, pinching her with the needle. "Ouch," she laughed.

At that moment, every sad thought disappeared from my heart, and I bent over and kissed her. "I love you so much."

She looked at me, her eyes bright. "I love you too."

Once she was ready, everyone stood in awe of her beauty. She wore a stunning sleeveless white dress with a long trail behind her. A simple yet elegant dress. They pinned her hair up in a bun, leaving curls wrapped around her face and neck. A shoulder-length sheer veil crowned her look. Pearled earrings and a matching necklace completed the charm. Her best friend said, "Oh my God! I can't wait to see her dad's reaction when he sees her."

She stepped out, and they gawked at each other. Sobbing, they hugged, and every single person in the room dabbed their eyes. Everyone except me. The man she was marrying had a young daughter, and she peered at me. "You're not crying?"

I'd promised myself I would not ruin her wedding. It'd been eight years since I'd left her dad. It seemed to be a last desperate attempt to control my life. If not, if this was a decision he made purely out of hate for Andre, then I pitied him. I'd stayed polite and even made small talk with him and his girlfriend. I smiled and said hello while in my head, I knocked his teeth out. Of course, Sara was there. Some of my friends had stated if they did not invite Andre, she shouldn't be invited either. I wanted nothing to do with either of them, but it was such an important day for Jessi, I could stay calm and be happy for her. But I'd be damn if I was gonna cry over their emotional moment. I wrapped a thick wall around my heart to make it through the day, and I felt nothing when they embraced.

Both her hubby's daughter and Meagan were part of the wedding party, along with two of her friends. They wore simple fuchsia dresses that hung just below the knee.

My favourite colour is green, so I'd bought a three-quarter, green-flowered dress. I had sent her a picture before buying it, and she adored it. She bought me matching earrings and necklace. The men wore white shirts and grey pants, no tie.

Ben and Sara's son were ushers for the ceremony. Ben took me by the arm and said Jessi had instructed him to sit me right up in the first row by the aisle. Many conflicting emotions ran through me as I watched her stroll up the aisle holding her dad's arm. I was happy for her; her radiant smile took my breath away. Yet, a part of me felt defeated without Andre by my side. I was alone in the crowd, but I grinned as she peered at me. She let go of her dad's arm and reached to hug me. She handed me a small bouquet and leaned over. "I love you. Please don't throw away the bouquet. There is a message for you inside the stem."

I smiled. "You look stunning." I'd seen her scribbling on a piece of paper a few minutes before the ceremony, but she hid it when I approached. I hadn't given it much thought.

The weather was perfect for an outside wedding. Jessi cried the whole time, stuffing wet tissues in her cleavage.

After the wedding and all the pictures were done, I stood outside looking at the magnificent trees, and I broke down. All the emotions I had ignored throughout the day came bubbling to the surface. *It's not fair. It's not fair.* Her friend wrapped her arm around me. "You're doing so good," she said. I sucked it up and went inside.

When Jessi and I hugged goodbye, I saw both happiness and sadness in her eyes. A reflection of how I was feeling. I left before dinner and Andre and I savoured a fancy meal in an expensive restaurant, toasting to their happiness.

Before going to bed, I remembered the message hidden within the flower stem. I glanced at it and threw it in my bedside drawer.

Looking back, I realize how difficult it must've been for her to make such a decision. She loved me and cared deeply for Andre. He didn't really care about being invited or not. But she knew she broke my heart by choosing her dad. I was angry with her for a long time, but it was Oso who put her in such a hopeless position. Imagine being her and having to choose between your dad and your stepdad. It was a no-win situation because if she had chosen Andre over her dad, she would've been sad that day and therefore, I would've upset also. She made the only decision she could.

Meagan's 16ᵗʰ Birthday

In November of the same year, Meagan turned sixteen, and her mom planned a special birthday party. At Meagan's insistence, Jessi welcomed everyone for this special event. Oso agreed to go, even if they invited Andre. It broke Jessi's heart he would miss her wedding, but he would not miss his granddaughter's sixteenth birthday.

My job was to entertain Meagan while her mom and hubby got everything ready. I had instructions to blindfold her and take her to a spa. Of course, she knew something was up, but she didn't know the details. I held her hand and walked her inside the spa building. We each got the full spa treatment and then drove to our house.

While we were at the spa, her mom had secretly brought all her make-up and clothes to our house. Giggling, we got ready. Oso was going to be there, and I was not nervous, I was petrified. I blindfolded her again, and Andre and I took her to the party, held at Jessi's friends' apartment. Someone beautifully decorated it with sweet sixteen birthday balloons. I took her hand again and guided her up the stairs. I took off her blindfold, and all her friends and family yelled SURPRISE!

I held my breath when Oso and Andre crossed each other in the hall. They exchanged small nods. Sara and Andre are both smokers, so they met on the veranda, puffing a cigarette. Sara told Andre, "This nonsense has gone on long enough."

I wrapped sixteen birthday presents, one for each year of her life. During a stroll in the woods when she was much younger, she had wept, "We're poor." She had said, "My mom will never be able to pay for driving lessons when the time comes."

"Well," I replied, "if you do well in school, I will pay for your driving lessons." I wrapped a model car with a note that said: I cannot afford to buy you a car, but a promise is a promise, so I will pay for your driving lessons.

She cried and ran to give me a big hug. Oso laughed and said that I was making the streets safer.

Toward the end of the party, Jessi hugged me tightly. It had been an emotional day, and to settle my nerves, I drank too much cheap wine. I cried, and I thanked her for keeping me in the family. I divorced the dad, not the kids, but I realized that day, they didn't divorce me either. Jessi laughed and said, "Oh my God, Andre, your wife is so drunk."

A Different Mother's Day

The following year, on Mother's Day, Jessi and her husband invited everyone for a Mother's Day dinner. Her husband had a few stepparents, and they figured one special meal would cover everybody. It angered me she expected me to sit at the dinner table on Mother's Day with her dad and Sara after all the fuss he had put us through for her wedding. I realized she loved all of us and wanted to share the day with everyone, but this was Mother's Day!

We always celebrated Mother's Day together, just us. I couldn't do it. Especially since I already struggle with Mother's Day. I refused the invitation. She got upset. But I stood firm, and I said, "When it's your day, I will be there, but this is my day, and I will not spend any time with Oso on my day." I felt like screaming at her.

If the wedding fiasco had not taken place, I think I would've been okay with the dinner. Uncomfortable for sure, but okay with it. It felt like she disregarded my feelings by inviting both of us to what I called my special day.

I invited a couple of friends over for a Mother's Day lunch because I needed to fill the void. My son was coming over for dinner with us.

During lunch, the doorbell rang. There stood Jessi with a beautiful lily plant. I didn't know what to say. She heard the laughter in the house and said, "Oh, you have company."

I dryly replied, "Yes."

"I wanted to bring you a gift. Happy Mother's Day." She cried and hugged me. I hugged her back, fighting tears. She left, and I softly closed the door behind her.

Looking back on that day, I'm still unsure how I feel about it. I understand why she did it. She wanted everyone she loved to be there, and since Oso and Andre had made a kind of truce, she assumed it would be okay for everyone. I simply did not have the strength to be with Oso on Mother's Day.

The Christmas after their wedding, we celebrated dinner at our house with Jessi, her hubby, Meagan, and Ben as we did every year. She grinned when she handed over their present. I unwrapped it, and I stared at it. She had addressed it to Andre and me. It was their wedding album. Why would she give Andre a photo album of a wedding she forbade him to attend? I glanced at it and put it aside. After they left, I took out all the pictures of Oso from the album and burned them.

In March, they flew to Curacao for their honeymoon. Meagan spent the week with us. She was sixteen by then, and although she did not need babysitting, her mom felt better if she was not home alone. When they came back from their honeymoon, they invited us for dinner. Jessi seemed surprised and happy that I wanted to look at their honeymoon pictures. Oso was not in those pictures.

For a while after the wedding and Mother's Day, things were chilly between us even though, deep down inside, we both knew that no matter what, we had each other's back.

PART FIVE

The Surgery

Jessi's stomach pain appeared in the spring of 2009. She blamed her fibroids. Fibroids are non-cancerous tumours that develop in or around the uterus. They can expand significantly and cause a woman to hemorrhage each month during her periods. They usually generate discomfort, but not extreme ache. Still, she blamed them for her pain and wanted a hysterectomy.

I stopped by her house to pick up a book I had lent her. She squirmed on the couch, moaning. My heart ached to see her writhing in agony. I kicked off my shoes and rushed to her side. We wept together. I was genuinely worried. It seemed like a déjà vu. The next day, her husband called to say they had admitted her to the hospital. I dashed over and found her with an intravenous line pumping strong medication into her.

Meagan and I had shopped for a basket full of goodies for her, but her pain was such that she hardly glanced at it. I laid a bouquet of her favourite flowers, gerbera daisies, by the windowsill.

A gynecologist stepped into her room, and Jessi introduced me. "This is my mom." The doctor nodded politely. She explained to us that fibroids did not cause pain and that no gynecologist would grant her a hysterectomy. Jessi was only thirty-five years old. The doctor stated that the fibroids were insignificant and could not be responsible for her symptoms.

I asked, "If it's not the fibroids, then what is it?"

She replied, "I don't know. She will have to consult her family doctor for more tests."

"I don't understand. Is this not a hospital?" She shook her head and left. Jessi wept softly. I helplessly held her hand. They had not taken her seriously when she was seventeen and pregnant, and they were doing it again.

They released her from the hospital on the Monday, three days after admitting her. One doctor agreed to treat her with strong hormones. He suggested that if the pain dissipated, it meant that endometriosis was possibly the cause. He would then agree to do the surgery. Her pain quickly diminished.

Andre and I visited my family in New Brunswick for a week in August. She sent me an email. Relieved, she had a surgery date the fifteenth of September.

The evening before her surgery, I was home relaxing in a bath when I suddenly remembered she was going in the next day. Lounging in the tub, I called her. "How are you feeling?"

She replied, "I'm nervous, but I know how good you felt after your hysterectomy."

"Best thing I ever did," I said. "You'll see. Everything will go well. You'll feel so good once you are rid of those fibroids and endometriosis." I had the same surgery two years before because of massive fibroids. Although the recovery time was long, they considered it a routine surgery. Just before hanging up, I said, "I love you."

She replied, "I love you too."

The specialist performed her hysterectomy on September 15th, 2009. That evening, I expected to hear from her husband. I didn't call her. She would probably be out of it. I presumed that, like me, she had general anesthesia, but it turned out they gave her an epidural. Since I heard nothing, I figured she was sleeping, and the surgery went well.

The next morning, I stayed home from work to study for an exam scheduled for the next Saturday. I was still in school part-time, completing my business degree.

The phone buzzed at eight o'clock while I sipped my coffee. My son was calling from his dad's house, and he sounded frantic. "Mom, go to the hospital now. Jessi's husband called. You have to go now."

"Oh my God, what's wrong?" I asked.

He said, "I don't know, go now."

I hailed Andre from my cell phone as I sprinted to my car. Our house is approximately twenty-five kilometres from the Ottawa General Hospital, a trip that would normally take thirty min-utes. But it was traffic hour, and I got caught in the downtown Ottawa morning commute. I wiped my eyes, driving through my tears. *Please do not die until I get there... Please do not die until I get there... Please do not die until I get there...*

My cell phone rang, and I grabbed it. "Where are you?" her husband asked.

"Trapped in traffic. On my way. What happened?"

He said, "I will explain it when you get here. Do not drive like crazy, but get yourself here." He hung up.

Please do not die until I get there...

I pleaded for the cars to move out of my way.

I remembered rushing to the hospital when she swallowed the pills after her fight with her dad. I recalled our shock when she was seventeen, pregnant, and losing her hair to cancer. What

I did not remember is ever considering she might die. During those ordeals, it had never crossed my mind that she could die. But this time was different. I knew it in the deepest part of my soul, yet the thought of her dying after all she'd been through was inconceivable.

I parked the car and raced to the Intensive Care Unit. I froze before the door, my eyes locked on the ICU sign.

Please do not die until I get there...

My hands shook as I pushed the button. Through the intercom, a female voice asked who I wished to see. I controlled my voice. "Jessi," I said.

"And you are?" she asked. I didn't hesitate.

"Her mom." I heard a click. My heart pounded so hard she surely heard it. I nudged the door open. The nurse walked from her desk, and she hugged me.

Through my daze, I overheard her say, "Poor thing."

Please do not die until I get there...

She gently placed her arm around my shoulder and guided me to a small private room.

"Her husband will explain." She squeezed my shoulder and returned to her desk. I entered the narrow room where Jessi's husband sat in one corner, Meagan in the other. Why I thought of a boxing ring, I don't know. Each team, in their respective corner, both cheering for the same fighter. For that's what she was, a fighter. Powerful, she would whip this, whatever this was.

In a low voice, while Meagan wept quietly in her corner, her husband revealed what happened.

"She was comfortable and chatting after her surgery. She had a good night's sleep, considering she had a major operation." He worked at the hospital, so he saw her before his shift that morning. He told her he would come back during his morning break.

He continued. "Twenty minutes later, the doctor checked on her and found her in cardiac arrest. They got her heart beating again, but she can't breathe on her own. She's on a ventilator. She has not regained consciousness. They are conducting tests."

"What? How? Why did this happen?" I said.

"We don't know yet," he said.

"Do you want to see her?" he asked. Confused and shocked, I couldn't speak. I nodded.

They organized the ICU in squares. The sounds of beeping and humming accompanied us through the hall. He led me to a square room in the centre. I vaguely noted white lab coats clustered around her. Her husband nudged me into the room. "This is Jessi's mom." A female white lab coat wrapped her arm around my shoulders and drew me closer to the bed.

She lay on a hospital cot. The doctors and nurses whispered to each other, shaking their heads. As if they were trying to solve a puzzle. A tube pushed up her nose while another one stuck out through her mouth. Liquid slowly dripped in her right arm from a line secured to a plastic bag on a post by her cot. Her other arm was connected to another distressing machine. I heard the heart beeps, confirming she was still alive. She was alive. Her eyes closed, her mouth open. Her struggle to bring air into her lungs caused her upper body to lift off the bed. With each inhale, her entire torso lifted off the mattress. Then, with each exhale, it heavily crashed down. Inhale... Thump... Inhale... Thump... Inhale... Thump...

Bubbles softly emerged from the corner of her lips, some almost floating up, others sticking to her wet skin. I stared at the bubbles. Why is she blowing up bubbles? How big would they grow before popping? Some grew to almost the size of a Canadian loonie, others burst on the edge of her mouth. Drool rolled on her chin. I was vaguely aware that a nurse was stroking my back. *It was supposed to be a routine surgery.* I didn't realize I said it out loud until she asked me to repeat it. "It was supposed to be a routine surgery." She sadly nodded.

They hushed us out of the room, wanting to perform more tests. We returned to the private room. Oso, Sara, and Ben waited at the table. Numb, we glanced at each other, shaking our heads. Jessi's husband briefed them on the situation. When they finally allowed us into her room again, Ben and I stood by her side. His hand settled on my shoulder, bringing me some comfort.

I knew that no matter what happened, those memories would haunt me for the rest of my life. Bubbles flowing out of her mouth. Her body lifting, then the thump, dropping back down hard on the bed. They finally pushed a drug into her IV bag, and her body relaxed. Then we only heard the sounds of the machines, the buzzing and the beeping and, of course, the bubbles.

They performed more tests, brain scans, heart scans, lung scans. The nurse explained, "The bubbles result from water accumulating in her lungs." The specialists notified us of their approach, which was two-fold. They were desperately working to figure out what had gone so terribly wrong. And they were desperately trying to bring her back.

The doctors targeted the swelling in her brain. They packed ice around her body to reduce her core temperature. She remained in this state for twenty-four hours before they gradually warmed her to normal temperature. "It's like when you have a bruise and you set ice on it to bring down the swelling," the doctor explained. "While she is in this state, it's very important to not move or even touch her."

Her husband reassured me she could not die while the machine pushed air into her. Therefore, each evening, around ten pm, Andre picked me up from the hospital, and I went home to get some rest. I've suffered from insomnia all my life; it can easily take me hours to fall asleep. Strangely, I would go to bed and immediately sink into a deep dreamless sleep.

For the next three days, Andre left me at the hospital in the morning and then waited at home. I didn't need him to hang with me. I preferred to be alone with her.

I stayed beside her as much as they allowed me. I whispered to her, but most often, I remained quiet. We had gone through a lot together. I did not ask her to forgive me for not going to the Mother's Day dinner. But I asked her, "Jessi, please forgive me for taking too long to get over it. I know you were just trying to make everyone happy." I stared in awe as a teardrop appeared in the corner of her eye, then softly rolled on her cheek, toward her ear. "She heard me!" I peered at the nurse, hope filling my heart.

She smiled gently. "It might be her body releasing liquids, but we never know for sure, so keep talking to her."

The kind older nurse discreetly took care of Jessi while I sat there. In ICU, each patient has his or her own nurse. I appreciated the soft way she spoke to her. "Jessi, I'm going to wipe your mouth now." Each time, explaining what care she was going to provide.

They only permitted two visitors at a time, so, once in a while, I had to leave her side. Her husband asked me how I could do that, sit there for hours. He found it so depressing. I simply needed to be beside her. She couldn't die, yet I knew she was going to die. I was not ready; I would never be ready.

The hospital specialists tested the machine that had been used to provide her with morphine. They analyzed the morphine itself. So far, nothing was conclusive.

I kept telling her, "You've been through hell and back. You can fight this!"

Goodbye

Meagan accosted me Friday morning as I entered the ICU. "My mom would not want her here," she said, her hands on her hips. Susan had flown in from British Columbia to spend a few days with her daughter. Jessi and Susan had not spoken since Jessi's wedding two years prior. But I knew it would make Jessi happy to have her mom near her.

I reassured Meagan, "Your mom is pleased she's here."

I faced her for the first time. The notorious biological mother, the one who sent birthday cards and broken promises. The woman I envied every time the kids' faces lit up at the sound of the telephone. The woman I detested when she crushed their hearts. The one I felt sorry for because she missed seeing her children grow up. Her blond hair was cut short, and she carried a few extra pounds. I'd seen pictures of her. She had been pretty once, but life had not been kind to her and/or she had not been kind to herself. As we met in the hall, we both knew instantly who the other one was. I paused and stared at her, unsure of what to do. Without hesitation, she reached out and wrapped her arms around me. She sobbed. Her words shattered me. Every negative thought toward her evaporated. "I can never thank you enough for having been there for my kids. They love you so much. They and I regard you as their mom."

I hugged her, and we wept together. "Jessi and I are relieved you're here."

I devoted as much time as I could to Jessi for the next three days. Her music played softly in the background. "Eminem?" I questioned her hubby with a weak smile.

"Hey, it's her music," he replied.

After the doctors raised her temperature, they did more tests. Nothing had changed. The nurse told us we no longer needed to restrict visitors to two people. I crossed her in the hall on my way to Jessi's room, and she asked me, "Do you understand what is going on?" She was telling me it was over, but I didn't get it.

I said, "Yes, I do." She smiled sadly and kept walking. What I'd thought was that the procedure failed, and they were going to investigate other strategies. I was wrong.

It was late in the day on Friday, September 18. Jessi's husband informed me that the doctor wanted to speak to the family in private. We gathered in a cramped room. I still had no idea they were surrendering, that she was gone. I figured they wanted to discuss other options. Her father and Sara, Susan, Jessi's husband, Meagan and I listened as the young black doctor sat with us. He seemed kind. He spoke in a slow, soothing voice, rubbing his hands together, his eyes on the floor.

"It's always so sad when a young person dies, but it's even worse when it's one of our own. I'm so sorry; we did all we could. I'm so sorry, but she is brain dead." I heard a scream and several gasps. My heart stopped.

The doctor shook his head, answered a few questions, then left, softly closing the door behind him. He'd done his job, now off to the next patient.

We scattered in various directions. Dazed, I stepped outside the hospital and wandered a fair distance from the building. I squatted on a cement block, away from everyone. I hugged and rocked myself back and forth, moaning softly. A guy strolling by asked me if I was okay. I shook my head. I would never be okay again. Later, I called Andre, and he came immediately. As we walked into the hospital, we faced Oso on the stairs. Our eyes locked with an understanding of our love for our daughter and the deep loss we both suffered. We sank into each other's arms. No words required. We shared the pain.

I wanted to be alone with her one last time. They kept her body "alive," plugged into the ventilator, to flush out all medications in case they could transplant her organs. I realized it was the first time that I had introduced myself as her mom. She used to present me to her friends as her stepmom until one day, she casually changed it to mom. Her friends gave us a strange look; Jessi was much taller than me, and we didn't look alike at all. I was only twelve years older than she. Each time, I thought she would explain, but she never did. To her, I was her mom.

I stroked her face, nuzzled a strand of hair off her forehead. It reminded me of her cancer and her lonely string of hair. During the day, her friend had painted her nails and braided her hair. She seemed peaceful, serene. I kissed her, told her how much I loved her. I murmured my goodbyes. "Thank you, Jessi, for teaching me to seize the moment, to live life to the fullest and always work on improving myself."

We drove home that evening, knowing they wouldn't pull the plug until late the next day. We agreed to meet again in the emergency room on Saturday morning. Again, I fell into a deep, dreamless sleep. The next morning, when we arrived, her husband informed us they had officially pronounced her dead that morning. The date was September 19, 2009.

The in-laws arrived from Montreal that day. My sister-in-law hugged me, crying, calling me la petite maman. We remained in the waiting room, her cousins recounting funny stories about her life. Susan said that Chris and Catherine were coming to Ottawa on a late flight from Vancouver. She asked if anyone could pick them up. She didn't have a car, and I don't expect she had a valid driver's license either. The Ottawa airport is approximately thirteen kilometres south of the hospital. Everyone stared at each other, too exhausted to volunteer. I glanced at Andre, and he nodded. "We'll get them."

We drove to the airport directly from the hospital, and I rushed inside while Andre stayed in the car. I hadn't seen Catherine since she visited us at Christmas seventeen years before. I'd seen Chris occasionally, every time he came to town. His hair was now razor-short, and he bore a moustache and beard. Large round earrings stretched holes in his ear lobes the size of a toonie. He still wore long, colourful hippie clothes and had tattoos on his face. Catherine had her long dark hair in a bun, and she also displayed a tattoo on her forehead. I understood why they were so close. Jessi might have felt she was the outsider. They were hippies; she was a city girl.

We parked at the hospital door, and although I yearned to go in, my body would not budge. The thought of being there when they pulled the plug paralyzed me. Catherine peered at me. "You coming in?" I shook my head.

"I can't, I just can't." I've often thought about it and I tell myself that I should've been there. But even today, more than ten years later, I know that my heart could not bear it.

Her husband and siblings were with her when they shut off the machines. I prayed they were wrong, that they would pull the plug and she would breathe on her own. She was such a powerful fighter; she would fool everyone. Such a drama queen. I smiled.

Jessi was thirty-five years old; she was not supposed to die. I often wonder if she died instantly and was only kept alive by the machines? Or did she peacefully slip away when we were sitting with her? I want to believe she was alive when she shed a tear. Did she pass alone at night? Did she die when they switched off the machines and her heart stopped? Why did she die? So many questions, no answers.

For many people, the next day was a normal Sunday morning. The hardest thing for me was waking up and not having to go to the hospital. I drifted around the house, lost.

Around midday, her husband called, and he sounded excited. For a moment, my heart raced; she's alive, they were wrong, she's laughing at us. But it was not so.

He said that the preliminary autopsy had shown a large gash on both her liver and pancreas. "What does that mean?" I asked.

"She had an aggressive cancer."

"Is that why she died?"

"No, it was not advanced enough to cause death. We don't know why she passed."

Mourning

"If Sara hugs me one more time, I'm gonna punch her," I tearfully told my mom on the phone. My mother looked at my dad.

"We're going to Ottawa. Liette needs us." My parents, Bert and his wife, Suzanne, drove from New Brunswick to spend a few days with us. I sat on the porch outside, waiting for them to arrive. I wept when they hugged me. Our house has two spare bedrooms, so they stayed with us.

"Eat," Suzanne kept telling me. Some people feed on their emotions, but I'm the opposite. If I'm angry or sad, I lose my appetite.

How could I swallow food when my heart was stuck in my throat?

The second day they were here, I opened the newspaper, and I read Jessi's obituary. Her friends wrote it. A few people considered her their daughter, so it wasn't easy to compose. I'd divorced her dad ten years before she died. What if they didn't mention me in the obituary? Would that mean that I was irrelevant? That I didn't matter?

I pleaded with her husband to include my name in the obituary. He said, "Of course." It's weird how these little things become so important. If they didn't have my name, it was as if I hadn't been important in her life. As if I'd been irrelevant. I didn't care whether they described me as her mother, but my name had to be there.

I held a small get-together for her at our place. I needed to be surrounded by people who loved her. It was easier to deal with the pain with other people around me. My parents could see Chris again and meet Catherine. I invited Oso and Sara, but they didn't come. One of my nieces drove from Laval, two hours away, and she had us laughing hysterically. I offered Catherine a fur coat that my mother-in-law had given me a long time ago. She had been so proud to hand it to me. I didn't have the heart to tell her I did not like wearing animal furs.

Catherine, Chris and Susan left before the celebration of Jessi's life. "I'm not attached to such things," Catherine said. I hugged them tightly, and as I waved, tears rolled down my cheeks. Jessi's husband drove them to the airport. Ben, now eighteen, gave me a puzzled look.

"But Mom," he said, "Why are you upset? it's not like they are your children." He had never seen me spend much time with them, as they lived far away. He didn't understand that I had fallen in love with Chris when he was nine years old. That I loved Catherine since she was ten and spent the summer with us. It's true the bond with them was not as strong as with Jessi because we didn't spend as much time together. But they were a part of her and she was a part of them. If only I'd known I'd never see Chris again....

My parents stayed for almost a week and then returned home the day before the reception. I didn't want them to stick around. It was going to be a long, stressful day, and I know they would've wanted to stay by my side during the entire time. My parents were older, and I didn't want them to wear out. As I waved them goodbye, I felt immense gratitude for their support.

Her husband held the reception in a lovely resort in Cantley, a twenty-minute drive from Ottawa. It was the same place they held their wedding. We drove to the building down a pleasant dirt road flanked by maple trees on each side. They completely covered the charming building in a dark stained wood. It accommodated forty guests; therefore, the family from Montreal stayed the weekend.

Inside, the place was rustic, with large wood beams on the ceiling. In the main hall, we displayed framed pictures of Jessi around the room. The funeral director had piled her ashes into two wine bottles, and we perched them on a table at the entrance. Meagan offered me a small urn with some of her ashes in it. "A leg maybe," she said with a sad smile.

It was a stunning fall day, sunny and warm. Her favourite season. I spent much of the time sitting outside on a picnic table. I knew most of her friends, having been to many birthday parties and other events. Her best friend introduced me to a woman I had never met before. She grabbed my hand. "Oh my God, you are Liette! Do you know Jessi worshipped the ground you walked on?"

Meagan's dad was from Toronto. He did not come, but his sister and mom showed up. They hadn't told him; they stated he was in a bad place. I hugged Jo's sister and told her Jessi claimed she was the only sane person in that family. She laughed and agreed.

I drank wine all day, trying to numb the pain. It made it worse. When everyone left, I grabbed a few of her pictures, and Andre and I got into the car. Every fibre of my body exploded with grief. There are no words to describe the immense suffering that engulfed my entire being. Even my skin hurt. I curled up in a fetal position on the couch and bawled for hours.

A few days later, Andre came home from work to find me sitting on the floor, inconsolable. Papers, photos, letters, and empty drawers surrounded me. "I can't find it; I've looked everywhere, and I can't find it."

"What are you looking for?"

"The note! The note she wrote me on her wedding day, I have to find it."

"We'll find it; I will help you." We searched everywhere, emptied all the drawers, my souvenir boxes, but I had this sinking feeling in my stomach that I threw it out. I'm like my mother; we don't hang on to material things.

I retreated to bed with a broken heart over not finding the note. The next morning, I opened my night table drawer, and there it was. The day before, Andre and I had completely emptied that drawer, and we had shaken every piece of paper in it. I read the note again.

> *Liette,*
> *Thank you so much for being here today. I really needed to have you with us on this day. I would not be who I am today without you. You have brought so much 'good' into my life and I will always always love you as my mom.*
>
> *Xox*
> *Jessi*

Two weeks after Jessi passed, I went back to work. To make sense of this new life without her, I had to stay busy and be with people. I saw myself take the bus and make my way to the office. I watched myself enter my cubicle, greet my colleagues. The blinking light on my phone caught my attention. In a fog, I pushed the button and entered my password. The first message dated from three weeks before. It was from Jessi's husband, telling me to rush to the hospital. I sobbed quietly, looking out the window.

Nothing had changed outside. The Canadian flag hovered on the tower on Parliament Hill, overlooking the city of Ottawa. The revolving restaurant on top of the building next to ours still rotated. Although my life would never be the same, life outside just proceeded with its business.

Mourning is such a personal thing. You learn about the various stages and how people say that time helps you heal. Colleagues and friends dropped by and offered their condolences.

One colleague interrupted my thoughts as I stared out the window, my back to the door. She asked, "Hey, how are you?"

I turned around, my eyes wet. "Not well. My stepdaughter passed away, and I'm a mess."

"Oh, I am sorry to hear that," she replied. Then she continued, "Huh, do you have a son?" "I do."

"How old is he?" she wanted to know.

"He's eighteen. Why do you ask?"

"Well, my son is dating this girl, and I don't like her mom. I'm afraid they'll get married, and I'll be stuck having to deal with her." I thought this conversation had taken a weird turn.

"How old is your son?" I politely asked.

"He's ten."

Fuck you and get out of my office!

Days turned into weeks, and I remained at my desk, floating in an ocean of sorrow. Once in a while, without warning, an immense wave snatched me and pulled me under. I couldn't breathe. As I panicked, feeling the water rush into my lungs, I'd send a quick email to my friend, Claudie. She worked a few floors below me. She'd drop everything, bolt upstairs and race to my cubicle. I'd grab her and she'd hold me. She did not let go until I breathed normally again. I'm not sure how I would've survived those days without her. Until I told her it was okay to stop, she sent me an email every morning, just to say hello.

On such a day, when sorrow threatened to destroy me, I took off. I headed toward Parliament Hill. A cool, windy October day meant that not too many people bustled on the streets. I needed to be alone. I sat down on the side of a monument behind the parliament building and I raised my arms in the air in desperation. *What am I supposed to do?* I cried out.

From the corner of my eyes, I saw him approaching. Dark sunglasses shielded his eyes, and he wore long dreads covered by a scarf on his head. Well dressed, he sported a brown jacket with frills on the bottom, black jeans, and white sneakers. He was dark-skinned.

Smiling, he sat near me and asked, "Are you lost?"

"Excuse me?" I replied. He repeated his question. "Are you lost?"

I answered, "No, are you?" I thought, this is one weird guy.

He smiled kindly at me and then said, "The sun sets, the moon hides, but the stars, they shine forever." And with that, he got up and walked away. I stared as he left, astonished. He turned around, grinned, opened his hands in a knowing fashion, and left.

I looked up again. What the hell was that? I stumbled back to my office. Was I lost? Of course, I was lost. Lost in a deep intense grief. Why did she die? Not knowing why or how tore me apart. The answer was simple. Yes, I was totally lost.

But what the hell was she trying to tell me?

I emailed Claudie, who immediately google searched. She wrote back. It's simple; Jessi's body is the sun that has set. The moon is hiding; you are clouded, not knowing what to do, lost. But like the stars, you shine in Meagan's life, and she knows you will always be there for her.

Susan

A few months before Jessi passed away, Susan sent me a friend request on Facebook. I wasn't sure how to respond, so I mentioned it to Jessi. She raised her shoulders. "What harm can it do?" I'd accepted Susan as a friend.

Until I met her at the hospital, Susan was almost like a mystical creature to me. She called on birthdays, but I didn't remember ever actually talking to her. I'd seen pictures of her and Oso when they were still together, but nothing since then.

He nicknamed her Sunny, and I understood why. She had been pretty once with long blond hair.

I had been envious of her for so long because the kids worshipped her.

When I faced her in the hospital hall, it surprised me that my reaction was relief. Although they had not communicated for two years, I knew Jessi would embrace having her biological mother with her while she fought for her life.

The nurse at the hospital asked her who she was. She raised her eyebrows when Susan said she was Jessi's mom. The nurse told me Susan had pointed out she was Jessi's biological mom, but I was the one that raised and loved her all these years.

After she returned to British Columbia, she sent me messages about Jessi. She wrote on her Facebook page about how much she missed her daughter every day. She shared her sorrow with me as a mother to another mother. I felt she was a hypocrite since they hardly ever spoke, let alone visited one another. There was that twinge of resentment again. I ignored most of her messages.

Five months after Jessi passed away, I received a message from Oso informing me that Susan had committed suicide. It's always tragic when a person takes her own life. A part of me wondered if the drama would ever end. I should not have ignored her messages. Jessi was her daughter, and she cared for her. Somehow, life prevented her from being a mom to her kids. I knew she was sick, and I was not responsible for her death, but I should've acknowledged her pain.

Jessi's death left me numb. I could not grieve for Susan. I grieved for her life. I ached for the family. A mother estranged from her children. A mother trying to make it through life, doing the best she could with what she had. A mother who not only recognized the love of another mother for her offspring but was immensely grateful for it.

I reached out to Catherine in British Columbia to extend my sympathy. Chris lived there, so I spoke to him as well. I will never forget his words when I offered him my condolences.

"I'm okay, Liette. You were much more of a mom to us than she ever was."

First Grandson

In February 2010, shortly after Susan died, we received a call from Andre's son, Max. Our first grandson was born. A week before the birth, I'd told Andre I felt nothing for this baby who was about to come into this world. How could I? My heart was closed with sadness and pain. Grief is a witty beast. It doesn't just invade your heart; it grabs every molecule of your body. Even when you don't know it, grief lurks around every corner, surfacing when you least expect it, reminding you it controls your soul.

Andre claimed it was normal for me to feel this way. After all, Max was not my son, not my blood. As we walked toward the hospital's front door, I lugged my feet. It was my first time inside a hospital since Jessi. I had no idea what my role would be with this new baby. He would have his two grandmothers cherishing him. What name will he call me? By the time we reached the room, my anxiety had mingled with my grief to form a potent cocktail in my stomach, a cocktail that threatened to come up.

Max held his newborn baby boy. "Oh, look," he beamed, "Here's grand-papa and grand-maman." He gently placed the baby in my arms. The result was instantaneous. Three things occurred at once. First, I exhaled all my anxiety, and my shoulders softened. Max called me grand-maman. I was grand-maman. Second, the moment I peered at our grandson's handsome face, my heart cracked open. I was in love. Third, the healing begun. I'd been numb for five months, drifting in a sea of sorrow.

It took several years for me to move through all the stages of grief. I hopped from one phase to the next without a compass. Eventually, I overcame my grief. I still miss her every day, but the sharp pain rarely surfaces, the wonderful memories triumphing over the sad ones.

Three years later, a second grandson was born. This time, I knew exactly who I was with this little one.

Andre has two sons. My relationship with them is not the same as with Jessi and Chris. There were adults when Andre and I moved in together. Their biological mom is very present in their lives.

As for my grandsons, I can't help but smile when the oldest one picks up a new Lego toy and points out each step in the manual. He's growing into a teenager. His younger brother often runs on the trails ahead of me, hunting for mushrooms. He calls out when he finds one, "Grand-Maman, Grand-Maman, look at this one!" We pull out our guidebook to identify it. He always wonders, "Is it edible?" He asked me, "How did this mushroom obsession begin?"

I laughed. "I guess since I'm retired, I've had more time for new passions."

I love them to pieces.

Life After Jessi

Jessi died in September 2009. It's been almost twelve years. I think about her every day, and most days, I smile when I recall a funny story or event we shared. Sometimes, the grief catches me off guard, and my heart performs a backflip. For example, if I visit a bookstore and I suddenly recognize a book she loved. Or whenever I spot a young woman jogging with a bouncing ponytail, I can't help it and I turn my head to stare.

They claim the first year is the hardest, the holidays, her birthday, my birthday, Mother's Day. We dined at her favourite restaurant on her birthday. Her best friend texted me on Mother's Day for several years after her death. It made me smile through my tears. I consulted a grief counselor, to not only make peace with her parting but also with the fact that I would never know why she died.

I reached out to her husband for the autopsy results. He told me they were inconclusive. Andre often teases me because I have to understand everything. Yet I still do not know why she passed. I've gone over it so many times in my head, I almost made myself sick, grappling to find some explanations for it. A routine surgery that went terribly wrong. I don't think I could've made peace with it without therapy and lots of love and support from my friends and family. Letting her go is the most difficult thing I've ever had to do. Letting go of the obsession to know why – I'm not sure how I've come to terms with it. It took seven years for me to not be fucked up on the anniversary of her death.

A year after Jessi died, I finally completed my university degree. I took twelve years to finish it, working full time through a divorce, through becoming a single mom, and through losing Jessi. When I asked my parents if they would attend my graduation, my dad would smile and say, "Hurry, we're not getting younger, you know."

I called them in August 2010. "I did it, I did it!" They agreed to come to my November graduation. After speaking to my parents about my graduation, Andre and I headed out to a movie. I said, "I have a crazy idea." He gave me a worried look. "My parents are coming to my graduation in November. We should surprise them and get married while they're here."

He glanced at me and shrugged. "Sure," he replied.

I screamed, "Do you mean it? We'll get married in less than three months?" He smiled and nodded. I giggled all the way to the movies. We kept it a surprise for my parents. It was hard to keep it a secret. I also struggled with the rest of the family. Should I invite them? It was the second wedding for both of us, and Andre preferred a modest wedding. I didn't want people to spend money on a plane ticket, so I kept it a secret. Marianne has a Ph.D. in Education, and she was my motivational board through my sweat and tears of the last twelve years. Writing exams after a night shift, finishing assignments after Ben had gone to bed, depressed in front of an empty Word document. She came to my graduation, so I confided to her about the wedding.

My parents flew in the day my dad turned eighty-four. I'd warned my mom that we were going to eat at a chic restaurant in Ottawa for my graduation so to bring her elegant dress. She said, "Okay, but we're paying for the meal." I smiled through the phone. We took my dad out for his birthday and I ordered wine and cake. My mom said, "This will cost you a lot of money. Remember, we'll pay for your graduation dinner." I nodded. She did not know that my graduation dinner was our wedding dinner with thirty-five of our closest friends and some of Andre's family who lived near us.

On Friday night, Marianne showed up, and we sipped wine after dinner. I said, "Mom, I'm happy you offered to pay for dinner tomorrow night because there will be a few more people."

She looked surprised, and my dad looked up. My mom is very generous, but my dad has always been tighter with his cash. "Oh, Ben?" she asked.

"Yes, and more," I replied.

"Meagan?" she added. My dad's eyes opened wider when I said more.

"How many?" he asked.

"Well, Mom, Dad, we haven't been exactly honest with you." Both of them raised their heads. "Dad, do you remember Kevin's wedding (my nephew)? You said you had never walked one of your daughters up the aisle? Well, Mom, Dad, tomorrow, will you escort me up the aisle?"

My two sisters were married, and this was my second wedding, but it had become a thing where the bride and groom strolled up together. Therefore, my dad had never walked up the aisle with any of his daughters. He watched with envy as my nephew's bride strode up the aisle with her dad.

My parents' mouths dropped open, and my mom said, "What? Are you getting married tomorrow? For real?" She stared at my laughing sister. "Did you know about this?" Then she said, "Oh, now I understand about the dress." She laughed, and my dad's eyes welled up. My parents really appreciated Andre. They stood up, giggling, and gave us big hugs.

I'd gone to a locally made candle store, and I told them I needed a special candle to represent Jessi's light during the wedding. The sales lady asked me what she was like. I recalled the words from her friend when she passed: Jessi, thank you for never doing anything halfway. You laughed hard; you cried hard, and sister, you danced HARD!

She offered me a magnificent colourful candle, a mix of oranges and yellow shapes. Fitting, as Jessi had passed during the colours of the fall, her favourite season. Meagan happily accepted to be my maid of honour. To begin the ceremony, she lit the candle. We bowed and held a minute of silence to honour her mom and acknowledge her presence with us.

We enjoyed the wedding in an old, renovated barn near where Andre and I live. My parents beamed when we strolled up the aisle. When Andre slipped the ring on my finger, I realized it was one of the happiest days of my life.

After the wedding, I laid the candle on a stand in our living room. A few days later, we came home, and it had not only fallen to the ground, but it was standing upright a couple of feet from where it had landed. Jessi had approved my choice of the candle.

AIDS

May 2015

My brother passed away tonight.

It was one simple sentence. No *hello*. No *how are you*. No *goodbye*. The message had appeared in my inbox at five-thirty that morning, but it was my Friday off, and I had slept in late.

I'd just finished eating my favourite breakfast, homemade granola cereal with plain yogurt, sweetened with maple syrup. Still wrapped in my robe, I sat in my rocking chair, clutching my cup of steaming black coffee, its powerful aroma tickling my senses to awake.

Andre and I had been married for five years now, living together for fifteen. He was retired, although he still worked on a few contracts here and there. I still had two more years to work before I joined him.

I opened my laptop. Although a few clouds drifted in the sky, the morning sun glared on my screen through the large living room window. The birds, returning from their southern refuge against our cold Canadian winter, chased the bees, themselves hiding in the budding flowers of the trees. Hmmm, a perfect day for a long run.

The brief message blinked: *My brother passed away tonight,* and instantly, my heart recoiled.

Catherine sent me the message. It was the first day of May 2015.

Thirty years before, I met and fell in love with two messed-up kids. I was young, and I figured I could handle anything life threw at me. Confident my parents had equipped me for everything. I was convinced I was going to give these kids the same life I had received. It would be great.

Thirty years later, both children are gone, wiped from the planet. Jessi had died six years ago, and now the universe had taken Chris. They both departed this earth the way they lived. Jessi, out with a bang, Chris slowly drifted off.

Losing Jessi had felt like losing a leg. One day, you're walking, running, dancing, and then you wake up the next morning without a leg. At first, it's the shock. What? How? Where did my leg go? Then, of course, denial. I must be dreaming. I had two legs yesterday. This cannot be real? Then anger. I want my leg back. This is not fair. Then sadness. What am I gonna do without my leg? Will I ever dance again? Of course, these are not linear emotions; you randomly bounce from one to the other. For a long time, you dwell and refuse to accept the leg is gone. Then someone suggests you try walking with crutches. At first you resist; you want your leg back. But then, you try it, and you find you can take a few steps. Then a friend offers a prosthesis and again, you resist. But eventually, you try it, and you discover you can walk again.

After a few years, with a lot of love and support, you dance again.

Losing Chris was different. I closed my eyes. It felt like I had no legs to begin with. Like it had all been a dream.

Life is like a book; we have a beginning and an end and if we are lucky; we have several chapters in between. A fierce storm roared and tore all these chapters out of my life. Everything we lived through, the hurt, the love, the despair and the hope, all these pages shredded into a million pieces and scattered all over the earth.

On May first, 2015, the universe laughed at me. The universe declared all these chapters irrelevant.

The universe can kiss my ass.

Lost Soul

Chris had become a drifter, a searcher of truths. He travelled the world with very little money. After he passed away, I learned he had been a porn star at one time in his life. Nothing surprised me anymore.

During our annual dinner, when he'd come back to Ottawa for a visit, he'd tell me about his visions. He spoke to the spirits, and they warned him of another flood coming. He wished to gather his family and take us to a towering mountain peak in British Columbia. My stepson was going to save us all.

In 2014, Ben had alerted me that Chris had stopped his HIV medications. I heard various reasons for him doing that. Chris's friend, with whom he had a baby, told me that Catherine urged her to come to force him to swallow his medications. But the friend said she couldn't go against Chris' decision. Catherine was adamant that dementia clouded her brother's mind, and he no longer could make good decisions. She reached out to Oso, who flew to British Columbia to help both his daughter and son. But he could not persuade Chris to accept the drugs.

He was getting sicker, and I knew I should go to him. But I kept postponing it. When Ben and his girlfriend decided that year to move to British Columbia, I planned to visit them and Chris and Catherine at the same time. A month before they left, Ben told me Chris didn't have much longer to live. I prayed I would make it in time. Why did I not go sooner? Honestly, I don't know. I think a part of me didn't believe that he would pass. Jessi was gone. He would not leave as well. It just seemed so improbable that they would both die before reaching forty. Chris was thirty-nine years old when he passed away.

At first, Catherine didn't invite me for the celebration of his life. I understood why. What kind of stepmom had I been? He'd been sick for an entire year, and yet I never visited him. It's not that I didn't want to. I don't know how to explain why I didn't go. It was a day's flight across the country. I was certainly not as close with him as I was with Jessi. We hardly ever saw each other, and he never reached out to me except when he came to Ottawa. A part of me still suspected he'd hurt Ben when he was a baby. I kept making excuses for not going. The truth is, I really don't know why I didn't go. I have to live with that decision.

Oso and Sara followed Ben and his girlfriend to British Columbia to attend the ceremony.

Finally, Catherine reached out and invited me to attend. I could've flown out there, but I felt I didn't deserve to be there. I didn't belong.

Ben described Chris's life celebration. They cremated him, and they divided his ashes among all his friends in order to spread him all over the globe. Catherine and her friends built a pyre and laid a maquette on it. They poured gasoline, and then Catherine struck it with a flaming arrow. Everyone placed personal objects on a table, souvenirs that reminded them of Chris. The party continued all night with intense testimonies from all who knew and loved him. Approximately forty people showed up. I'm sure Chris loved it.

During an appointment with my doctor, I told her both my stepchildren had died. She was aghast. "What happened?" she asked. When I explained, she said, "But, Liette, nobody dies from AIDS anymore in Canada."

"He stopped taking his meds," I said. Her response blew me away.

"Oh, it was a suicide." The thought had never even crossed my mind. When I questioned Catherine recently, she said it was not true. He wished to live, but he could no longer bear the medications' side effects.

I saw Chris's friend in the Ottawa market. She said that Chris had travelled the world, and he had nowhere else to go. He was ready to sail over to the other side. I pray that in the end, he found the peace he searched for all his life.

MeToo

If a person has to look up the definition of rape, can they honestly say they were raped?

Tarana Burke started the MeToo Movement in 2006, but it exploded in the fall of 2017 with the hashtag #Metoo and the Hollywood denunciations. The movement bombarded every social media platform. It broke my heart to see some of my friends typing #Metoo on their social status. I wrote it down many times, but I deleted it each time. Was I raped?

I spent hours and hours researching various definitions of rape and sexual assault. I read parts of Canada's Criminal Code and compared it with the American laws. I researched women's support group websites. Was I raped? When I asked Andre, his reply was quick and firm: *Yes.* Still, I could not make myself believe it. He never physically held me down. Each time, I let him do it to me.

Canada's Criminal Code defines consent in section s. 273.1(1), as the voluntary agreement to engage in the sexual activity in question.

It's true. He never physically forced me. He would have stopped if I had said no. I had a choice, didn't I? I could either let him fuck me or endure his temper. Most times I said yes, I hated myself for it. It's not because he was my husband that I question whether I was raped or not. It's because each time he did it, I did not verbally say no. I said yes because I was terrified of his reaction. I was a second-degree Taekwon-do black belt holder. Raised in a loving, peaceful home, I was not a victim. I was not raped by my husband.

I learned an unfamiliar word: coercion.

Merriam-Webster defines *coerce* as:

> 1: to compel to an act or choice
> was coerced into agreeing
> abusers who coerce their victims into silence
> 2: to achieve by force or threat
> coerce compliance
> coerce obedience
> 3: to restrain or dominate by force
> religion in the past has tried to coerce the irreligious
> — W. R. Inge

When I sent my initial draft story for a professional manuscript evaluation, the editor wrote a seven-page, very helpful review. Within her evaluation, she noted: You suffered multiple rapes at the hands of your husband. I shook my head; I was still skeptical.

I could not resign myself to write #MeToo on my status. It seemed unfair to women who had been physically/forcefully raped. Women who had feared for their lives. Of course, I had sex many, many times when I didn't want to. I argued with Oso about rape. I smiled when I told the therapist that I pretended to be somewhere else during sex.

In the end, #MeToo never appeared on my status. Admitting he had raped me meant admitting that I had allowed myself to become a victim. A rape victim. A domestic abuse victim. I was better than that. I'd cried when my doctor informed me I had high blood pressure because I'd done everything right. It wasn't fair. How can a person who believes having high blood pressure is a failure admit to letting her partner abuse and rape her? When a specialist declared I could never run because of my bad hips, I began training for a ten-kilometre race. I did not fit the pattern of growing up in an abusive home, and I certainly did not choose an abusive partner. I was not abused. I was not raped.

A month before I retired from work, I walked to my car when a couple whizzed by me. They were not holding hands; he was pulling her by the hand. His angry demeanour frightened me as he lugged his girlfriend forward. The terror in her eyes grabbed my attention. I froze, not knowing what to do. I did nothing. The look in that woman's eyes still haunts me today. I felt what she was feeling.

On the eve of my sixtieth birthday, as I'm writing the closing words on my story, my body remembers the intense pounding of my heart, the bruises on my arms. I remember my white knuckles as I held on to the bedsheets.

He did not violently rape me; he raped me under the threat of violence.

#MeToo.

The Circle of Life

February 2018

"Push! Push! Push!" the midwife said calmly but urgently. Then she looked at me and whispered, "Are you ready to catch this baby and put it on mommy's stomach?"

I received the text around ten o'clock that evening. *Labour has begun, meet us at the birth centre.* I grabbed the bag I'd prepared in anticipation of this wonderful moment, and as I raced to join them, I prayed to Jessi. *Your daughter, my granddaughter, will need your help tonight as she delivers her first baby, your grandson. You better step up and be there for her. She needs you.*

Meagan grew up and married her sweet love. She got pregnant shortly after the wedding, and they were very excited. They had a gender reveal party, so we knew it was going to be a boy.

When I stepped into the birth room, Meagan, her face twisted in pain, said, "I don't think I can do this." She wanted to have a natural childbirth with a midwife, no drugs, no hospital. She prepared for this.

I said, "Yes, you've got this. I had a chat with your mom on my way over here, and she's going to help you."

Her face shifted. Hope and determination replaced fear and pain. She could do this.

Her husband and I worked as a support team. He helped her from the front, and I pressed on her hips to widen the road for this little person coming into the world. Her bum in my face, I glanced up. "You have a cute butt." They laughed.

At around three o'clock in the morning, her water broke with such a powerful boom that I looked on the floor, thinking the baby blew up. The midwife ran in and told her it was time to push. The baby's head poked out, ready to face the world.

Meagan lay on the bed sideways, and her husband sat near her head. I kneeled near the midwife, prepared to catch this little baby, my great-grandson. My mom later asked me if I felt queasy, but I was in such awe, I only felt pure love and joy. I'd had a cesarian with Ben, so it was my first time witnessing such a miracle. Meagan was awesome, and she delivered that baby as if she'd done this many times.

The midwife told me she was going to pull the head out, and then I could lay him on mommy's stomach. I was delirious with love for this little one coming into our lives. My mood abruptly switched to horror when his head appeared with the cord wrapped around his neck. The midwife plunged her hands inside Meagan's vagina and yanked him out. Within a few seconds, she had the cord unwrapped, thrust the baby in my arms, earnestly telling me to lay him on mommy's belly. His lips had already turned blue. His mouth was open, but no sound was coming out. A terrifying silence. Meagan grabbed a towel and rubbed his back. Baby made a cooing sound, and we exhaled loudly.

I stayed with them for the next hour. Every time Baby produced a sound, we looked at each other and grinned.

The irony is not lost on me. I know that if Jessi were alive, it would've been her sitting on the bed holding her new grandson. I hope that wherever she is, she viewed the miracle birth. She'd be so proud of her daughter, and she'd be a wonderful grandma.

I drove home in the wee hours of the morning with the stupidest widest smile on my face.

Catherine

2020

In January 2020, not having heard of Covid-19 yet, I flew to British Columbia to visit Catherine. I'd written most of my story, but a few pieces were missing. She was ten years old when she visited us, and I wondered what she remembered. I planned to discuss Chris' illness and apologize for not going. I wanted to talk about her mom. But mostly, I earnestly needed to beg for forgiveness for saying no to the social services when they asked us to take her. I wanted her to release me from my guilt. To say that somehow, it was okay.

After agreeing on a date, I bought a flight ticket from Ottawa to Castlegar, British Columbia. From there, I would pick up a rental car and drive the thirty minutes to Nelson. I've had a bucket list for more than thirty years, and I've always wanted to ride across our beautiful country on the VIA train. I purchased a train ticket to come back. It would be the perfect opportunity to finish my book. I'd have four days to reflect on our conversations and write while enjoying the lovely winter scenery.

Andre drove me to the airport. As the plane took off, I smiled, but I also took a few deep breaths. I love travelling, but I didn't know what to expect. Catherine had invited me to stay with them, but I needed my space. I booked an Airbnb room in Nelson.

After a few cancelled flights, I finally made it to Nelson a day late. The weather caused every flight to Castlegar to be cancelled, so I had to land in Cranbrook, rent a car, and drive three hours to Nelson. I was dog-tired, and I desperately wanted a glass of wine. Early that evening, I texted Catherine, and she responded, *are you coming now? We have food if you're hungry.* I was more tired than hungry, but I'd already lost a day because of the flight cancellations, so I wrote back, *on my way.*

She instructed me on how to get to her house, which she said was the highest house on the side of the mountain. She said to park on the road, and her boys would come get me.

As we climbed the abrupt hill to her house, I understood why she suggested I park on the road. Her boys held my arms so I wouldn't slip on the ice. Her adult daughter lives in Vancouver. One of her sons is a teenager, the other one just a few years shy of becoming one.

I hesitated for a few seconds before following her boys into the house. I didn't know how she would react. Would she welcome me? She'd seemed happy that I was coming when we talked on the phone, but now, I wasn't so sure if this was a good idea. I'd seen her in the summer of 2015, the year her brother died. I'd made it to Nelson to visit Ben and his girlfriend. Catherine had dinner with us. She looked good, and we mostly made small talk. Ben's apartment was small, so she invited me to stay with them, but I wasn't comfortable imposing on her. I visited her clothing store. Both she and her husband are artists, and they design their own clothes. They have a cute shop in downtown Nelson. I fell in love with Nelson. The town sits beside the beautiful Kootenay Lake, surrounded by gorgeous mountain peaks on all sides. With a population of slightly over ten thousand people, it is known as The Queen City because of its three hundred and fifty restored heritage buildings from the silver rush days. It has a hippy atmosphere. Ben and I strolled to a local cafe to savour its organic taste on a terrasse. He and his girlfriend stayed in Nelson for six months.

As I stepped onto the porch, Catherine rushed to greet me at the door. She wrapped her arms around me. She cried. I looked at her. "Oh no, is this a bad time? Should I come back tomorrow?"

She said, "I can't believe you're here; I can't believe you've come to see me." Her reaction both touched and saddened me. I honestly didn't think she really cared that much about me coming. I later understood that she'd always felt left out, far from the family.

The inside of the house was as I'd imagined. The warmth of wood everywhere, the walls, the furniture, every room breathed a rustic, cozy atmosphere.

She introduced me to her husband, her two boys, and her friends who rented the downstairs. I met their two dogs, a huge one trained to protect them from grizzly bears and a small Chihuahua that made me fall in love with the breed. We spent three days together, mostly relaxing on the couch near the wood stove in the log house they rented. We drank wine, and she smoked pot. I had to drive back to the Airbnb each evening, so I stayed sober. The more she drank, the more she talked, and the more she wept.

She brought it up first. The rapes. Lodged in her soul like many other cruel injustices life had thrown at her. I'd carefully prepared my story, my explanation of why I'd made such a difficult decision ages ago. When I saw the raw pain in her eyes, in her whole body, I knew my words were irrelevant. Between sobs, she spoke about the assaults. I realized there were not enough words in the dictionary to fix the damage done to her or to ease my guilt. As my mom often says, all I could do was love her.

Catherine told me her brother had hitchhiked across the country to save her after she called him following the abuse at the youth shelter. She said, "I walked out to find him standing on the front lawn. He wanted to rescue me." I understood then how close they had been. He went to her when she needed him the most. She said she understood; she held no grudge. Everyone had made hard decisions in order to survive.

We sat on the couch, a fire glowing in the woodstove in their rustic living room. "Hang on," I told her, "I brought you something." I grabbed my purse and pulled out a small plastic container. I handed her the box filled with some of her sister's ashes. "It's not much," I said, "but it's part of her."

Her hands trembled as she held the container close to her. "It's all I have of her. It's all I have." She sobbed. Then she got up and grabbed a similar container from the cupboard in the kitchen and gave it to me.

"And here is a part of him," she said. I couldn't speak. All three siblings, in the same room. Now, I also had a part of him.

She talked about her mom, how much she tried to give her daughter a better life yet kept failing at it. "She loved us with all her heart, but she was broken." I understood why she changed her mind every summer after promising Jessi and Chris they would go to British Columbia. She had good intentions, and she missed her children. But Catherine explained they were so poor, some days they had no food to put on the table. How could she bring her other children into her hell? When I asked her what she remembered about her visit with us when she was ten years old, she replied it had been the best summer of her life.

Chris died an awful death, long and agonizing, and I wonder if I'll ever forgive myself for not going to him. A whole year it took him to die. He slowly rotted away. When I told Catherine that I used to tell people these kids had done everything you don't want kids to do, except kill someone, she said, "That's not true." Apparently, Chris had sex with six men near Nelson, knowing he had AIDS, and four of them died from the same disease.

"Why did he do that?"

She replied Chris wanted desperately to be loved, and when partners did not want to use condoms, he obliged, although they both knew the risks. I suspect these partners were also desperate for love. Catherine said her brother had a heart of gold. I told her about my fear that he had harmed Ben when he was a baby. And that my parents had suspected the same thing. My mom only revealed the story after Chris passed. The first year we took Ben to New Brunswick, my parents agreed to babysit while Oso and I went out with friends. They'd left Ben with Chris while they took a short walk. When they came back, Ben was in Chris' arms, and he was screaming. My dad had grabbed Ben and said, "What did you do to him?" Ben had quickly calmed down in my dad's arms. Chris swore he only changed his diaper. My mom had suspected otherwise, and she'd even peered inside the diaper in the garbage can. She said the diaper was clean. When I mentioned all of this to Catherine, she shook her head. "My brother was a strange dude, but he would never hurt no one."

She asked me if her dad physically abused me. I told her about the few times he'd given me bruises. How he sometimes thought hurting me was funny. He would stick his thumb up my anus while I sat on the bed. I'd jump and yelp, "Ouch! That hurts."

He'd giggle and say, "I know."

Catherine shook her head.

I rented cross-country skis, and we skied with her husband and a family friend. The Chihuahua rode in the side pocket of the gigantic dog's backpack. People laughed and stopped to take pictures of this tiny dog hopping a ride with his colossal friend.

I drove three hours from Catherine's house to the Cranbrook airport. I could hardly see the road as my eyes overflowed with tears. Nobody should have to bear such pain.

I told her I loved her when I left. I hope she meets us in Dawson City, Yukon, when we bring Jessi and Chris's ashes next summer. Jessi was born in the Yukon, and Chris was born in northern Alberta. They left the Yukon on an old school bus. They will go back in our camper. I want to see them dance in the northern breeze.

Epilogue

A split-second decision altered the course of my existence. After the breakup with my fiancé, I yearned to leave my old life behind. I drove to the high school to apply to the St John, New Brunswick Community College in order to learn computer programming. It was 1984 and people stated computers were the future. I grabbed a pen to fill in the proper papers when I noticed a different form on the table. A two-year course in environment technology at the Bathurst, New Brunswick Community College. It took me less than ten seconds to change my mind. I've always cared for nature and animals and studying about them seemed way more enticing than computer work.

I sometimes wonder what my story would've been like if I had moved to St John instead of Bathurst. I certainly would not have met Oso, not lived on a bus, and not fallen in love with three messed-up kids. I've never regretted that choice I took so long ago. Of course, I would never choose to be abused and raped. But I would not want to trade the love I found with Jessi, Chris, and Catherine. Surviving those painful experiences made me the person I am today. I know it's cliché, but so be it. For many years,

I'd assumed my parents had not prepared me for real life because they raised us with much tenderness and patience. Today, I know that my upbringing allowed me to not only survive all the hardships but to grow and thrive.

I want to believe that if Jessi and Chris had not been there, I would've left Oso sooner. But then, after the kids moved out, I made other choices, and I stayed. I even had a son with this man.

Domestic violence is an ugly and devious beast. For years, I worked hard to forgive myself for allowing my partner to abuse me. What I've finally come to understand is none of it was my fault. Domestic violence can affect anyone, regardless of race, age, education, or upbringing. A friend who also suffered assaults at the hands of her spouse told me she felt she had done something wrong and somehow deserved her partner's wrath. I cannot speak for other abused victims. No behaviour ever justifies being yelled at, bruised, insulted, or raped. Nobody merits such brutalities. However, I'd blamed myself for tolerating his abuse. Somehow, I'd felt I should've been stronger, fought back, or left sooner. Women stay because, for most of us, leaving means something worse, or we believe we can fix it. I was fortunate. I never feared for my life.

How can anyone judge a woman for not taking off after her partner brandishes his fist in her face, yells at her, warns her that if she leaves, he will kill her and her kids? We all have our stories, our reasons, our decisions. But it is never, never, ever the victim's fault.

We carry shit on our sleeves for years without realizing it.

Men can suffer abuse also, but women are more often the victims. I'm not an expert on stepparenting nor domestic violence, but I've experienced both, and I not only survived, I've grown. I recently had breakfast with my friend, Claudie. She read the first draft of my book and provided me with invaluable comments.

She asked me the tough questions I needed to improve my story. After reading a subsequent draft, she said she only had one question. "Five months after you left Oso, you jumped right in with Andre. I understand you knew him and worked with him for a long time, but were you not hesitant to embark on another relationship? After your awful experience, did you not fear the same might happen? Did you at least hesitate? How could you trust another man so soon after your breakup?"

I looked at her. It was a valid question. "You know, I never even considered that possibility. I knew in my heart that Andre was a good, gentle man." She smiled and nodded her head. Later that night, twenty years after our first date, I watched Andre sleep. I pondered her question. It's true, I never believed for one second Andre could hurt me, and he never has. My father treated my mother with love and respect and although Oso had almost convinced me of the opposite, that is my normal. I want to believe that Oso was the exception, the anomaly. I need to trust that most men are good men. No, I'm not naïve; I know that domestic abuse is still very present in our society. I mourn every woman killed by her partner.

After leaving Catherine in Nelson and spending one additional night in Vancouver, I hop on the train where the agent shows me to my cabin. The room measures two meters by one meter. In that narrow space, I have a small couch-like seat that painfully lowers into a bed. When I sit on it, I have no choice but to prop my feet on the toilet cover. Measuring slightly more than five feet tall has some advantages. I brush my teeth in the tiny sink by the latrine. I stare out the wide window, where I contemplate the rolling scenery. Maybe I will glimpse wildlife, a deer or bear? It's perfect.

As we travel through the majestic Canadian Rockies, I think of Jessi, Chris, and Catherine. Like the horizon, many obstacles marred our lives, and yet I remember the good times. When they joined us on a college outing. The entire class travelled on the old school bus for a school trip. Some students played cards on the table as others chatted in the back. It was our first year of college; it must've been a PD Day. Jessi was ten, and Chris was eight. It was the first time I met them. Jessi crawled on her hands and knees; Chris perched on her back. They giggled as they crashed to the ground. Oso sprawled down on the soft earth, smelling a strand of hay. The kids gathered large bundles of dried-up hay. They tiptoed behind their father and buried him under the withered grass. He turned around laughing, and instantly, everyone took part in a hay fight.

During the few months we lived on the bus, we played the board game Risk on those long rainy afternoons. Oso consistently on the warpath, brutal, no mercy, winning on his mind. The three of us ganged up on him, aiming to eradicate him, while he snickered and shuffled the dice.

As the train rumbles through the flat prairies, I hold the small plastic container with Chris' ashes. I lay it on the narrow table in front of me. I quietly stare at it. *Chris, I will never know if you harmed Ben or not when he was a baby. But when Ben speaks of you, he says you were one weird brother who had the most captivating life ever. The pride shines in his eyes, and I hear the admiration in his voice. Your brother loved you dearly. When you initially became sick, Catherine called your dad, and he flew to British Columbia to help you. I wondered why she hadn't reached out to me, then I figured she might not want me there. Ben updated me on your condition, but I refused to acknowledge you were that ill. When I received the message from Catherine saying you had passed, a piece of me collapsed that day.*

Catherine had told me, "You should've come to his life celebration."

I'd shaken my head. "I didn't deserve to be there."

She'd nodded. "He loved you so much."

I have a few regrets, but I've come to terms with most of them. I still mourn the two dreadful decisions I took: refusing to take Catherine when she was twelve and not reaching out to Chris when he was sick. If I could go back . . . These days, I'm working on being kind to myself.

The train continues through the remote woods of northern Ontario. My memories switch to Meagan's cadet's parade, how proud I was, cheering in the stands beside her mom, not even trying to hide my tears. I recall Jessi, Joe, and Meagan camping with us, building sandcastles together. My face glows at the memory of my great-grandson being born and how he's turned into this fearless, smart, and curious toddler.

I think about Ben, who lives within an hour of our house with his silly dog Chuck. He works in construction and owns a nice bungalow with a small pond in the backyard. He loves to send me pictures of the turtles and ducks enjoying the water. Chuck races ahead of us in the woods, chasing squirrels, when we snowshoe together.

I reflect on my father, who passed away from complications related to Alzheimer's in 2016. Andre and I rushed home from a holiday in Newfoundland and Labrador to spend one last week with him. It was such a privilege to walk this last mile together. Early one morning, I ate my breakfast in his hospital room. He dozed, and I'm not sure he understood me. "Papa, thank you for being the best dad ever, but mostly, thank you for making me your favourite." Watching my father lose his memory from such a despicable disease is the second hardest thing I've ever done. My mom gently stroked his forehead when he drew his last breath. She loved him enough to let him go in peace. Powerful, she inspires us to be better people, to remain kind, positive, and to enjoy living to the fullest. Still independent and strong, she soars into her nineties. We talk every day on the phone.

I think about Andre, with whom I've been sharing my life with for over twenty years. His love and patience help to keep my anxiety under control, most of the time. He supports me in all my crazy goals, such as training for a marathon (he's never missed a single race I've done), camping across the country, learning Spanish, and foraging for wild mushrooms. He's my best friend.

My cell phone brings me out of my reverie as we approach Sioux Lookout in northern Ontario. It's Meagan. Now a single mom, she's in a tight bind and needs a place to crash with her two-year-old son. "Just for a month," she says.

"I have to ask Andre," I say, but I already know his answer.

The train comes to its final stop in Ottawa, and I wave to Andre from the platform. I hug him tightly and we head home.

I open the door to our house, and I pull my great-grandson into my arms. My heart gushes with love.

Acknowledgments

Several people helped me while I wrote this book. I wish to thank my family and friends who shared their memories with me. My friend Chantal St-Pierre who drove with me to the old farmhouse, where we sat in the car, remembering past events. Jessi's friend, Chantal Smith-Piepers, who took the time to sit and have coffee with me and share her memories. Lisa Meunier-Hickey who researched the information on the Bathurst Campground and shared her recollections of those years. My best friend in college, Joanne Landry, who reminded me how I chased Oso like a groupie. A special thanks to Catherine, who welcomed me into her house and spent hours talking about her siblings and her mom. I owe a debt of gratitude to the people who read parts or all of my manuscript and provided me with invaluable constructive comments. My cousin, Andrea Bureau, and my friends Jan Gardiner and Natalia Kudryashova. A special thank you to Leona Yantha who generously provided me access to her reading friends, Corrie Fransen, Karen Dacey, Laurie Bernard, Erin Cull, and Joan Simpson. Their comments helped me make my story into a better book. Thank you very much. I'm not sure I would've reached my goal without the help of my friend Claudie Ouellet. I trusted her with my first and following drafts. Sitting together on the couch, wrapped in our blankets, she asked me the tough questions I needed to improve my story. Thank you to my family for their unwavering love and support. My brothers and sisters who welcome me with delicious meals every time I go home. Your encouragement and memories helped me throughout this process, and I am forever grateful. Thank you to my brother, Louis M Cormier. You paved the way with your book, *From Addiction To Fitness*, three years before me and then patiently answered my tons of questions. Dad, I miss you, always. A special thank you to my mom, Thérèse Cormier, who not only helped me remember, but shared her wisdom with me. Mom, your confidence in my abilities to pull this through means the world. I love you so much. I want to thank my husband and best friend, André. You heard me rattle off my story so many times, you could've written this book. Your patience and love help me in so many ways.